Race(ing) Intercultural Communication

Race(ing) Intercultural Communication signals a crucial intervention in the field, as well as in wider society, where social and political events are calling for new ways of making sense of race in the 21st century. Contributors to this book work at multiple intersections, theoretically and methodologically, in order to highlight relational (im)possibilities for intercultural communication. Chapters underscore the continuing importance of studying race, and the diverse mechanisms that maintain racial logics both in the U. S. and globally. In the so-called 'post-racial' era in which we live, not only are disrupting notions of color-blindness crucially important, but so too are imagining new ways of thinking through racial matters.

Ranging from discussions of new media, popular culture, and political discourse, to resistance literature, gay culture, and academia, contributors produce incisive analyses of the operations of race and white domination, including the myriad ways in which these discourses are reproduced and disrupted.

This book was originally published as a double special issue of the *Journal of International and Intercultural Communication*.

Dreama G. Moon is a Professor in the Communication Department at California State University San Marcos, California, USA. Within a human rights framework, she studies the varied communicative processes by which relations of domination are constructed, negotiated, reproduced, and resisted, with special attention to race and white supremacy.

Michelle A. Holling is a Professor in the Communication Department at California State University San Marcos, California, USA. From a critical rhetorical lens, she advances the study of Chican@ rhetoric, and examines the ways that racial-ethnic individuals rhetorically challenge reigning ideologies, systems, or representations that contribute to their continued marginalization.

NCA Studies in Communication

The National Communication Association (NCA) advances Communication as the discipline that studies all forms, modes, media, and consequences of communication through humanistic, social scientific, and aesthetic inquiry.

NCA serves the scholars, teachers, and practitioners who are its members by enabling and supporting their professional interests in research and teaching. Dedicated to fostering and promoting free and ethical communication, NCA promotes the widespread appreciation of the importance of communication in public and private life, the application of competent communication to improve the quality of human life and relationships, and the use of knowledge about communication to solve human problems.

NCA publishes 11 academic journals that provide the latest research in the discipline and showcase diverse perspectives on a range of scholarly topics. These journals are:

- *Communication and Critical/Cultural Studies*
- *Communication Education*
- *Communication Monographs*
- *Communication Teacher*
- *Critical Studies in Media Communication*
- *First Amendment Studies*
- *Journal of International and Intercultural Communication*
- *Journal of Applied Communication Research*
- *Quarterly Journal of Speech*
- *Review of Communication*
- *Text and Performance Quarterly*

The *NCA Studies in Communication* book series contains special issues from these journals, edited by leading scholars. The main aim of publishing these special issues as a series of books is to allow a wider audience of scholars from across multiple disciplines to engage with the work of the National Communication Association.

Available book titles in the series:

Cultural Studies of Rights
Critical Articulations
Edited by John Nguyet Erni

The Future of Internet Policy
Edited by Peter Decherney and Victor Pickard

Race(ing) Intercultural Communication
Racial logics in a colorblind era
Edited by Dreama G. Moon and Michelle A. Holling

Race(ing) Intercultural Communication
Racial logics in a colorblind era

Edited by
Dreama G. Moon and Michelle A. Holling

LONDON AND NEW YORK

First published 2016 by Routledge

2 Park Square, Milton Park, Abingdon, Oxfordshire OX14 4RN
711 Third Avenue, New York, NY 10017

Routledge is an imprint of the Taylor & Francis Group, an informa business

First issued in paperback 2017

Copyright © 2016 National Communication Association

All rights reserved. No part of this book may be reprinted or reproduced or utilised in any form or by any electronic, mechanical, or other means, now known or hereafter invented, including photocopying and recording, or in any information storage or retrieval system, without permission in writing from the publishers.

Notice:
Product or corporate names may be trademarks or registered trademarks, and are used only for identification and explanation without intent to infringe.

British Library Cataloguing in Publication Data
A catalogue record for this book is available from the British Library

ISBN 13: 978-1-138-92176-4 (hbk)
ISBN 13: 978-1-138-30632-5 (pbk)

Typeset in Minion
by RefineCatch Limited, Bungay, Suffolk

Publisher's Note
The publisher accepts responsibility for any inconsistencies that may have arisen during the conversion of this book from journal articles to book chapters, namely the possible inclusion of journal terminology.

Disclaimer
Every effort has been made to contact copyright holders for their permission to reprint material in this book. The publishers would be grateful to hear from any copyright holder who is not here acknowledged and will undertake to rectify any errors or omissions in future editions of this book.

Contents

Citation Information — vii
Notes on Contributors — ix

Introduction—A Politic of Disruption: Race(ing) Intercultural Communication — 1
Dreama G. Moon & Michelle A. Holling

1. The Rhetorics of Racial Power: Enforcing Colorblindness in Post-Apartheid Scholarship on Race — 9
   Marzia Milazzo

2. Queer Intercultural Relationality: An Autoethnography of Asian–Black (Dis)Connections in White Gay America — 29
   Shinsuke Eguchi

3. The Construction of Brownness: Latino/a and South Asian Bloggers' Responses to SB 1070 — 46
   Anjana Mudambi

4. Resisting Whiteness: Mexican American Studies and Rhetorical Struggles for Visibility — 65
   Chad M. Nelson

5. Our Foreign President Barack Obama: The Racial Logics of Birther Discourses — 83
   Vincent N. Pham

6. New Media, Old Racisms: Twitter, Miss America, and Cultural Logics of Race — 105
   J. David Cisneros & Thomas K. Nakayama

7. (Net)roots of Belonging: Contemporary Discourses of (In)valuability and Post-Racial Citizenship in the United States — 125
   Megan Elizabeth Morrissey

8. Problematic Representations of Strategic Whiteness and "Post-racial" Pedagogy: A Critical Intercultural Reading of *The Help* — 144
   Rachel Alicia Griffin

CONTENTS

9. "My Family Isn't Racist—However. . . .": Multiracial/Multicultural Obama-ism as an Ideological Barrier to Teaching Intercultural Communication   164
Yea-Wen Chen, Nathaniel Simmons & Dongjing Kang

Conclusion—Continuing a Politic of Disruption: Race(ing) Intercultural Communication   184
Michelle A. Holling and Dreama G. Moon

Index   187

Citation Information

The following chapters were originally published in the *Journal of International and Intercultural Communication*, volume 8, issue 1 (February 2015). When citing this material, please use the original page numbering for each article, as follows:

Chapter 1
The Rhetorics of Racial Power: Enforcing Colorblindness in Post-Apartheid Scholarship on Race
Marzia Milazzo
Journal of International and Intercultural Communication, volume 8, issue 1 (February 2015) pp. 7–26

Chapter 2
Queer Intercultural Relationality: An Autoethnography of Asian–Black (Dis)Connections in White Gay America
Shinsuke Eguchi
Journal of International and Intercultural Communication, volume 8, issue 1 (February 2015) pp. 27–43

Chapter 3
The Construction of Brownness: Latino/a and South Asian Bloggers' Responses to SB 1070
Anjana Mudambi
Journal of International and Intercultural Communication, volume 8, issue 1 (February 2015) pp. 44–62

Chapter 4
Resisting Whiteness: Mexican American Studies and Rhetorical Struggles for Visibility
Chad M. Nelson
Journal of International and Intercultural Communication, volume 8, issue 1 (February 2015) pp. 63–80

The following chapters were originally published in the *Journal of International and Intercultural Communication*, volume 8, issue 2 (May 2015). When citing this material, please use the original page numbering for each article, as follows:

CITATION INFORMATION

Chapter 5
Our Foreign President Barack Obama: The Racial Logics of Birther Discourses
Vincent N. Pham
Journal of International and Intercultural Communication, volume 8, issue 2 (May 2015)
pp. 86–107

Chapter 6
New Media, Old Racisms: Twitter, Miss America, and Cultural Logics of Race
J. David Cisneros & Thomas K. Nakayama
Journal of International and Intercultural Communication, volume 8, issue 2 (May 2015)
pp. 108–127

Chapter 7
(Net)roots of Belonging: Contemporary Discourses of (In)valuability and Post-Racial Citizenship in the United States
Megan Elizabeth Morrissey
Journal of International and Intercultural Communication, volume 8, issue 2 (May 2015)
pp. 128–146

Chapter 8
Problematic Representations of Strategic Whiteness and "Post-racial" Pedagogy: A Critical Intercultural Reading of The Help
Rachel Alicia Griffin
Journal of International and Intercultural Communication, volume 8, issue 2 (May 2015)
pp. 147–166

Chapter 9
"My Family Isn't Racist—However. . .": Multiracial/Multicultural Obama-ism as an Ideological Barrier to Teaching Intercultural Communication
Yea-Wen Chen, Nathaniel Simmons & Dongjing Kang
Journal of International and Intercultural Communication, volume 8, issue 2 (May 2015)
pp. 167–186

For any permission-related enquiries please visit:
http://www.tandfonline.com/page/help/permissions

Notes on Contributors

Yea-Wen Chen is based in the School of Communication Studies at Ohio University, Athens, OH, USA.

J. David Cisneros is an Assistant Professor in the Department of Communication at the University of Illinois, Urbana-Champaign, IL, USA.

Shinsuke Eguchi is an Assistant Professor in the Department of Communication and Journalism at the University of New Mexico, Albuquerque, NM, USA. His research and teaching interests are in queer intercultural communication, performance studies, and critical autoethnography.

Rachel Alicia Griffin is Associate Professor in the Department of Communication Studies at Southern Illinois University, Carbondale, IL, USA.

Michelle A. Holling is a Professor in the Communication Department at California State University San Marcos, California, USA. From a critical rhetorical lens, she advances the study of Chican@ rhetoric, and examines the ways that racial-ethnic individuals rhetorically challenge reigning ideologies, systems, or representations that contribute to their continued marginalization.

Dongjing Kang is a Teaching Associate based in the School of Communication Studies at Ohio University, Athens, OH, USA.

Marzia Milazzo is Assistant Professor of English at Vanderbilt University, Nashville, Tennessee, USA. She is currently completing a book that examines the rhetorical contours of color-blindness and their implications for literary imaginaries, antiracist politics, and the production of knowledge in a transnational context.

Dreama G. Moon is a Professor in the Communication Department at California State University San Marcos, California, USA. Within a human rights framework, she studies the varied communicative processes by which relations of domination are constructed, negotiated, reproduced, and resisted, with special attention to race and white supremacy.

Megan Elizabeth Morrissey is an Assistant Professor of Rhetoric at the University of North Texas, Denton, TX, USA.

Anjana Mudambi is Visiting Assistant Professor of Communication Studies at Randolph-Macon College, Ashland, Virginia, USA.

NOTES ON CONTRIBUTORS

Thomas K. Nakayama is Professor in the Department of Communication Studies at Northeastern University, Boston, MA, USA.

Chad M. Nelson is a Lecturer at Pennsylvania State University, PA, USA. His dissertation is titled 'The Violence of Scarcity, Rationality, And School Choice: Ideology and Race in the Closing Southwestern High School in Detroit'.

Vincent N. Pham is an Assistant Professor of Communication at California State University San Marcos, California, USA.

Nathaniel Simmons is an Assistant Professor based in the Department of Communication at La Salle University, Philadelphia, PA, USA.

Introduction
A Politic of Disruption: Race(ing) Intercultural Communication

Dreama G. Moon & Michelle A. Holling

> "Attention to the absences in the development of the field [of intercultural communication] can be disruptive"
>
> (Nakayama & Martin, 2007, p. 113).

> "We must examine and attend to the specifics of race, as it emerges in concrete conflicts and practices, communities and cultures if we are to uncover the mechanisms that sustain its logic"
>
> (Flores, Moon, & Nakayama, 2006, p. 184).

The insights of the scholars quoted above give us pause as we think about this special issue on race. Following Flores et al., we note that to commit to identifying mechanisms that sustain racial logics requires drawing attention to the absences that enable inequities and inequalities to persist in society and in our scholarship. In contemplating racial logics, two recent examples call attention to absences that surface not only in intercultural communication but also in global and domestic contexts. Concomitantly, the conflicts and practices examined by the examples we discuss, along with the essays composing this special issue, underscore the continuing importance of studying race and the diverse "mechanisms" that maintain racial logics.

Our first example harks back to the call for this special issue wherein we referenced the United Nations' World Conference against Racism (WCAR) in 2001, citing the following passage from the Durban Declaration:

> racism, racial discrimination, xenophobia and related intolerance, where they amount to racism and racial discrimination, constitute serious violations of and obstacles to the full enjoyment of all human rights and deny the self-evident truth that all human beings are born free and equal in dignity and rights, are an obstacle to friendly and peaceful relations among peoples and nations, and are among the root causes of many internal and international conflicts.

Clearly, the Declaration established in no uncertain language that global racism, as a major threat to human rights, peace, and dignity, is foundational in terms of intercultural and intracultural conflicts around the world and as such, need to be addressed. We failed to mention the unfortunate reality that WCAR has not enjoyed strong support from many Western nations including the United States. Western countries have opposed a number of the proposed agenda discussion items including the construction of slavery as a "crime against humanity," the lingering effects of the transatlantic slave trade, reparations, prohibition of hate speech, and critiques of Zionism. Unable to dictate the conference agenda, the United States and its European allies—those who have benefitted greatly from racism (and continue to do so)—have either walked out of or boycotted the conference, and when some have deigned to attend, they have sent low level dignities (another way of signaling a lack of serious engagement with racism, xenophobia, and related intolerances). Accusing the conference organizers of permitting "hateful language" against Israel and opposing the term "reparations," the West, who has been the greatest beneficiary of global racism, has offered little support to WCAR and, in these important conversations, Western voices have been primarily absent.

Looking inward to the U.S., shortly after the shooting of yet another unarmed Black youth, Michael Brown, six Black children of Ferguson, Missouri participated in the making of a video entitled, "Hey White People: A Kinda Awkward Note to America by #Ferguson Kids." The objective was to educate those who do not or will not "get" the racial reality in the United States for people of color and by association, for themselves. Blogs posted in response to the video call into question the success of that educational attempt given the vitriolic tone of some of the posts by self-identified white people. Rather than use the video as an opportunity to gain insight into peoples of color's realities, some positioned the video as "racist" pointing to the title ("Hey White People"), referring to the children in the video as "haters" and to the video itself as "raceterbation" (injecting racism where it does not exist) (http://vimeo.com/105147740).

These two seemingly disjointed events led us to reflect upon the contours that race and racism—in global or domestic contexts—assume in political and social landscapes. Evident to us are the ways in which those in power are accustomed to setting the terms of the debate, deciding what gets discussed, if and how issues get discussed, and so forth. On this point, we are reminded of the stalled conversations on race instigated by former President Clinton that represented a bold undertaking to centralizing race in the U.S. imaginary. The examples mentioned thus far were opportune moments to have radically different kinds of conversations about race and the practice of racism; inevitably and regrettably, those opportunities escaped and continue to escape a collective "us." A danger inherent in disengaging, opting out of, and/or faltering in such significant conversations is the surfacing of an insidiousness belief that individuals, internationally or domestically, live in a post-racist era that an ideology of colorblindness backs.[1] Of concern are the varied repercussions stemming from such beliefs that recent scholarship examines (i.e., Milazzo, 2015; Holling et al., 2014).

As we think about intercultural communication as a field, it has had its own historical experience with the privilege to set the agenda. Given the context in which the field emerged, for much of its history intercultural communication has served dominant interests (Moon, 1996). While Moon notes that briefly in the 1960s and 70s, intercultural scholarship evidenced more heterogeneous notions of culture including race, by 1980 race-related scholarship in the field had all but disappeared. What began to surface is the "white problem" in intercultural communication. Nakayama and Martin

(2007) observe that much of what we have come to understand as "intercultural knowledge" has been driven, implicitly and explicitly, by a white, Western agenda (albeit often unconscious) in which the experiences of the dominant are centered. While this agenda-setting function may not have been driven by a conscious effort to exclude, regardless of intent, the intellectual agenda has been framed in very particular and limited ways for most of our history. For instance, take the notion of race. Intercultural communication scholars have been notoriously silent on issues of race. Even during historical moments such as the Civil Rights era, few intercultural scholars took up what was certainly the most important issue of the day. When we explore the field's history, we note that there has not been a special issue in *any* NCA journal exploring the nexus of intercultural communication and race. Given the importance of race as a social and political marker, we are troubled that no journal has attended to the intersection of race and intercultural communication across the 70+ years since its inception. We thank the current editor of *JIIC*, Rona Halualani for allowing us to fill that gap.

> "To engage in a serious discussion of race in America, we must begin not with the problems of black [sic] people but with the flaws of American society – flaws rooted in historic inequalities and longstanding cultural stereotypes. How we set up the terms for discussing racial issues shapes our perception and response to these issues" (Cornel West, 1994, p. 6).

How have we, the guest editors, "set up the terms for discussing racial issues?" As detailed in the call for submissions, we sought

> "submissions that investigate or examine issues of race, racism, nativism and xenophobia that aim to intervene in post-racism rhetoric and show the variety of ways that race continues to matter both in the United States and abroad. . . . The contributions to be garnered from this special issue on race are to challenge the myth of post-racial societies, domestically or internationally, and to reaffirm the saliency of race within intercultural and international relations."

Quite explicitly then, we desired essays that interrogated "the flaws" of any society in hopes that authors would be able to conceive of hopeful communicative possibilities and of ways through and out of global racial denial systems. More broadly, we committed to and envisioned this special issue on race as a politic of disruption. "Politic" highlights the delicate balance of politics that come with pursuing race and the shrewdness of a scholar needed to apprehend the connection between race and intercultural communication. "Disruption" offered an enticing means to underscore a need to interrupt an event, activity or process by causing a disturbance or problem in order to destroy the normal continuance or unity of a process. Combined, a politic of disruption is about calling for the race(ing) of intercultural communication. Through a double special issue on race, a politic of disruption begins to manifest in the field, in intellectual work on race, and in intercultural communication. As guest editors our intentions were certainly to challenge the field's neglect of race but moreover we wished to push the intellectual boundaries of theorizing race. In the so-called "post-racial" era not only are disrupting notions of colorblindness crucially important, but also are imagining new ways of thinking through racial matters. The first set of essays composing one of two special issues² sets us, readers, and the field afoot on a politic of disruption.

In this set of papers, we observe authors enacting a politic of disruption as they levy a host of challenges to the study of "race as usual" in the context of intercultural communication. For example, several authors centralize marginality and/or marginal identities that is a noteworthy intervention in the study of the norm(al) populations evident in much intercultural scholarship. Authors' scholarship also draws from robust and complex methodological and theoretical frameworks that showcase the creativity required to disrupt traditional approaches to the study of race in the field and racially oppressive practices and ideological systems. Next, the topics and racial subjects pursued by the four scholars gesture toward a rhetoric of dispensation, which "counters hegemonic positionings and/or narratives of a subjugated citizenry in an effort to secure rights ..." (Holling, 2012, p. 66). Phrased differently, the work undertaken by the four authors herein implicitly calls for "dispens[ing] with dominant narratives" (such as the notions that society exists in a post-racial era or that colorblind ideology can address structural racism) so that "dispensing of political rights" (Holling, p. 72) might ensue. Moreover, in different ways, these papers speak to the ways in which white dominance communicates (dis)belonging through positioning people as "forever foreign," "enemy of the State," or "Asian=bottom" and through resurgence of colorblind discourse that disingenuously suggests that race is no longer of importance despite many examples to the contrary. Finally, the papers illustrate how targeted groups negotiate a space of belonging within white supremacy via resistance and/or vernacular discourse, eschewal of white desire, talking back to colorblindness, and construction of potential coalitional spaces.

The ordering of the essays is intentional; order is another way of carrying out a politic of disruption. Paralleling the introduction that begins with an international focus to a U.S. based domestic focus to the sub-field of intercultural communication are the four essays that mirror such an order. In so doing, our hope is that readers read across and between the essays to discern how each informs the other and to identify overlapping points where race is concerned regardless of the context or locale of its situatedness.

In "Rhetorics of Racial Power," Milazzo takes on post-Apartheid academic scholarship in South Africa, tracing the reproduction of colorblind discourse in economics, education, literature, philosophy, and sociology. Although outside the scope of her essay, she acknowledges a similar move within communication. Reading colorblindness as a global discourse and disrupting the often assumed "objectivity" of the academy, she demonstrates how academe often participates in the reproduction of racialized privilege. She demonstrates how post-colonial societies all too quickly move from a goal of racial reconciliation to colorblind rhetoric where horrendous racial pasts get buried under class analysis—this move aided by its (usually white) intellectuals. In the post-colonial era, the push back from whiteness in the form of colorblind discourse threatens racial reconciliation and recovery.

In "Queer Intercultural Relationality" Eguchi works at the intersection of race and desire, demonstrating the complexities of intercultural contact in gay communities. He interrogates his queer intercultural production of desire through an examination on intraqueer Asian/Black (dis)connections that call into question White (homo)normative constructions of a straight/gay binary. Showing how imperialist relations inform desire, he notes that a form of empowerment can be located in Western obsession with Orientalism and the "other's" rejection of white desire. At the same time, he highlights how desiring Black bodies is both a means of disrupting whiteness and a potential problematic political strategy.

Next, Mudambi in "The Construction of Brownness" breaks apart the Black/white binary showing how brownness poses challenges to Arizona's SB 1070. She examines how "brownness" emerges as a highly contextualized racial formation that is aligned with constructions of "illegal" immigrants that does not fit neatly into a traditional Black/white racial structure. Her work illustrates how shared experiences of discrimination among Latina/os and South Asian constitute them as a racialized group that experiences unique forms of racism. Disrupting the Black/white racial binary enables potential cross coalitions of people of color around brownness and develops brownness as a racial project in its own right.

Lastly, Nelson in "Resisting Whiteness" offers a critique of whiteness discourse involved in criticisms of Mexican American Studies in the Tucson Unified School District in Tucson, Arizona through the political lens of Santino Rivera's collection of Chicana/o literature. His paper demonstrates how racial discourse threatens spaces of liberation demonstrated in resistance rhetoric as Chicana/os define themselves against Arizona's construction of Mexican American studies.

These first four essays play critical roles in race(ing) intercultural communication by bringing to our attention international discourses and domestic voices and communities not often, or consistently, heard in social or scholarly arenas. Thus, we thank the authors for the meaningful work they undertook.

Continuing *A Politic of Disruption: Race(ing) Intercultural Communication*
Michelle A. Holling and Dreama G. Moon

Complementing the above are the five essays closing this second special issue on race. The final set of essays continue the work of race(ing) intercultural communication— an impetus behind a politic of disruption. The essays enact a politic of disruption by revealing the subtle (and, perhaps not so subtle) ways that race and racism inflect various discourses that permeate websites, web based campaigns, social media sites such as Twitter, popular films, and classroom spaces. What unites these five essays is how they expose the presence of post-racialism and colorblindness in discourses that ultimately shape, preclude or inhibit intercultural possibilities. For instance, some authors identify the machinations of racial logics and ideology (e.g., "new racism," "Birther logics," and "multicultural/multiracial Obama-ism"). Other authors expose the ways that whiteness surfaces in narratives produced by dispossessed and excluded subjects that undercut prospects for cross racial-ethnic identifications and conversely, in the processes by which film facilitates social desires for a post-racial society even as whiteness is valorized. Taken together, the essays race intercultural communication through their interrogation of the inter/cultural operations of race(ing) and a post-racial society in innovative ways.

As in the prior issue, we organize the essays deliberately and thoughtfully in order to bring to the fore a particular progression that we did not expect when finalizing the second issue. Opening the issue are two essays that take to task discursive questioning of the nation through its national figures that begins first and foremost with the President of the United States to another socially coveted role of Miss America (i.e., Pham, and Cisneros & Nakayama, respectively). The work of these scholars critique Birther and social media discourses that racialize treasured figures subsequently indicating desires for a nostalgic return to a clean white past or a "better time." Of course, we know that although such a past has never existed, despite acts of violence, conquest, colonization, etc., our nation's history implicates an idolized notion of citizenship premised on being white (as in the President or Miss America) and/or whiteness. Gaining access to citizenship relies upon expressing one's desire for national belonging such as what surfaces in Morrissey's essay. Her essay demonstrates how migrant Others access whiteness as invaluable through their espousal of a value system (e.g., ownership or paying dues) arguably based on a system of white domination. Amongst these scholars' analyses, an implicit narrative of progress politically, socially, and economically begins to surface—whether attributable to the election of the first Black president or the crowning of the first Indian American—albeit one rife with ruptures, which the authors named deftly unpack. When turning to the realm of popular culture, a similar narrative of progress surfaces but this one requires refashioning white supremacy in the Jim Crow south. Griffin's essay adroitly unpacks the ways in which a popular film represents racial consciousness and white-Black female friendships as a means of transcending racism that come at the expense and de-valuation of Black women. The public pedagogy of film examined by Griffin segues into the narrative pedagogy produced by students, who write about their own cultural identities, examined by Chen, Simmons and Kang. Their analysis provocatively identifies a perception among students who narrativize progress as "multicultural/multiracial Obama-ism." Interestingly, the final essay circles back to the first essay that implicated President Obama. To illustrate the ordering discussed, we offer brief comments about the individual essays.

In "Our Foreign President," Pham examines birther discourse especially in its questioning of the citizenship of President Barack Obama and thus the legitimacy of his presidency. En route, he unpacks the racial logics of how Birther constructions of the "natural born citizen" positions President Obama as an inscrutable foreigner without legitimacy and activates xenophobic fears regarding an increasingly multi-racial and global society. Articulated with longstanding (white) racial logics around anti-Blackness and Yellow Peril, Birther discourse activates other racial logics around leader acceptability regarding all non-white groups.

Next, in "New Media, Old Racisms," Cisneros and Nakayama argue that rather than seeing old racism and "new" (colorblind racism) as oppositional, the relationship between them is one of coexistence, continuity, and complementarity. Taking the win of Davuluri's crowning as the first Indian American Miss America in 2014 as a case study, the authors show that the emergence of racist tweets in response to her victory provided an opportunity for the re-assertion of colorblind and race-neutral ideologies.

In her essay, "(Net)roots of Belonging," Morrissey argues that in an era of post-racism, raced migrants in the United States must prove their value to the nation in order to be integrated or accepted by the dominant culture. Analyzing the We Are American campaign, migrant testimonials perform desire for national belonging and de-valuing of U.S. minorities, thus demonstrating their (in)valuability to/for whiteness. Morrissey argues that in their efforts to establish credibility, migrants must manage their intersectional subjectivities in ways that service (U.S. national) whiteness and reproduce the value of the category.

Next, in "Problematic Representations," Griffin performs a critical reading of the popular film *The Help* as a way of unpacking the public pedagogical impetus of popular culture. She illustrates the ways in which the centralization of whiteness and the redemption of white racists are manifestations of a strategic whiteness that operates at the expense of Black women. In so doing, she argues that the film functions as a site of racial apologia for whites and provides momentum of post-racial ideology.

Finally, Chen, Simmons and Kang in "'My Family Isn't Racist" analyze undergraduate data on cultural identity in order to unpack the challenges of teaching race to millennials reared in a "post-racial" period. They identify the emergence of an ideology they coin, "multicultural/ multiracial Obama-ism" (MMO) that is supported by three frames of individualism, meritocracy, and universalism. They conclude their essay by offering pedagogical suggestions useful for unpacking MMO in terms of classroom interaction and self-reflexivity about their identities.

For now, we delay offering concluding comments. Our intention will be to unite the essays through a series of themes, questions, and directions for the continued race(ing) of intercultural communication. Meanwhile, we invite readers to mull the arguments, contemplate the implications stemming from the essays, and participate in a politic of disruption.

Notes

(1) As we argue elsewhere, "colorblindness is conceived of as an ideology that denies that white privilege or contemporary institutionalized racial discrimination exist thus facilitating the belief that the U.S. is post-racial (Risman & Benejee, 2013). As such, we do not view the terms—colorblindness and post-racial—as interchangeable. However, we do see that colorblind ideology supports the claim of post-racialism as conceived as an era in which race does not matter in any methodical or socially significant manner (Bonilla-Silva, 2010)" (Holling, Moon, & Jackson Nevis, 2014, p. 22, fn1).
(2) Following this first special issue, the second one was published in May 2015.

References

Bonilla-Silva, E. (2010). *Racism without racists: Color-blind racism & racial inequality in contemporary America* (3rd ed.). Lanham, MD: Rowman & Littlefield.

Flores, L. A., Moon, D. G., & Nakayama, T. K. (2006). Dynamic rhetorics of race: California's racial privacy initiative and the shifting grounds of racial politics. *Communication and Critical/Cultural Studies, 3*(3), 181–201.

Holling, M. A. (2012). A dispensational rhetoric in "The Mexican Question in the Southwest." In D. R. DeChaine (Ed.), *Border Rhetorics: Charting Enactments of Citizenship and Identity on the U.S.-Mexico Frontier* (pp. 65–85). Tuscaloosa, Alabama: University of Alabama Press.

Holling, M. A., Moon, D. G., & Jackson, A. N. (2014). Racist violations and racializing apologia in a post-racism era. *Journal of International and Intercultural Communication, 7*(4), 1–27. doi: 10.1080/17513057.2014.964144

Milazzo, M. (2015). The rhetorics of racial power: Enforcing colorblindness in post-apartheid scholarship on race. *Journal of International and Intercultural Communication, 8*(1), 7–26. doi: 10.1080/17513057.2015.991075

Moon, D. G. (1996). Concepts of culture: Implications for intercultural communication research. *Communication Quarterly, 44*, 70–84.

Moon, D. G., & Holling, M. A. (2015). A politic of disruption: Race(ing) intercultural communication. *Journal of International and Intercultural Communication, 8*(1), 1–6. doi: 10.1080/17513057.2015.991073

Nakayama, T. K. & Martin, J. N. (2007). The "white" problem in intercultural communication research and pedagogy. In L. M. Cooks & J. S. Simpson (Eds.), *Whiteness, pedagogy, performance: Dis/placing race* (pp. 111–137). Lanham, MD: Lexington Books.

Risman, B. J., & Banerjee, P. (2013). Kids talking about race: Tween-agers in a post-Civil Rights era. *Sociological Forum, 28*(2), 213–235.

West. C. (1994). *Race matters*. Boston, MA: Beacon Press.

The Rhetorics of Racial Power: Enforcing Colorblindness in Post-Apartheid Scholarship on Race

Marzia Milazzo

This article examines the reproduction of colorblindness discourse in selected post-1994 South African studies in economics, education, literature, philosophy, and sociology. It argues that the presence of dominant racial ideologies in this scholarship is emblematic of an active investment in maintaining racialized privileges. As it illustrates some of the rhetorical mechanisms that inform the articulation of colorblindness discourse at large, it shows that unpacking colorblind rhetoric is itself necessary if we are to make sense of the research emphases, arguments, logics, and findings of a significant body of South African scholarship on race published since the advent of democratic rule.

Testifying to the ongoing *killability* of the Black person in post-apartheid South Africa, in August 2012 police opened fire on a group of striking workers who were demanding living wages, killing 34 and injuring at least 78.[1] The event at the Lonmin platinum mine in Marikana starkly resembled the 1960 Sharpeville massacre, which also occurred in Gauteng after a protest that challenged the status quo, and speaks to striking continuities between the apartheid past and the democratic present. That the police force carrying out the executions today is multiracial rather than predominantly white does not make this incident disconnected from institutional racism, but it does give ammunition to colorblind arguments that deny the central role that racial power played in the tragedy and the demonstrations preceding it.[2]

Twenty years after the official end of apartheid, racial inequality remains rampant in South Africa. White people, less than 10 percent of the population, own approximately 85 percent of the land, 85 percent of the entire economy, and over 90 percent of the largest companies.[3] Undeniably, whites "still act as gatekeepers for the majority group who are in power politically but certainly not economically" (Steyn in Grant, 2007, p. 94). The differential life expectancy of less than 50 years for Blacks and over 70 years for whites also speaks to a ghastly politics that does not value Black life. Yet, despite these noticeable realities, as Tukufu Zuberi and Eduardo Bonilla-Silva (2008) show, not unlike in the United States, the "declining significance of race" myth also permeates South African sociology.

A significant body of scholarship on race produced in post-apartheid South Africa demonizes the employment of racial categories, underemphasizes or silences white advantage, and vilifies policies that attempt to redress racial inequality. It is crucial that we give close attention to these studies because, as Howard Winant (2001) explains, "The rearticulation of (in)equality in an ostensibly colorblind framework emphasizing individualism and meritocracy, it turns out, preserves the legacy of racial hierarchy far more effectively than its explicit defense" (p. 35). Of course, this is not only relevant in the South African context. Colorblindness is a transnational discourse deployed also in Europe and in other former European settler colonies—from Australia to Brazil and from Cuba to the United States, places in which racial inequality remains pervasive.

In South Africa, during the anti-apartheid struggle, the nonracialism promoted by the African National Congress (ANC) represented a practical antiracist strategy aimed at fostering unity across racial lines while still privileging the interests of Black people (see Motlanthe & Jordan, 2010). However, as Achille Mbembe (2014) writes, "Reactionary and conservative forces have co-opted nonracialism, which they now equate with colour-blindness. They use nonracialism as a weapon to discredit any attempt to deracialise property, institutions, and structures inherited from an odious past" (n.p.). Although nonracialism is rooted in a history of decolonial resistance, today it represents a regressive tool that supports white privilege. The terms "nonracialism," mainly used in the South African context, and "colorblindness," used more frequently in the United States, have become de facto interchangeable.

This study identifies the discursive presence of colorblind ideology in selected post-1994 South African studies on race in economics, education, literature, philosophy, and sociology. In the process, it makes visible some of the rhetorical mechanisms that inform the repertoire of colorblindness at large and shows that the discourse permeates both social sciences and humanities. Precisely because colorblind strategies traverse disciplinary and even national boundaries, it would be impossible to proceed analytically by ascribing each one to a specific discipline, topic, or scholar. In fact, I aim to illustrate precisely the malleability of colorblind rhetoric. Understanding the rhetorics of colorblindness is itself necessary if we are to make sense of the research emphases, arguments, logics, and findings of a considerable body of South African scholarship on race produced in the last two decades.

I interrogate South African scholarship in light of the interdisciplinary tools provided by critical race studies and the works of Black radical thinkers. So far, most research on colorblindness has focused on U.S. cases (Ansell, 2006, p. 335). Given the transnational dimensions of colorblindness, some U.S. scholarship provides a useful lens for understanding the discourse elsewhere. Still, it is necessary to remain attentive to national particularities. The primary methodology I employ for unpacking colorblind rhetoric is *close reading*. In doing so, I build upon Critical Race Theory, which has long established the desirability of using literary methods to interpret legal texts (see Lawrence, 1995, p. 347). Scholars in other fields have also recognized the importance of "looking at whiteness as critical readers" (Ratele & Laubscher, 2010, p. 86). While this study is grounded in an extensive engagement with post-apartheid scholarship on race, performing close rather than distant readings requires privileging depth over breadth and therefore presenting only a limited number of studies.

The studies examined herein have three fundamental things in common: (a) they advance arguments about racial relations, racial inequality and/or racial discourse in post-apartheid South Africa, (b) their interventions are *not* obviously racist but are framed as antiracist or concerned with racial justice, and (c) they are often widely cited and written by scholars who are influential voices in their fields. However, I do not intend to generalize and suggest that most South African academics who work on racism are committed to the same agenda, for this is certainly not the case. Instead, I hope to call attention to the urgent reality of racial domination, a reality that is too often mystified in academia. While I contend that works in the specific disciplines I examine—in particular sociology and education—have become central venues for the reproduction of colorblind doctrines in South African universities, I acknowledge that no field is immune to the phenomenon and hope that this study will pave the way for analyses that tackle colorblind logics within alternative studies and disciplines.[4]

Recognizing that the production of knowledge is a key site for the protection of racial power across national boundaries, this article thus turns the lens to academic scholarship itself. In doing so, it is indebted and contributes to a substantial body of interdisciplinary scholarship (for example, Conway, 2008b; Lipsitz, 2006; Mills, 1997; Morrison, 1992; Shome & Hedge, 2002; Zuberi & Bonilla-Silva, 2008) that shows how whiteness "is built into our disciplines, our institutions, our professions … and in our methods as researchers" (Steyn & Conway, 2010, p. 286). Originally monopolized by the United States (Steyn & Conway, 2010, p. 285), whiteness studies have gained traction in the South African context (see Steyn & Conway 2010; West & Schmidt, 2010). For example, significant studies on white identity (Distiller & Steyn, 2004; Drzewiecka & Steyn, 2012; Steyn, 1998, 2001, 2005), white advantage (Ratele & Laubscher, 2010; Steyn, 2007), or antiracist whiteness (Conway, 2008a; Matthews, 2012) show that the field is wide-ranging and growing.

This study has benefited in particular from Melissa Steyn's work on "White Talk" (Steyn, 2001, 2004, 2005, 2010), which Steyn and Foster (2008) define as a set of discursive practices that "attempt to manage the positionality of white South Africans to their (perceived) greatest competitive advantage, within an Africanizing context"

(p. 26). The authors contend that, although not all white people resort to "White Talk," its repertoire is nevertheless characteristic of white South African discursive approaches to race (p. 26). There is much overlap between "White Talk" and "colorblind talk" (Kim, 2000, p. 17). Although I am interested primarily in texts rather than authors, it seems relevant to disclose that most of the works examined in this study are written by white scholars and that I myself am one. Only a few studies examined herein are authored by scholars of color. Mentioning this is not an attempt to "share the blame" (Steyn & Foster, 2008, p. 32) and deflect attention from white people's primary responsibility for the perpetuation of racial inequality. It means noticing that, for example, in South Africa and beyond, a commitment to colorblindness can signify a larger chance to succeed in white-dominated academia, which tends to reward scholars who embrace colorblind doctrines (Zuberi & Bonilla-Silva, 2008, p. 281). It also implies recognizing that everyone, especially people in positions of power, can have an interest in maintaining the status quo.

In contesting the idea that any emancipatory vision for a New South Africa can be undertaken without speaking of race and making racial inequality visible, I acknowledge that, as Toni Morrison (1992) writes, "The world does not become raceless or will not become unracialized by assertion. The act of enforcing racelessness ... is itself a racial act" (p. 46). Beyond raising uncomfortable questions about the meaning of justice in the post-apartheid present, the location of colorblindness ideology in South African scholarship reveals the impact of racial consciousness onto the production of racialized meaning. Established theories of racial epistemology argue that white ways of knowing, and privileged positionalities in general, are primarily defined by *ignorance* (see Mills, 1997, 2007; Steyn, 2012), as exemplified by the statement "lack of insight into its own privilege ... is the trademark of privilege" (Steyn & Foster, 2008, p. 30). Yet, racialized knowledge, agency, and intentionality are central to the reproduction of colorblindness discourse in South Africa and beyond. I argue that the presence of colorblind rhetoric in the studies analyzed herein is neither the product of ignorance nor coincidence, but is indicative of what George Lipsitz (2006) calls a *possessive investment in whiteness*; that is, an active interest in reinscribing white privilege. In the pages that follow, I aim to show that the investment in silencing race within scholarship *about* race, particularly racial inequality, is a paradox of great significance.

Reading Racial Power

In October 2010, a number of leading South African scholars gathered at Wits University for a colloquium titled Revisiting Apartheid's Race Categories, which was inspired by a debate about admission criteria and affirmative action that had taken place at the University of Cape Town in 2007 (Erasmus, 2012, p. 1). Co-hosted by the School of Human and Community Development, the Transformation Office, the Faculty of Humanities at Wits University, and the Centre for Critical Research on Race and Identity at the University of KwaZulu-Natal, the colloquium featured many papers that critiqued the employment of racial categories. Ongoing academic efforts to revise and silence apartheid categories beg the question that Harry Garuba (2012) posed in the closing remarks of the colloquium: "What are the conditions of possibility for the emergence of a particular problematic concerned with bureaucratic and administrative classification and not another, say, one concerned with the material and discursive production of race?" (p. 174). While more empirical research on institutional racism is sorely needed, numerous South African studies focus on racial categories per se. This emphasis is not accidental.

The institutionalization of colorblindness in South African academia becomes evident if we consider that the theoretical deconstruction of racial categories frequently goes hand in hand with the explicit demonization of race-based affirmative action policies. Several studies brand measures which are meant to *redress* racial inequality as "new policies of racial discrimination" (Seekings, 2007, p. 1) or as "pro-African racial discrimination" (Seekings, 2007, p. 26), while the racial categories needed to implement these policies are vilified as having "negative effects" (Ruggunan & Maré, 2012, p. 56), causing "separation" (Maré, 2003, p. 23) or "entrenching racial prejudice" (Alexander, 2007, p. 94). Jonathan Jansen (2009a) goes as far as attacking affirmative action as follows: "Black nationalists are doing after apartheid exactly what Afrikaner nationalists did under apartheid: promoting people on the crude basis of colour, this time to meet employment equity pressures and through a misguided sense of parity with white academics" (p. 149).[5] This statement compares white supremacist policies with measures intended to compensate for them. It also suggests that white academics are somehow superior to Black scholars. In a noteworthy body of South African scholarship on race—especially scholarship produced in disciplines with a direct impact on public policy such as sociology and education—racial categories themselves, and not institutional racism, are routinely endowed with the power of maintaining apartheid logics, reproducing colonial violence, and creating racial conflict.

A conspicuous number of South African sociological studies about race ironically argue that race should no longer be the object of discussion. The scholarship of Gerhard Maré (2003) is a case in point. In "Non-Racialism in the Struggle against Apartheid," the sociologist argues that in order to "come to grips" (p. 13) with the racist past, South Africans should now stop thinking racially. Maré argues that *"the very notion of 'race' must be deliberately undermined"* (p. 14—italics in the text). However, how does "not thinking racially" contribute to dismantling institutionalized racism? If race is automatically suspended as a category of analysis, how do we confront racial inequality? The article in actuality does not propose any remedy to racial inequality. Maré argues that racism "continues to draw on the banal perpetuation of notions of race in everyday life, as well as in political practice in a democratic South Africa" (p. 13). Since "[r]ace still exists because racism persists" (Lipsitz, 2011, p. 21) and not vice versa, Maré here reverses cause and consequence. The depiction of racism in Maré's statement is in agreement with what Neil Gotanda (1995) defines as *formal-race unconnectedness*; that is, racism viewed merely as "individual prejudice" (p. 257). Such an individualized conceptualization, Gotanda explains, excludes "an understanding of the fact that race has institutional and structural dimensions" (p. 265).

Another key rhetorical strategy that Maré's article employs is *aggregation*. The scholar writes: "we have continued with *an acceptance that there are races* ... and then the discussion is really just about the relevance of race: should this determine citizenship, land ownership, cultural funding, census categories, etc; does it apply to intelligence, physical ability, cultural traits ...?" (p. 29; italics in the text). Here, Maré conflates issues that are vital for the achievement of racial equality ("citizenship, land ownership") with biological-deterministic notions of race that are obviously fallacious ("intelligence, physical ability") in order to discredit the category 'race' per se, a move commonly employed in colorblind talk. In the meantime, the scholar does not mention how racism continues to define everyday life for most Black South Africans.

As Maré argues that racial categories are divisive, an action that further stigmatizes their employment in affirmative action policies, he also relies on a de-politicizing appeal to a "shared humanity" that precludes any critique of white privilege (see Steyn & Foster, 2008, p. 32). Separation, he writes, "can make people forget their shared humanity, with suspicion then generating racism" (p. 23). Referring to a common humanity allows Maré to obscure racialized particularity. Although it appears to express concern for collectivity, the discourse of liberal humanism that Maré reproduces is entwined with a liberal ideology that "purportedly judges individuals on the basis of their own individual actions" (Bauman & Briggs, 2003, p. 59). The appeal to liberal humanism as a means to silence racial inequality also transcends disciplinary boundaries. For example, literary scholar Rosemarie Jolly (1995) insists on "the resurrection of the scholar's 'I'" and the "reference to the self" (p. 25) as conditions that enable the intellectual to speak about the Other. Claiming a neutral subjectivity, Jolly assumes that a "reference to the self" can occur without interrogating and historicizing its positionality.

An especially powerful strategy for silencing racial grievances across disciplines, the evocation of liberal humanism is facilitated by the appropriation of antiracist thought in general and the co-optation of Edward Said's work in particular. For instance, citing Said's *Culture and Imperialism*, education scholar Crain Soudien (2012b) argues that Said called for a historiography that was attentive to "human experience in all its diversity and particularity" (p. 35). While Soudien considers this positive, the abstract valorization of human diversity is here accompanied by efforts to silence the concrete reality of racialized particularity. Comparably, in "Confronting the Categories: Equitable Admissions Without Apartheid Race Classification," sociologist Zimitri Erasmus attacks affirmative action by opening with an epigraphic citation from Said's *Humanism and Democratic Criticism*. Paradoxically, as they appeal to humanity itself, these studies fail to recognize Black humanity as in need of redress.

It is not a claim to universal subjectivity—the belief that 'we are all just people'—that will make racism disappear. Racism is not produced by suspicion, as Maré (2003) contends, neither is it a pathology that can be cured through behavior modification, as philosopher Samantha Vice (2010) suggests. The dismantling of racial regimes requires concrete institutional actions, not arguments about the commonness of humanity that disregard collective advantages. Andile Mngxitama (2009) explains that liberal humanism is deliberately invoked to concurrently mystify and reinforce white dominance:

> Whiteness [in South Africa] is so pervasive it has become invisible, that is to say normalized—the "normative state of existence." This normative state of existence is also a powerful tool of silencing. "Why can't we all just get along?" someone asks innocently, while another claims that "colour is just skin deep, in fact we are human beings ultimately." Blacks are under pressure to accept this, and therefore fail to bracket off whiteness. ... The arsenal of strategies which function to normalize and make invisible whiteness (with all its unearned privileges), generally falter when whiteness is exposed, because to point out that whites are white is to call for accounting. (p. 16)

Far from encouraging accountability, much post-apartheid scholarship minimizes or completely disavows white privilege. For instance, Jolly (1995) contends that white South African academics enjoy a position of "relative privilege" (p. 24) while philosopher David Benatar (2011) mystifies racial advantage by resorting to the discursive minoritization of white people. White South Africans, who are "a minority of the population," Benatar argues, "are hardly capable of *managing* and *shaping*" the political landscape (n.p.—emphasis in the text). According to the philosopher, during apartheid only "some 'whites' were benefited from discrimination against 'blacks.'" The irony of affirming that whites "are better off now that apartheid has ended" to demonstrate that white people did not benefit from apartheid must have escaped Benatar. For these arguments to be effective, any reference to economics must be elided.

In *Class, Race, and Inequality in South Africa*, one of the most influential book-length studies on inequality in post-1994 South Africa, Jeremy Seekings and Nicoli Nattrass (2005) also rewrite apartheid history, a technique frequently deployed in "White Talk" (Steyn, 2010). The study, which in over four hundred pages examines changes in economic inequality from the beginning of apartheid until the present, argues:

> that the distributional regime in South Africa has long served to privilege one section of the population while excluding others, but the composition of the privileged group and the basis of privilege has changed over time. Initially, under apartheid, insiders and outsiders were defined primarily in racial terms. ... But the very success of [the apartheid distributional regime] in advantaging white people allowed the basis of exclusion to shift from race to class: white South Africans acquired the advantages of class that allowed them to sustain privilege in the market and cease to be dependent on continued racial discrimination. (p. 6)

As the passage illustrates, merely six pages into the volume, the study detaches white privilege from ongoing exploitation. It treats white privilege as residual, as produced in a racialized past with no bearing on the present, and ironically contends that *apartheid itself* enabled its alleged demise. The authors separate white economic advantage from its causal connection to racial domination, obfuscate the intersectional relationship between race and class, and silence racial power in the present.

Seekings and Nattrass's study also detracts attention from the reality of white economic power by focusing on income gap and class differences *among* Black South Africans. In the attempt to demonstrate "the steadily declining importance of interracial inequality and rising importance of intraracial inequality" (p. 308), the scholars write that "by 2000, there were about as many African people as white people in the top income quintile" (p. 45). However, we could use the same statistics to prove exactly the opposite. A very simple fact is mystified in the text: Whites are less than 10 percent, and not 50 percent, of the South African population. This inclusion of statistics, and the analysis thereof, reveals the employment of what Zuberi and Bonilla-Silva (2008) call *white methods*, defined as "the practical tools used to manufacture empirical data and analysis to support the racial stratification of society" (p. 18). According to Seekings and Nattrass, the fact that white people occupy approximately 50 percent of the top earning quintile does not demonstrate that racial inequality remains rampant, but shows that class alone constitutes an adequate indicator of inequality.

Yet, if class can autonomously explain inequality in post-apartheid South Africa, as the authors argue, then why direct the reader's attention to racialized phenomena such as intraracial inequality? Seekings and Nattrass's study exhibits contradictions inherent in scholarship that enforces colorblindness while producing knowledge about racial inequality. The book does not provide detailed data about the racial composition of the poorer classes, nor does it examine the significance of the striking difference in life expectancy for Black and white people. Rather than speaking to a "shift from race to class" (p. 6), these realities demonstrate that the South African class structure remains deeply racialized and that institutional racism impacts not only economic distribution, but also people's very chance to reach adulthood.

Seekings's (2007) *Race, Discrimination, and Diversity in South Africa* also manipulates apartheid history. The study argues that the apartheid system required racial classification to maintain its three main objectives, which Seekings considers to be: first, ideological (maintaining 'racial purity'); second, economic (protecting the economic privileges of whites); and third, political (maintaining the political dominance of whites; pp. 3–4). The text here denies the primacy of economics in explaining apartheid categorization and instead provides a "revisionist history" that literally "whitewashes apartheid" (Steyn, 2010, p. 542). Although Seekings admits that the 1950 Group Areas Act "led to the forced removal of almost one million people," spatial segregation is represented primarily as a way to preclude inter-racial mixing by preventing "temptation" (p. 3). Seekings represents racist ideologies as independent from, and more important than, the economic structures they sustain. This strategy portrays segregation mainly as the consequence of white people's misguided ideas and fears about miscegenation, rather than the deliberate attempt to manage difference so as to make white economic dominance and Black poverty permanent.

Seekings's study goes as far as depicting whites as the new victims of racism while announcing the end of anti-Black racism in South Africa, writing:

> Racial discrimination in economic life against black people has been largely ended in South Africa. Some lingering discrimination by white employers against black people no doubt persist, but it is probably more than offset by the effects of affirmative action. Persistent racial inequalities reflect class stratification rather than racial discrimination. (p. 1)

Seekings concedes that, in compensating for discrimination in the labor market, affirmative action has had a positive effect. Still, the "probably" indicates conjecture and a reluctance to provide empirical evidence. Racism is here also individualized and represented as the personal prejudice of certain employers. The institutional racism that enables these "white employers" to be a racialized group in a collective position of power is not addressed. As Steyn affirms, "top positions in the country remain very much in the hands of White males, who have actually increased their stake at the top in corporate South Africa in recent years" (in Grant, 2007, p. 94). While Black people are 87 percent of the economically active population, as Khaya Dlanga (2010) shows, 91 percent of South African chief executives are white. Facts such as these, which challenge Seekings's contentions, are omitted in the study.

In colorblind talk, individualization is deployed to obfuscate the causes of white advantage and to portray Black disadvantage as unrelated to racism. For example, Seekings affirms that many Black workers in South Africa are unemployable because of a long series of hindrances that begin during childhood. Black children, Seekings maintains, are raised in "home environments which are not conducive to educational success, and attend schools where the quality of education is very poor" (p. 25). In instantly locating the causes of Black poverty in the home, Seekings constructs a narrative that risks pathologizing the Black family. As Zuberi and Bonilla-Silva (2008) explain, "[a]nother way to minimize the effects of racial stratification is by portraying the effects of poverty as the causes of poverty; specifically, by focusing on the 'culture of the natives' as the problem" (p. 144). As Seekings's study intimates that deficiencies in the Black home could explain Black poverty, it fails to acknowledge poor schooling as the product of institutional racism.

Even as it announces the demise of racism, Seekings's study contends that empirical research on patterns of discrimination in the South African labor market has yet to be conducted. Rather than calling for such investigation, the scholar predicts that this research *would* find that "racial discrimination is practiced in favour of black applicants through affirmative action and BEE [Black Economic Empowerment] policies" (p. 24). Although Seekings states that "being white apparently continues to earn a premium in the labour market" (p. 24), he nevertheless represents white people as victims of discrimination. White South African children, Seekings asserts, are subjected to the "disadvantage of being white in an affirmative action environment" (p. 26). The unemployment rate in South Africa, as Dlanga (2014) shows, is only seven percent for whites and over 30 percent for Blacks. Still, Seekings blames affirmative action for allegedly foreclosing working opportunities for white people, arguing that whites are increasingly migrating "to avoid unemployment" (p. 25). Reproducing a "rhetoric of injured self-righteousness" (Steyn, 2010, p. 8), Seekings's work hence concludes by postulating a complete reversal in relations of power: White people, who continue to own 85 percent of South Africa's wealth, are depicted as the new victims of racism.

Although much South African scholarship that enforces colorblindness is produced in the social sciences, the humanities are similarly susceptible to the seduction of hegemonic racial ideologies. Proving that any discipline offers both racist and antiracist tools, literary criticism, which provides important methods for the textual analysis of colorblind rhetoric, also features works that reproduce colorblind doctrines. Examining an important piece of early post-apartheid literary criticism shall probe this contention. In "Rehearsals of Liberation: Contemporary Postcolonial Discourse and the New South Africa," Rosemary Jolly (1995) argues that it is necessary to undertake "a critical evaluation of the terms used to phrase condemnations of racism" (p. 17) in post-apartheid South Africa. The literary scholar envisions this task as a "massive critique" (p. 17) that should occur in several intersecting domains, including the economic and political spheres, both at home and abroad. In an attempt to contribute to this critique, Jolly's article takes on postcolonial scholarship as it has been applied to the South African context. Examining primarily anti-apartheid theatre and Jacques Derrida's essay "Racism's Last Word," Jolly argues that the strategies some postcolonial critics employ to denounce South African racism are misguided and represent a "reactionary measure" (p. 17). As Derrida's essay depicts South Africa as a "spectacularly other" (p. 19) and retains Manichean oppositions, Jolly contends, its effects are "neo-colonial rather than counterdiscursive" (p. 20). Because Derrida names the colonizer and the colonized, Jolly considers Derrida's essay to be at odds with its intended goal of condemning racism.

Contesting the alleged failure of deconstructionism to deconstruct Western subject–object binarism, Jolly rejects any theoretical approach that "requires the maintenance of the binary colonizer/colonized as an essential racial opposition" (p. 22) in post-apartheid South Africa. Jolly states that upholding racial categories and racial identities represents a hindrance in the quest to "triumph over the history of apartheid" (p. 22). Yet, the ambiguity of Jolly's essay provokes several questions: What does it mean to "triumph over the history of apartheid"? Is this a purely rhetorical maneuver? Who are the primary beneficiaries of the "liberation" (p. 22) that Jolly envisions? And if all binary oppositions are to be removed, how can oppression be articulated and how is resistance possible? Can scholars speak of colonialism without speaking of colonizer and colonized?

Vilashini Cooppan (2000) challenges arguments such as those presented in Jolly's article and argues that postcolonial scholars need to continue theorizing race and nation. She writes:

> For many South African intellectuals and activists schooled in the ANC's non-racialist tradition, to speak of race now is tantamount to the retention and promulgation of old apartheid classificatory categories. Not to speak of race and ethnicity, however, is to risk elision of apartheid's legacies; it is to commit that very error which 'the post-colonial' is so frequently found guilty, namely the premature announcement of the end of a system of domination and the erasure of its contemporary traces. (p. 30)

Although Jolly contends that the past should be used "as a resource for a different future" (p. 21) she does not explain how the legacies of apartheid continue to affect lives and economies in the present. In relegating racism to the past, Jolly's study disavows the centrality of white privilege in contemporary South Africa.

Jolly advocates a multiculturalism that silences race through the strategic valorization of ethnic difference. Recreating another dichotomy, she stipulates that speaking of difference in general is progressive, but focusing on racial difference in particular is reactionary. She argues that in order to achieve a "postapartheid era" it is necessary to highlight the "multiple differences among and within racial groups" (p. 23). Jolly stresses in particular that "there are marked differences within the black community in South Africa" (p. 23) and argues that eliding these differences would mean maintaining "the hegemony of apartheid" (p. 23). However, racial domination in South Africa, as in the rest of the African continent, has relied precisely on fabricating and highlighting ethnic differences among Black people as a fundamental divide-and-conquer strategy. In South Africa, Mahmood Mamdani (1996) explains, white domination was imposed by means of a "system of ethnic pluralism (institutional segregation), so that everyone, victims no less than beneficiaries, may appear as minorities" (p. 7). Since ethnic categories in South Africa remain embedded in racialized structures of power, highlighting ethnic differences, far from being a viable antiracist strategy, remains a powerful technique for silencing white economic dominance.

Jolly's essay is unable to escape the paradoxes of colorblindness. Whereas she asserts that it is necessary to "avoid essentially racial oppositions in contemporary South African literature" (p. 22), Jolly does speak of "black illiteracy," a "black majority," or a "generation of black Afrikaans writers" (pp. 27–28). In various instances, Jolly speaks of Black people by referring to "culture" (p. 24) instead of race. Employing racially coded language, however, does not mean transcending race altogether for language can sustain racial meanings also when racial terms are not explicitly used. Expressing differences in cultural rather than racial terms, as Claire Jean Kim (2000) explains, is yet another typical move of colorblind talk. Appeals to culture, which have served to refer surreptitiously to racialized Others since colonial times, continue to be a central device for the occlusion and concurrent reproduction of racial power.

Minimizing white privilege, Jolly asserts that it is "profoundly irresponsible" for white South African academics to "assume that their position of relative privilege renders them politically disabled" and that therefore "their work is futile, since it does not affect the 'masses'" (p. 24). Who are the masses that Jolly mentions here? And if these masses are not to be understood in racial terms, as Black masses, then why do they stand in opposition to *white* critics? The article exposes white anxieties about being "politically disabled" (p. 24) in a democratic South Africa. Despite Jolly's request that scholars do away with race, her work cannot transcend it.

Jolly is not the only literary scholar who views acknowledging difference in general as emancipatory, but recognizing the specific reality of racial difference as reactionary. In *Entanglement: Literary and Cultural Reflections on Post-Apartheid*, one of the most important books on post-1994 literary and cultural production, Sarah Nuttall (2009) writes:

> South African studies have, for a long time, been overdetermined by the reality of apartheid. ... A theory of entanglement can be linked in important ways to a notion of desegregation. One could argue that the system of racial segregation in the political, social and cultural structure of the country paradoxically led to ... a form of segregated theory. Segregated theory is theory premised on categories of race difference, oppression versus resistance, and perpetrators versus victims ... (p. 31)

In this work, as in "City Forms and Writing the 'Now' in South Africa," Nuttall (2004) argues that scholarship on creolization produced abroad proves useful to theorize South African social relations in the present, particularly in light of the need to grapple with "a legacy of violence in a society based on inequality." Nuttall (2009, p. 31) conceptualizes postcolonial theory's emphasis on difference as "a political resource in struggles against imperial drives to homogenize and universalize identity politics" and constructs hybridity and entanglement as intrinsically progressive categories.

Given that apartheid confined writers and critics into a persistent engagement with Black–white conflict, the abandonment of racial dualism in post-apartheid scholarship and the pursuit for alternative ways of reading is often seen as intrinsically positive. Importantly, in "Preparing Ourselves for Freedom" Albie Sachs (1998) lamented the fact that in Black apartheid literature frequently "ambiguity and contradiction are completely shut out," for he believed that "the power of art lies precisely in its capacity to expose contradictions and reveal hidden tensions" (p. 240). It is thus not surprising that Nuttall conceptualizes the move toward hybridity and away from an engagement with racial difference, literally, as an instance of "desegregation" (p. 31). However, this obfuscates the fact that hybridity is itself the historical product of racialized violence and that the eagerness to abandon notions of "oppression versus resistance" in favor of a colorblind heterogeneity is itself a racial move.

While the concept of hybridity is useful to describe the de facto historical, racial, aesthetic or sociocultural characteristics of post-colonial societies, it is not a neutral signifier. An emphasis on hybridity or entanglement can open up theoretical spaces for rethinking both apartheid and contemporary social relations. Still, it is necessary to foreground that notions of hybridity in South Africa and other post-colonial societies are inscribed within hierarchies of power that remain racially defined.[6] Discursively detaching racial and cultural mixture from the institutional racism that produced them entrenches the structures of domination that the move purports to challenge. As Cooppan (2000) explains, "to imagine, as contemporary post-colonial studies sometimes seems to do, that we can simply choose one (hybrid) model of identity over another (particularist) one ... is to forget precisely the ways in which these conceptual categories are collectively bound to one another" (p. 29). Rather than being progressive per se, as Joshua Lund (2006) writes, hybridity is often invoked to undercut affirmative action policies, arguments for reparations, and land redistribution in Latin America, South Africa, the United States and elsewhere. Not only are celebratory notions of hybridity unable to create a "genuinely post-colonial future" (Jolly, 1995, p. 21), but the example of Latin American societies in which *mestizaje* is the dominant national ideology teaches us that invocations of 'mixture' often serve merely the interests of elites attempting to protect their racial privileges.

In *Entanglement*, the valorization of hybridity and critique of scholarship that emphasizes racial power are accompanied by attempts to rescue white people from stigmatization. It should not be taken for granted that Nuttall's study, comparable with what we saw in Seekings and Nattrass (2005), directs the reader's attention towards the growth of the Black middle-class and increase in intraracial inequality but silences white economic dominance. As Steyn and Foster (2008) affirm, "black elites are a decoy, drawing attention away from where to bulk of the country's wealth is still to be found: middle- and upper-class white South Africa" (p. 42). Scholarship that idealizes abstract notions of hybridity, mixture, créolité, entanglement, or difference while refusing to acknowledge Black people's concrete experiences of racial oppression, further reinforces the normativity of whiteness.

The enforcement of colorblindness through the appropriation of deconstructionism and postcolonial theory is not confined to literary scholarship. In "The Modern Seduction of Race: Whither Social Constructionism?," Soudien (2012b) also cites Derrida in an attempt to demonize racial categories. While Jolly (1995) accuses Derrida of reproducing colonial logics, Soudien co-opts Derrida to argue that the employment of the category 'race' constitutes a challenge much more serious "than its manifestations in apartheid" (p. 20). Appropriating Derrida's powerful definition of apartheid, Soudien contends that *race itself* is the "most racism of racisms" (p. 20). Although Derrida's writing is condemned in one case and valued in the other, its strategic location in Jolly and Soudien's texts fulfills the same function: antiracist thought is decontextualized in these studies and put at the service of racial power.

Even the writings of Black Consciousness leader Steve Biko are distorted and appropriated. In *Realising the Dream: Unlearning the Logic of Race in the South African School*, Soudien (2012a) co-opts Biko's reconceptualization of apartheid racial categories in order to demonize affirmative action. Correspondingly, in "Apartheid Race Categories: Daring to Question their Continued Use," Erasmus (2012) invokes the Black Consciousness Movement to enforce colorblindness. She states that in the 1970s the Movement defined blackness "*not* as a race category or classification, but rather a global political identification premised on resistance to oppression in contexts of white supremacy" (p. 1—emphasis in the text). Erasmus here misinterprets the gesture. Biko's politicized understanding of blackness was not a theoretical intervention in the rethinking of apartheid racial categories per se. Biko was concerned with the concrete need to forge solidarities among people of color that could lead to the dismantlement of apartheid. Biko's definition of blackness is intrinsically related to racial oppression. For Biko (1971/2002), Blacks are "those who are by law or tradition politically, economically and socially discriminated against as a group in the South African society and [identify] themselves as a unit in the struggle towards the realization of their aspirations" (p. 48). Biko makes clear that being racialized as "non-white" is a necessary precondition to claiming blackness. Given that he envisioned "complete ownership of land" (p. 149) for Black people, Biko would radically oppose any attempt to silence racial dispossession today.

In "How Do I Live in This Strange Place?", a philosophical essay that sparked heated debate about whiteness in the South African press and in online forums, Samantha Vice (2010) also cites Biko. Arguing that white privilege is "nonvoluntary in its origins" (p. 325), Vice invokes Biko to further corroborate her claims. "It is not as if whites are allowed to enjoy privilege only when they declare their solidarity with the ruling party," Biko claims in Vice's quote. However, Biko's understanding of racial power speaks to a different concern: not to white privilege as something that "may be more or less consciously embraced or rejected" (p. 325), as Vice defines it, but as something that *cannot* be simply rejected through an act of will. Biko explains that profiting from white privilege does not require active allegiance to white supremacist parties or ideologies. At the same time, he sustains precisely the opposite of what Vice asserts: that white privilege is not a somatic habit that can be minimized by changing our mindsets. It is not the prelapsarian innocence of whites that Biko articulates, but rather white people's collective responsibility for the reproduction of the racist status quo.

Emphasizing the primacy of economics in understanding and combating racial domination, Biko made clear that in a democratic South Africa "for meaningful change to appear there needs to be an attempt at reorganizing the whole economic pattern" (p. 149). Although Vice recognizes that in post-1994 South Africa "materially nothing much has changed for anyone, black or white" (p. 332), she does not suggest that one appropriate reaction to privilege would be to work towards relinquishing some of the *material* benefits of whiteness. Vice's project presumes that white moral regeneration can occur prior to, and irrespective of, wealth redistribution. The task of 'lessening' whiteness need not cost white people anything. In collapsing white habits and white advantages, Vice silences white agency and fails to make visible white privilege as something *wanted* and guarded through the ongoing exploitation of people of color. The location of antiracist thought within much South African scholarship that enforces colorblindness—whether in literature, education, sociology, or philosophy—reveals the ongoing currency of appropriation as a technique of silencing and the centrality of active investment in the production of racialized knowledge across disciplinary boundaries.

Conclusion

On June 6, 2014, the South African Institute of Race Relations (IRR) issued a press release titled "Affirmative Action is Killing Babies and must be Scrapped." Citing the death of three children after they drank contaminated water in the municipality of Bloemhof, the CEO of the IRR Frans Cronje argued that "the officials responsible for these deaths were appointed, at least in part, on grounds of race-based affirmative action and that *a direct causal link therefore exists between the policy and the deaths*" (IRR, 2014, n.p.—italics in the text). The demonization of affirmative action detracts attention from white responsibility for the ongoing abject life conditions faced by most Black South Africans and speaks powerfully to the *possessive investment in whiteness* (Lipsitz, 2006). Although the consequences of racial domination in the present are nowhere as evident as in the differential life expectancy for Black and white people, even the IRR today publishes colorblind life expectancy statistics that do not once mention the word *race* (see IRR, 2012a, 2012b). Rather than enabling racial justice, the Institute funds scholarship that enforces colorblindness (see Holborn, 2010). It is troubling that institutions allegedly devoted to making racism visible silence institutional racism.

The IRR is not an exception. Strikingly, South African scholars who embrace colorblind doctrines are appointed to administrative positions created to rectify racialized imbalances in the student and faculty body. Crain Soudien, for example, condemns affirmative action policies (see Soudien, 2012a), yet he formerly chaired the Ministerial Review Committee into Transformation in Higher Education and is currently deputy vice-chancellor in the area of transformation and social responsiveness at the University of Cape Town (UCT). The term 'transformation' in the post-apartheid context has come to indicate official and unofficial attempts to redress racial inequality, especially in educational institutions and the workplace. That the scholarship of an official who should guarantee desegregation demonizes measures needed to make deracialization possible speaks powerfully to the institutionalization of colorblindness in South African academia.

This has serious material consequences. Concerned about racial inequality and ongoing incidents of overt racism on campuses around the nation, in July 2014 the South African Human Rights Commission hosted a national hearing that addressed the lack of transformation in South African universities. In the meantime, UCT unveiled a new admission policy that took a step away from race-based affirmative action, with 75% of incoming students now being "selected without race being taken into account" (Price, 2014a, n.p.). If most Black students remain excluded from access to higher education, South African faculty of color fare even worse. In 2012, there were merely 34 Black and 29 Coloured full-time female professors *in the entire country* (Price, 2014b, n.p.). As if that was not enough, Afrikaans universities such as Stellenbosch and North West continue to vehemently resist change (De Vos, 2014, n.p.).

In a society in which racial inequality is rampant, the desire to suppress race as a category of analysis, as we have seen, always creates textual paradoxes. It also produces meta-discursive contradictions. It is ironic, for example, that Gerhard Maré should direct a Centre for Critical Research on Race and Identity while insisting that we should no longer talk about race. If "race thinking," as Maré argues, is not "appropriate in a democratic 'non racial' South Africa" (Maré, 2003, p. 27; see also Maré, 2001, 2013), then why study race? If race does not matter in South Africa, then what is the value of engaging it academically? The fact that Maré has devoted most of his recent scholarship to examining race, implies that, at least to the scholar himself, race does matter a great deal.

As has hopefully become clear through this study, the recurrence of racial disavowal and the rhetorical contradictions it textually produces need to be adequately accounted for in the assessment of post-apartheid scholarship and beyond. The presence of dominant racial ideologies in the works examined herein cannot be considered fortuitous and much less the product of ignorance. It is the consequence of racialized knowledge and is emblematic of an active investment in maintaining the status quo. Although many white people may "[take] for granted unearned entitlements that come at the expense of racialized others, and generally [lack] insight into the normalized racial order" (Steyn, 2012, p. 11), ignorance cannot explain the *systematic* promotion of colorblindness across national contexts, disciplines, and discourses that continues to sustain white hegemony across national borders (see Lipsitz, 2011; Mngxitama, 2009; Nascimento, 1989; Winant, 2001). Importantly, although ignorance was structurally produced by the apartheid regime through segregation, Steve Biko insisted on bringing white people's knowledge about their privilege to the forefront of analysis, rather than their alleged obliviousness about racial domination (see Biko, 2002, p. 19). Scholarship on whiteness that does not account for *knowledge* and *agency* risks reinscribing colorblindness, "an ally to White supremacy" (Simpson, 2008, p. 142). In grappling with the rhetorics of racial power and the reality of racial inequity in the present, it is useful to shift the academic lens from white ignorance to deliberate disavowal.

Since colorblind doctrines dominate South African academia, too few courses today give adequate attention to apartheid and even fewer engage Steve Biko's writings. Revealingly, during the first semester of 2010 the Department of Historical Studies at the UCT offered three graduate courses on the Jewish experience, one of them specifically on anti-Semitism, but *none* on anti-Black racism in South Africa or explicitly on apartheid. In the meantime, not unlike Ethnic Studies programs in Arizona and the United States at large, the UCT Centre for African Studies has to battle to ensure its continuing existence. As white domination persists, the South African case reveals itself as symptomatic of an ongoing *global* assault on the knowledges and lives of people of color. Millions of students of all backgrounds are being indoctrinated into naturalizing and reproducing racial inequality.

Acknowledgments

This study is indebted to the scholarship, insights, and invaluable support of Carl Gutiérrez-Jones, George Lipsitz, Francisco Lomelí, and Abdul JanMohamed for which I am deeply thankful. Thank you Pallavi Benerjee, Ulrike Muench, Alison Reed, and LaTonya Trotter for reading the manuscript and providing many helpful suggestions. Special thanks to Neica Michelle Murray, who read two different versions of this article and improved both. I am grateful to Harry Garuba for providing resources and inspiring conversations. I thank Mark Schoenfield and the Department of English for providing me with the time and resources to complete this article. I thank the librarians in the African Studies Library at UCT and Vanderbilt University for their help and professionalism. Thank you, Zama Hadebe, for the support and generosity. Last but not least, I thank the anonymous reviewers for their constructive critique and invaluable comments, and Dreama Moon and Michelle Holling for their helpful suggestions and support with this project.

Notes

[1] In line with its South African usage, herein I employ the term *Black* both to denote specifically the Indigenous African population (approx. 79.4% of the total South African population) and to include the Coloured community (8.9%) and the Indian/Asian population (2.6%). This does not mean ignoring that, historically and presently, there are significant differences among and within these groups. *Black* is herein thus sometimes used as synonymous with *people of color*, a term much more common in the U.S. context than in the South African. This usage of the term "Black" also recognizes that Black people represent the vast majority of the South African population. For racial demographics see: Statistics South Africa (2012). On the Marikana massacre see, for example, Alexander, Lekgowa, Mmope, Sinwell, and Xezwi, (2013) and Nhlabathi (2013).

[2] I borrow the term *racial power* from Claire Jean Kim (2000) who defines it as follows: "Racial power refers to the racial status quo's systemic tendency towards self-reproduction. It finds concrete political, economic, social, and cultural processes that tend cumulatively to perpetuate White dominance over non-Whites" (p. 2).

[3] On racial inequality in South Africa see, for example, Ansell (2006), Dlanga (2010), Emery (2008), Levenstein (2010), Ratele and Laubscher (2010), and Winant (2001). On the land question, see, for example, Ntsebeza (2011) and Ntsebeza and Hall (2007).

[4] For example, South African scholarship that enforces colorblindness also exists in communication (Bornman, 2011), demography (Moultrie & Dorrington, 2012), law (Stone & Erasmus, 2012), and most likely any other field that engages race and racism in some capacity.

[5] For book-length studies by the author that enforce colorblindness, see Jansen (2009b, 2011).

[6] See Gqola (2010) on white appropriations of 'racial mixture' discourses in post-apartheid South Africa.

References

Alexander, N. (2007). Affirmative action and the perpetuation of racial identities in post-apartheid South Africa. *Transformation, 63*, 92–108.

Alexander, P., Lekgowa, T., Mmope, B., Sinwell, L., & Xezwi, B. (2013). *Marikana: A view from the mountain and a case to answer*. Johannesburg: Jacana Media.

Ansell, A.E. (2006). Casting a blind eye: The ironic consequences of color-blindness in South Africa and the United States. *Critical Sociology, 32*(2/3), 333–356.

Bauman, R., & Briggs, C.L. (2003). *Voices of modernity: Language ideologies and the politics of inequality*. Cambridge: Cambridge University Press.

Benatar, D. (2011). Why Samantha Vice is wrong on whiteness. *Politicsweb*, 21. Retrieved from http://www.politicsweb.co.za/politicsweb/view/politicsweb/en/page71619?oid=256436&sn=Detail

Biko, S. (2002). *I write what I like: A selection of his writings*. Chicago: University of Chicago Press. (Original work published 1971).

Bornman, E. (2011). Patterns of intergroup attitudes in South Africa after 1994. *International Journal of Intercultural Relations, 35*, 729–748.

Conway, D. (2008a). Contesting the masculine state: White male war resisters in apartheid South Africa. In J. Parpart & M. Zalewski (Eds.). *Rethinking the man question: Sex, gender and violence in international relations* (pp. 127–142). London: Zed.

Conway, D. (2008b). Masculinities and narrating the past: Experiences of researching white men who refused to serve in the Apartheid Army. *Qualitative Research* 8(3), 339–346.

Cooppan, V. (2000). W(h)ither post-colonial studies? Towards the transnational study of race and nation. In L. Chrisman & B. Parry (Eds.), *Postcolonial theory and criticism* (pp. 1–35). Cambridge: DS Brewer.

De Vos, P. (2014). White, Afrikaans universities: When will they truly transform? *Daily Maverick*. Retrieved from http://www.dailymaverick.co.za/opinionista/2014-07-03-white-afrikaans-universities-when-will-they-truly-transform/#.U9N_N4229kg

Distiller, N., & Steyn, M.E. (2004). *Under construction: 'Race' and identity in South Africa today.* Oxford: Heinemann.
Dlanga, K. (2010). It's still too white at the top. *CSI: Year in review.* Supplement to the *Mail & Guardian, 26*(49), 12.
Dlanga, K. (2014). Affirmative action is here, deal with it. *Mail & Guardian.* Retrieved from http://mg.co.za/article/2014-01-31-affirmative-action-is-here-deal-with-it
Drzewiecka, J., & Steyn, M. (2012). Racial immigrant incorporation: Material-symbolic articulation of identities. *Journal of International and Intercultural Communication, 5*(1), 1–19.
Emery, A. (2008). Class and race domination and transformation in South Africa. *Critical Sociology, 34*(3), 409–443.
Erasmus, Z. (2010). Confronting the categories: Equitable admissions without apartheid race classification. *South African Journal of Higher Education, 24*(2), 244–257.
Erasmus, Z. (2012). Apartheid race categories: Daring to question their continued use. *Transformation, 79,* 1–12.
Garuba, H. (2012). Closing reflections on 'Revisiting apartheid's race categories.' *Transformation, 79,* 173–177.
Gotanda, N. (1995). A critique of 'our constitution is colorblind.' In K. Crenshaw *et al.* (Eds.), *Critical race theory: The key writings that formed the movement* (pp. 258–75). New York, NY: New Press.
Gqola, P.D. (2010). *What is slavery to me?: Postcolonial/slave memory in post-apartheid South Africa.* Johannesburg: Wits University Press.
Grant, T. (2007). Transformation challenges in the South African workplace: A conversation with Melissa Steyn of INCUDISA. *Business Communication Quarterly, 70*(1), 93–98.
Holborn, L. (2010). *The long shadow of apartheid: Race in South Africa since 1994.* Johannesburg: South African Institute of Race Relations.
IRR. (2012a). *The South African development index (SADI): Report for first quarter 2011.* Retrieved from http://www.sairr.org.za/services/development-projects/south-africandevelopment-index/2011/SADI-2011-02.pdf
IRR. (2012b). *The South African development index (SADI): Third update for 2011.* Retrieved from http://www.sairr.org.za/services/development-projects/SADI/Third%20update%20report.pdf
IRR. (2014). Affirmative action is killing babies and must be scrapped. 6 June 2014. Retrieved from http://irr.org.za/reports-and-publications/media-releases/affirmative-action-is-killing-babies-and-must-be-scrapped/view#.U7KsLo229kg
Jansen, J.D. (2009a). Intellectuals, the state and universities in South Africa. In W. Mervin Gumede and L. Dikeni (Eds.), *The poverty of ideas: South African democracy and the Retreat of intellectuals.* Auckland Park, South Africa: Jacana.
Jansen, J.D. (2009b). *Knowledge in the blood: Confronting race and the apartheid past.* Stanford, CA: Stanford University Press, 2009.
Jansen, J.D. (2011). *We need to talk.* Northcliff, South Africa: Bookstorm.
Jolly, R. (1995). Rehearsals of liberation: Contemporary postcolonial discourse and the new South Africa. *PMLA, 110*(1), 17–29.
Kim, C.J. (2000). *Bitter fruit: The politics of Black-Korean conflict in New York City.* New Haven, CT: Yale U Press.
Lawrence, C.R. III (1995). The id, the ego, and equal protection: Reckoning with unconscious racism. In K. Crenshaw *et al.* (Eds.), *Critical race theory: The key writings that formed the movement* (pp. 235–57). New York, NY: New Press.
Levenstein, K. (2010). Let the Gini out of the bottle. *Mail & Guardian.* Retrieved from http://mg.co.za/article/2010-02-04-let-the-gini-out-bottle
Lipsitz, G. (2006). *The possessive investment in whiteness: How white people profit from identity politics.* Philadelphia, PA: Temple University Press.
Lipsitz, G. (2011). *How racism takes place.* Philadelphia, PA: Temple University Press.
Lund, J. (2006). *The impure imagination: Toward a critical hybridity in Latin American writing.* Minneapolis: University of Minnesota Press.
Mamdani, M. (1996). *Citizen and subject: Contemporary Africa and the legacy of late colonialism.* Princeton, NJ: Princeton University Press.
Maré, G. (2001). Race, democracy and opposition in South African politics: As other a way as possible. *Democratization, 8*(1), 85–102.

Maré, G. (2003). Non-racialism in the struggle against apartheid. *Society in Transition, 34*(1), 13–37.
Maré, G. (2013). The cradle to the grave: Reflections on race thinking. *Thesis Eleven, 115,* 43–57.
Matthews, S. (2012). White anti-racism in post-apartheid South Africa. *Politikon, 39*(2), 171–188.
Mbembe, A. (2014). Blind to colour—or just blind? *Mail & Guardian.* Retrieved from http://mg.co.za/article/2014-07-17-blind-to-colour-or-just-blind/
Mills, C. (1997). *The racial contract.* Ithaca, NY: Cornell University Press.
Mills, C. (2007). White ignorance. In S. Sullivan & N. Tuana (Eds.), *Race and epistemologies of ignorance* (pp. 11–38.). Albany, NY: SUNY Press.
Mngxitama, A. (2009). Blacks can't be racist. *New Frank Talk, 3.* Johannesburg: Sankara.
Morrison, T. (1992). *Playing in the dark: Whiteness and the literary imagination.* New York, NY: Vintage Books.
Motlanthe, K., & Jordan, Z.P. (2010). Social origins. In B. Turok (Ed.), *The historical roots of the ANC.* Auckland Park, South Africa: Jacana Media.
Moultrie, T.A., & Dorrington, R.E. (2012). Used for ill; used for good: A century of collecting data on race in South Africa. *Ethnic and Racial Studies, 35*(8), 1447–1146.
Nascimento, A. (1989). *Brazil, mixture or massacre?: Essays in the genocide of a Black people.* Trans. Elisa Larkin Nascimento. Dover, Mass: The Majority Press.
Nhlabathi, H. (2013). Witness admits to police blunder in Marikana massacre. *The Sowetan.* Retrieved from http://www.sowetanlive.co.za/news/2013/04/30/witness-admits-to-police-blunder-in-marikana-massacre
Ntsebeza, L. (2011). The land question: Exploring obstacles to land redistribution in South Africa. In I. Shapiro & K. Tabeau (Eds.), *After apartheid: Reinventing South Africa?* (pp. 294–308). Charlottesville: University of Virginia Press.
Ntsebeza, L., & Hall, R. (Eds.). (2007). *The land question in South Africa: The challenge of transformation and redistribution.* Cape Town: HSRC Press.
Nuttall, S. (2004). City forms and writing the 'now' in South Africa. *Journal of Southern African Studies, 30*(4), 731–748.
Nuttall, S. (2009). *Entanglement: Literary and cultural reflections on post-apartheid.* Johannesburg: Wits University Press.
Price, M. (2014a). UCT's new student admission policy explained. *UCT Daily News.* Retrieved from http://www.uct.ac.za/dailynews/?id=8735
Price, M. (2014b). Staff transformation at UCT. *UCT Daily News.* Retrieved from http://www.uct.ac.za/dailynews/?id=8752
Ruggunan, S., & Maré, G. (2012). Race classification at the University of KwaZulu-Natal: Purposes, sites and practices. *Transformation, 79,* 47–68.
Ratele, K., & Laubscher, L. (2010). Making white lives: Neglected meanings of whiteness from apartheid South Africa. *Psychology in Society, 40,* 83–99.
Sachs, A. (1998). Preparing ourselves for freedom. In D. Attridge & R. Jolly. (Eds.), *Writing South Africa* (pp. 239–248). New York, NY: Cambridge University Press.
Seekings, J. (2007). *Race, discrimination, and diversity in South Africa.* Rondebosch: Centre for Social Science Research, University of Cape Town.
Seekings, J., & Nattrass, N. (2005). *Class, race, and inequality in South Africa.* New Haven, CT: Yale University Press.
Shome, R., & Hedge, R.S. (2002). Postcolonial approaches to communication: Charting the terrain, engaging the intersections. *Communication Theory, 12*(3), 249–270.
Simpson, J.L. (2008). The color-blind double bind: Whiteness and the (im)possibility of dialogue. *Communication Theory, 18,* 139–159.
Soudien, C. (2012a). *Realising the dream: Unlearning the logic of race in the South African School.* Cape Town: Human Sciences Research Council.
Soudien, C. (2012b). The modern seduction of race: Wither social constructionism. *Transformation, 79,* 18–38.
Statistics South Africa. (2012). Mid-year population estimates, 2011. *Statistical Release P0203.* Retrieved from http://www.statssa.gov.za/publications/P0302/P03022011.pdf
Steyn, M.E. (1998). White identity in context: A personal narrative. In T.K. Nakayama & J.N. Martin (Eds.), *Whiteness: The communication of social identity* (pp. 264–278). Thousand Oaks, CA: Sage.

Steyn, M.E. (2001). *Whiteness just isn't what it used to be: White identity in a changing South Africa*. Albany: State University of New York Press.

Steyn, M.E. (2004). Rehabilitating a whiteness disgraced: Afrikaner *white talk* in post-apartheid South Africa. *Communication Quarterly, 52*(2), 143–169.

Steyn, M.E. (2005). White talk: White South Africans and the management of diasporic whiteness. In A.J. López (Ed.), *Postcolonial whiteness: A critical reader on race and empire* (pp. 119–136). Albany, NY: SUNY Press.

Steyn, M.E. (2007). As the postcolonial moment deepens: A response to Green, Sonn, and Matsebula. *South African Journal of Psychology, 37*(3), 420–424.

Steyn, M.E. (2010). "The creed of the white kid:" A diss-apology. In T.K. Nakayama & R.T. Halualani (Eds.), *The handbook of critical intercultural communication* (pp. 534–548). Chichester: Wiley-Blackwell.

Steyn, M.E. (2012). The ignorance contract: recollections of apartheid childhoods and the construction of epistemologies of ignorance. *Identities, 19*(1), 8–25.

Steyn, M.E., & Conway, D. (2010). Introduction: Intersecting whiteness, interdisciplinary debates. *Ethnicities, 10*(3), 283–291.

Steyn, M.E., & Foster, D. (2008). Repertoires for talking white: Resistant whiteness in post-apartheid South Africa. *Ethnic and Racial Studies, 31*(1), 25–51.

Stone, L., & Erasmus, Y. (2012). Race thinking and the law in post-1994 South Africa. *Transformation, 79*(1), 119–143.

Vice, S. (2010). How do I live in this strange place? *Journal of Social Philosophy, 41*(3), 323–342.

West, M., & Schmidt, J.M. (2010). Preface. Whiteness studies in South Africa: A South African perspective. *English in Africa, 37*(1), 9–13.

Winant, H. (2001). *The world is a ghetto: Race and democracy since World War II*. New York, NY: Basic Books.

Zuberi, T., & Bonilla-Silva, E. (2008). *White logic, white methods: Racism and methodology*. Lahnam, MD: Rowman & Littlefield Publications.

Queer Intercultural Relationality: An Autoethnography of Asian–Black (Dis)Connections in White Gay America

Shinsuke Eguchi

For this critical intercultural inquiry, I as an Asian/Japanese transnational cisgendered gay man write my autoethnography of queer (or non-heteronormative) Asian-Black (dis) connections. Specifically, I challenge, interrogate, and problematize my queer intercultural production of desire and attraction as I engage in my critical autoethnographic interrogation of dialogues with five Asian/Japanese transnational gay men who have previously engaged in queer Asian–Black relationality. In so doing, I intend to create a potential point of departure to decenter the discursive and material effects of White gay normativity in the knowledge production of Asian queer male desire and attraction.

[M]arking the territory of Whiteness is not only theoretically significant but crucial to social justice. (Moon & Nakayama, 2005, p. 88)

"American" has become nearly synonymous with [W]hiteness. (Holling, 2006, p. 92)

It is around 1 am on July 21, 2013. With my Black gay friend, Kenny, I open the door of a Korean restaurant's bar and lounge in the Hell's Kitchen district of Manhattan, New York. As a weekly Saturday night event, the bar/lounge offers a queer (or non-heteronormative) space for Asian men and their admirers. As soon as we enter into the bar, I recall the atmosphere of an Asian gay bar called The Web, which closed a couple of years ago. As I reimagine The Web, we are served by a topless, tall, and well-built Asian male bartender. While we order drinks, I take in the whole space. I realize there are some Black men I have previously met. After getting drinks, Kenny and I begin to chat with these Black men. We are also introduced to their Asian friends. The hours pass so quickly. It is little after 3 am. As we leave the bar/lounge, I say to Kenny, "Wow . . . I have not seen a lot of rice-queens (meaning White male admirers of Asian men) tonight."

From this personal, intellectual, and political space, I write my autoethnography of queer Asian–Black (dis)connections to illustrate the multiplicity of Asian queer male desire and attraction for this critical intercultural inquiry. Since I moved to the US from Japan in 2001, I have repeatedly observed *younger* and *feminine* Asian men desiring *older* and *masculine* rice-queens in multiple queer cultural spaces (i.e., bars, clubs, restaurants, and online sites). As Lim (2014) notes, "In the Western context, the [W]hite, urban, gay male youth is a generic icon of queer boys, while Asian boy is a subcultural category referencing the racialized fetishes of an older white male for the diminutive and effeminized Asian male" (p. 27). These Western queer subcultural productions of illusive binaries reveal the historical continuum of racial formation in a larger global and colonial context (e.g., Ayres, 1999; Fung, 2005; Han, 2006; Lim, 2014; Phua, 2007; Poon, 2006). That is, an ideological reproduction of Orientalism: "Asians were inferior to and deformations of Europeans" (Okihiro, 1994, p. 11). To disidentify with the ideological framing, I have *alternatively* engaged in my queer relationships with Black/African American men. My "oppositional" desire has emerged as I have internalized the Black–White binary paradigm that "one group, [B]lack, constitutes the prototypical minority group" (Delgado & Stefancic, 2012, p. 75). Given the US American cultural context in which Asian Americans have been historically positioned as *forever foreign* (Nakayama, 2012), I utilize the Black–White binary as a discursive strategy to measure my queer intercultural practices of belonging. The irony of my desire, however, is its reinforcement that I am actually a queer foreign subject who *desperately* wants to be a part of the (gay) US America.

To complicate my queer desire and attraction as an ideological product in this essay, I engage in my critical autoethnographic interrogation of dialogues with five Asian/Japanese transnational cisgendered gay men living in New York[1] who have previously been involved in queer Asian–Black relationships. As Chávez (2013) and Yep (2013) encourage, ongoing articulations of racialized, gendered, and classed knowledge(s) embedded in the material realities of GLBTQ (gay-lesbian-bisexual-transgender-queer) people of color remain relevant to the field of international and intercultural communication. For example, the previous collections of interdisciplinary literature on Asian queer male identities and experiences (e.g., Fung, 2005; Han, 2006, 2008, 2009a; Phua, 2007; Poon, 2006; Poon & Ho, 2008; Lim, 2014) pay particular attention to their homogenized and essentialized desires for Whiteness. Queer *color-to-color* connections between Asian American men and non-White men remain generally unknown and understudied. Such relationships are silenced. The overemphasis on the queer eroticism of Asian–White encounters reproduces aesthetic, intellectual, and political *disconnections* between *Asian* and *Black*. In addition to my own investment, however, my intercultural participation in New York's gay communities offered me multiple places/spaces to observe various forms of queer Asian–Black relationality. For that reason, I have revisited New York for a month in the summer of 2013 to conduct this autoethnographic writing to reconnect some of the disconnections between Asians and Blacks in White gay America. By interrogating such queer intercultural (dis)connections, I intend to create a potential point of departure to decenter the discursive and material effects of Whiteness in the knowledge productions of Asian queer male desires and attractions.

I employ my autoethnography as an autobiographical genre of performative writing that explicitly explicates, elucidates, and elaborates on the social, cultural, political, and historical. Alexander (2012) writes that autoethnography is "a critical methodology or approach to doing critical cultural examinations that might shape the mode of investigating experience but not establish a standard of experience" (p. 141). I recognize that autoethnography has not lacked controversy as a method of research. Some may argue that autoethnography is narcissistically about an individual, that it lacks the rigor of a critical/cultural research method. Muñoz (1999) replies to that claim by stating, "Autoethnography is a strategy that seeks to disrupt the hierarchical economy of colonial images and representations by making visible the presence of subaltern energies and urgencies in metropolitan culture" (p. 82). Adapting this line of thinking, I argue that autoethnography is a powerful and radical method to disrupt normative systems of knowledge productions to investigate historically marginalized experiences (e.g., Boylorn & Orbe, 2014; Spry, 2001). Autoethnography serves a political and intellectual move to call out the taken-for-granted idea and to diversify voices in the academy (e.g., Adams & Holman Jones, 2008; Calafell, 2012; Griffin, 2012). Thus, I value that the methodological praxis of autoethnography allows me to complicate the socially and culturally normative beliefs about Asian queer male desire and attraction.

To conduct this autoethnographic interrogation, I pay attention to simultaneous functions of what Yep (2010) would call my thick intersectionalities, multiple identity positionings that mirror macrostructural implications. I acknowledge that my immigration status offers me a space of privilege to critique the queer eroticism of Asian/Eastern-White/Western colonial encounters. I am a Japanese national who is a US university faculty member with a PhD. Given today's political alliance between Japan and the US, I have been able to quickly achieve my US permanent residency (also known as a green card). This ticket allows me to stay single, date men, enjoy my American gay lifestyle, and/or travel back and forth between Japan and the US. However, I can see that these choices of "freedom" would not exist if I didn't have the privilege. Yep (2013) notes, "We should attend to the lived experiences and biographies of the persons occupying a particular intersection, including how they inhabit and make sense of their own bodies" (p. 123). Thus, my critique is not to object to any Asian male migrants participating in the queer eroticism of Asian–White colonial encounters. My purpose with this autoethnography is to illustrate instead the multiplicity of Asian queer male desires and attractions.

Global–Local Circuits of White Gay Normativity

Having lived in a US–Japan borderland, I have seen how the social and performative constructions of White gay normativity circulate globally. Various scholars (e.g., Alexander, 2008; Calafell, 2009; Chávez, 2013; Eng, 2010; Johnson, 2001; McCune, 2008; Moreman & McIntosh, 2010; Snorton, 2014; Yep, 2013) have also argued that Whiteness hegemonically structures global and local formations of GLBTQ identities and spaces. Lee (2003) observed that "sexual minorities who are not [W]hite, male, and affluent remain relatively invisible in their different localities" (p. 160). Some of the Western knowledge structuring and organizing GLBTQ personal, institutional, and cultural lives does not address racialized and classed concerns and needs for GLBTQ people of color within and beyond the US (Chávez, 2013; Yep 2013). The White capitalistic hetero-patriarchal circulations of power reproduce the queer formations of homo-normative thinking and politics (e.g., Cohen, 1997; Ferguson, 2004).

The US queer cultural productions of bars, clubs, and neighborhoods illustrate the discursive and material effects of White US middle-class gay normativity (Nero, 2005). For example, White gay men are the aesthetic center of desire and performance (e.g., Calafell, 2009; Moreman & McIntosh, 2010). Black/African American men, perceived as a "threat" and/or "dangerous," are often denied entrance to the White middle-class normative gay bars and clubs (Han, 2009b). By gathering in corners of gay bars and clubs, Asian American men are often waiting to *be chosen* by White rice-queens (Han, 2008). Music played in queer bars and clubs reflects the US popular cultural trends of White gay men (e.g., McCune, 2014; Muñoz, 2009). The queer cultural areas, which are historically known as gay neighborhoods (e.g., New York's West Village and Chelsea, San Francisco's Castro, and Los Angeles' West Hollywood), continue to be overwhelmingly White and male (e.g., Nero, 2005; Han 2009b). Muñoz (2009) points out, "The contemporary [W]hite gay male clone" dominates major gay neighborhoods in metropolitan areas such as New York, Los Angeles, and San Francisco (p. 60). In this context, I maintain that marginalizing women and people of color from various queer cultural spaces is a discursive and ideological practice to systematically re/center Whiteness and normalize the material and aesthetic conditions of White gay male sexuality and experience.

Given the powerful circuits of White gay normativity, Western cultural discourses about coming out of the closet function as a hegemonic measurement to evaluate the progressivity of queer of color sexualities (e.g., Decena, 2008; Lim, 2014; McCune, 2014; Ross, 2005; Snorton, 2014; Yep & Lescure, 2014). As McCune (2008) suggested, "'Coming out of the closet' has been the contemporary niche phrase to articulate the universal threshold experience of sexual self-discovery and self-fulfillment" (p. 298).

The Western cultural production of a closet paradigm reinforces the idea that (homo)sexual identifications are singular and stable. The closeted paradigm also reinforces the discursive illusion of a rigid binary between heterosexuality and homosexuality. Moreover, the practice of being in the closet signifies oppressive conditions of non-normative sexualities in the post-Stonewall context of gay liberation movement era (Suganuma, 2012). However, the complex particularities of racialized and classed sexualities are overlooked. Ross (2005) critiqued the closet paradigm as raceless and classless. He continued, "This narrative of progress carries the residue, and occasionally the outright intention, borne with evolutionary notions of the uneven development of the races from primitive darkness to civilized enlightenment" (Ross, 2005, p. 163). The closet paradigm emerges from the epistemological world of White elite metropolitan gay men (Lim, 2014).

For example, US popular culture discourses about Black men on the Down Low (DL) have reproduced the images of Black sexualities as *backward*. Since men on the DL are assumed to cheat on their wives/girlfriends with other men, they are re/presented as closeted, secretive, and deceptive. However, McCune (2014) argued that "[t]he DL, like the culture of dissemblance, offers a way for men to navigate the complex web of gender, race, class, and sexuality" (p. 7). African Americans have historically practiced the performative mode of "quiet as kept" to survive under White supremacy (Snorton, 2014). The performative modes of Black masculinities and sexualities have been negotiated under the sociopolitical and economic constraints of White discipline and surveillance (McCune, 2008, 2014). In this historically oppressive context, men on the DL engage in the racialized, gendered, and classed practices of passing as straight for their survival (McCune, 2008, 2014; Snorton, 2014). DL men are neither in the closet nor coming out.

This contemporary discourse of coming out of the closet becomes the powerful signification of White/Western modernity in the historical continuum of US American cultural imperialism. Chávez (2013) witnessed that gay liberation rights "can both operate imperialistically by which all others are evaluated, and they can become a rationale for imperialist expansion" (p. 87). In the case of Japan, the advanced images of White/Western gay cultural liberation offer a discursive measurement to assess the backward positionality of queer Japanese culture (Suganuma, 2012). The cultural adaptation of White gay normativity is assumed to globalize the construction of queer Japan to be compatible with the West. Japanese historical and local knowledge about gender, sexuality, and body are erased, marginalized, and downgraded (Suganuma, 2012). In recent years, it has also become obvious that "Japan's male-queer culture is making increased reference to other Asian queer cultures" (Suganuma, 2012, p. 182). Simultaneously, other Asian queer cultural references serve as an alternative way to evaluate the Westernization of queer Japanese cultures. This discursive shift paradoxically perpetuates the colonial and imperialist production of an East–West binary (Suganuma, 2012). For that reason, I argue that White gay normativity is powerfully renegotiated across national and cultural boundaries.

In this context, I engage in my transnational performances of (dis)identifications with the global–local circuit of White gay normativity. As Muñoz (1999) defined, "Disidentification resists interpellating call of ideology that fixes a subject within the state power apparatus. It is a reformatting of self within the social" (p. 97). Disidentification is *neither* assimilation *nor* resistance. It is the performative fashion for minoritarian subjects to navigate the hegemonic circulations of power, oppression, and privilege. Minoritarian subjects are socially positioned to negotiate, resist, and reframe normalizing, dominant, and oppressive ideological forces within the complex webs of sociopolitical, economic, and historical contexts. As Muñoz (1999) articulated, "Disidentification is about recycling and rethinking encoded meaning" (p. 31). To showcase my complex and ambiguous nuances of disidentifications, I move forward to carefully interrogate my queer desires next.

(Re)Articulating My Positionality

Born and raised in Japan, I had not actively articulated my foreign-born Asian/Japanese cisgendered gay man (of color) identity or my transnational queer minoritarian positionality. I was given the societal privilege not to think of racial/ethnic/minority categories as I grew up in a middle-class Japanese mainstream cultural community. As Kinefichi (2008) observed, the hegemonic cultural and ethnic particularizations of Japaneseness remain powerfully sustained in various localities of Japan. In the material condition of Japanese ethnocentric hetero-patriarchy, my queer/non-heteronormative identification artificially appeared to be the only minoritarian identity variable in my everyday world. As I "crossed" the transnational border to the US as an international student, I dramatically experienced shifting to identify as a foreign-born "Asian/Japanese" gay man (see Eguchi, 2011). I have become visibly aware of how race/ethnicity, language, and minoritarian status intersected with nationality, sexuality, sex/gender, and class simultaneously to function in reproducing the material contents of my everyday intercultural contacts. As Muñoz (1999) suggested, "[queer minoritarian] identities are formed in response to the cultural logics of heteronormativity, [W]hite supremacy, and misogyny" (p. 5). Being stuck in the queer cultural spaces betwixt and between Japan and the US, I have internalized how the White capitalistic hetero-patriarchal relations of power politicize and historicize my Asian/Japanese cisgendered gay body as a feminine/foreign Other.

On a Friday night in July 2013, Taro, Shumpei, and I enter a gay sports bar in Hell's Kitchen in Manhattan, New York. We proceed to the rooftop of a two-story building and then locate a sofa for us to sit. Since there is a bar on the rooftop, Shumpei and I go to the bar. As we approach the counter, the tall, butch-looking African American female security guard says, "We are trying to close the bar here. Go downstairs to get drinks." So we go to the ground floor to get drinks. As we come back to the rooftop, we see that a couple of White macho-looking guys are ordering drinks from the White male bartender. All of us know what the situation means: We do not have White gay male privilege because, as Carbado (2005) explained,

"Our identities are reflective and constitutive of systems of oppression" (p. 191). Feeling frustrated with what I see, I then raise my voice to Taro and Shumpei: "What the F***! Why have we been sent downstairs?"

The cultural and communicative act of ordering drinks has been a repeatedly contested site of struggle in which I learned my positionality as an Asian/Japanese cisgendered gay man. When I stood in line to order drinks in multiple gay bars and clubs on several occasions, I was overlooked in favor of macho-looking White male clients. Calafell and Moreman (2010) write that "[a]s we repetitively answer the discursive call, our racial identity becomes naturalized for ourselves and for others" (p. 403). Right after I express my frustration, Shumpei responds that "people generally look down on gay Asians. They think that we are not going to complain about anything. We are automatically assumed to be *submissive feminine bottoms*." Taro nods his agreement with Shumpei's comment.

In this communicative moment, I rethink of my past, when I used to go out to San Francisco's gay bars and clubs with my previous partner, James, who is a Black gay professional. James is taller, muscular, and 10 years older than me. Whenever we ordered drinks together, the bartenders always talked to James when we asked for the check. Some bartenders looked surprised when I occasionally gave them cash or a credit card. These interactions illuminated the social and cultural frame that Asian gay men are framed like women in the hetero-patriarchal tradition. As Han (2006) wrote, "Much like the way that women are 'rewarded' for playing the feminine role, gay Asian men are 'rewarded' by the dominant [or White] gay community for performing their prescribed gender roles" (p. 17). Our queer intercultural pairing reinforced the imaginary binary thinking of (Black/US top) masculinity—(Asian/Japanese bottom) femininity that illuminates the homonormative gaze of White gay men. James temporarily bypasses the racial line to perform the US imperialist masculine narrative of a man who can afford to buy drinks for his foreign/feminine partner.

In our bar conversation, Shumpei continues, "I am a top. I do not like to be seen as a bottom. I have always dated someone who is smaller than me." To reframe the feminization and subordination of his body, Shumpei puts effort into working out his 5'10" tall, 165-pound body to look like a gym-going gay man. He presents his body by wearing jock-style clothes with a New York Yankees baseball hat. From my perspective, Shumpei conforms to the material significations of US male appearance norms. At the same time, "the assessment, or 'review' of the [Asian gay masculine] program, is met with disapproval by gay white men and is, therefore, invalidated" (Han, 2009a, p. 115). Asian gay men are sociopolitically and historically positioned as "feminized bottoms who serve [W]hite studs with asses" in the Western discourse (Browning, 1994, p. 196). The White capitalistic hetero-patriarchal relations of power ideologically patronize and discipline the material and aesthetic conditions of Asian queer male sexuality and experience.

The underlying functions of language further complicate the "authentic" significations of my foreignness as I navigate the everyday world. For example, both American-born and foreign-born Asians have historically been racialized and gendered as *perpetual foreigners*, regardless of their places of origin (Nakayama, 2012). In the continuation of our bar conversation, at the same time, Taro maintains that "we need to realize we are foreign-born Asians [or Japanese]. We are not American-born Asians [or Japanese]. The fact that we were not born and raised here matters." Taro continues, "It is hard for me to initiate conversations with other men in gay bars because the way Japanese socialize with one another at a party is very different from the way Americans do." I am surprised to hear this, as I observe that Taro's queer intercultural identity performance illustrates his Westernization/Americanization. At the same time, I relate to his feelings. I have frequently violated unwritten rules of White hetero-/homo-normative communication. In the context of gay bars/clubs, I was not sure whether or not other men are romantically interested in me because I could not read the social and cultural meanings of their non-verbal signs. Also, I have struggled to fully understand complex and ambiguous nuances of spoken words when they express their romantic interests. Moreover, I have struggled to choose the right words for what I want to express. As I have repeatedly experienced these queer intercultural miscommunications, I feel like I have hit the glass ceiling of becoming an (gay Asian) "American." The discursive and material effects of my words have always functioned as a contested site of ideological struggle through which I articulated my positionality in the context of my privileged and voluntary migration to the US. Thus, I will be always already constructed as an *Asian/Japanese queer feminine/foreign Other*.

I argue that the articulation of my transnational queer minoritarian positionality subconsciously began while growing up in Japan. Since the mid-nineteenth century, Japan has been a major site of globalization, in which various Western sociocultural, political, and economic elements were adapted, normalized, and naturalized into our everyday lives (Iwabuchi, 2002). I was born and raised in the historical and ideological context of the post-WWII period of Americanization. Growing up in Japan in the 1980s and 1990s, I consumed US/Western popular culture through music, films, and TV programs. My favorite singers were Madonna, the Spice Girls, TLC, Whitney Houston, and Mariah Carey. I saw the movie *Titanic* when I was in high school. I hung a poster of Australian swimmer, Ian Thorpe, who recently came out as gay in 2014. Also, I frequently visited Tokyo Disneyland with my parents or friends throughout late 1980s and 1990s. Moreover, the US continues to maintain a number of major military bases in cities (i.e., Tokyo, Yokohama, and Hiroshima) near where I was raised. In this material environment, the US imperialist relations of power were hyper-visible. I knew that I was not (White) American. Thus, I might have "naturally" internalized the US rhetorical production of Whiteness as power. My intersectional negotiation of my "queer man of color" identification might have started a long time ago.

Critiquing My Desire

After my privileged and voluntary migration to the US, I repeatedly chose to situate myself in queer color-to-color relationships. I utilized my queer Asian–Black relationality to disidentify from the homoeroticism of Asian–White colonial encounters and to perform a *unique* and *alternative* kind of "gaysian [gay Asian] fabulosity" (Lim, 2014, p. xiii). As Buckland (2002) reinforced, the act of "fabulousness" signifies that gay cultural constructions of fashion, music, and lifestyle associated with bars/nightclubs are quintessentially significant to the queer formations of personal and relational identities across various racial and ethnic lines. In this material condition, I have felt my empowerment as *a gaysian diva*—"the cream of crop" (McCune, 2014, p. 78)—by saying, "I don't do White men." Since I consumed and internalized the US capitalistic performance of "fabulousness," my queer Asian relational proximity to Blackness temporarily allowed me to feel that I am not Miss Asia in the beauty pageant for rice-queens.

For example, Yoshi, Takuya and I talk about our previous dates and relationships during dinner on a Tuesday night in July 2013. Yoshi starts, "I can't date White men. I do not feel any connection with them." Takuya echoes, "Macho Black men are so cool." So I question Yoshi's desire. He replies, "I fell in love with hip-hop and R&B (Rhythm & Blues) music while in Tokyo. That is why I do hip-hop dance as my hobby. I think I have a lot in common with many Black [gay/bisexual/queer] guys." Since Yoshi moved from Tokyo to New York in March 1998, he has realized that he can't really be the part of mainstream gay culture. He says, "Most gay clubs in Chelsea played house music. Also, Chelsea boys love high fashion and designer-brand stuff. I am not rich like them." Thus, Yoshi develops his relational web of a subcultural community that revolves around "the combination of hip-hop and queer space (or coolness and queerness)" (McCune, 2008, p. 302). Then Yoshi asks me, "Why do you like Black guys?"

In this dialogic moment, I reflect that I have developed my fantasized desire for *coolness* by internalizing the historical commodification of (heteronormative) Black masculinity in the US discourse. McCune (2014) asserted, "Coolness is a theory in practice—an embodied rubric that regulates and monitors what is and is not acceptable among [B]lack men under and outside of [W]hite surveillance" (p. 79). While I was growing up in Japan in the 1980s and 1990s, the stereotypical American representations of hyper-macho Black men were visible, available, and accessible. As Morris (2013) articulated, the global circulations of hip-hop music and fashion have been sensationally consumed in the Americanized contexts of the Japanese media over the last three decades. In this intercultural space, I internalized the historical and ideological product of (heteronormative) Black masculinity through my active consumption of Japanese media (e.g., Cornyetz, 1994; Condry, 2006). Given that race is a fundamental aspect of our lives, I am (inter)culturally socialized to subscribe to, internalize, and reinforce the White/Western hetero-/homo-normative imperialist productions of power. As I interrogate my construction of desire and attraction, I recall what James used to tell me when we were together in San Francisco. He felt uncomfortable when people related to him through the global circulations of hip-hop music and fashion in gay bars/clubs. Hip-hop music and fashion did not characterize how he made sense of who he was. As a (Black/African American) gay man, he was more familiar with the songs of Madonna and Beyoncé than with 50 Cent and Jay-Z. Reimagining James's struggle, I recognize that I have functioned as a queer intercultural agent reproducing the White capitalistic hetero-patriarchal hierarchy through my desire.

At the same time, the discursive expressions of coolness represent cultural and performative illusions of Americanness in a larger global context. The material significances of hip-hop music and fashion mirror aesthetic, political, and cultural products of African American tradition, identity, and performance (Morris, 2013). The racialized, gendered, and classed image of Blackness symbolizes an authentic US minority status (Delgado & Stefancic, 2012). In this discursive context, I identify with the hegemonic distributions of US cultural imperialist power. As I position myself within the queer eroticism of Japanese/African American encounters, my fantasized desire for coolness illuminates my internalization of the US as sexy and cool. The historical narratives of East–West binary have ironically reproduced the materiality of my desire. For that reason, my embodied performance of desire for and attraction to coolness illustrates the complex, contested, contradictory, and dynamic nature of my assimilation into and resistance to (White/Western) capitalistic hetero-/homo-normative America.

I simultaneously argue the intraqueer potentiality for my post-colonial articulations of Japanese cultural ethnic national identity through my desire for coolness. The intercultural connection between Japanese nationalism and African American racial politics emerged shortly after Japan's cultural adaptation of Western imperialism, starting from the middle of the nineteenth century (Morris, 2013). Subsequently, Japanese leaders in the early twentieth century assumed the legacy of African American politics as a powerful model of resistance to the White capitalistic hetero-patriarchal institution (Koshiro, 2003). However, "admiration of African American progress coexisted with a Japanese disdain for Black people, and a general desire to be seen as '[W]hite'" (Morris, 2013, p. 473). At the same time, the recent emergence of the Japanese hip-hop music and fashion scenes illustrates their post-colonial potential by critiquing and resisting the global distributions of White/Western capitalistic hetero-patriarchal imperialist power. In this larger ideological context, I am willing to critique my own aesthetic forms of desire for coolness. My self-reflexive turn is a potential point of intercultural reentry to unpack the Westernization/Americanization of my Japanese intersectional identities.

On a Sunday in August 2013, Taro hosts a dinner party at his apartment in Brooklyn. When Yoshi and I are chatting about dating, Taro's roommate Shumpei comes back from a pool party in New Jersey. I ask, "How was the party?" Shumpei responds, "It was okay. There were too many Asians who chase after White men." His observation historically and ideologically illustrates the Asian gay performance of *business as usual*. Ayres (1999) observed that "[Asian gay men] are competing for the attention of the limited number of Caucasian men who desire Asian men" (p. 92). Taro joins the conversation as he is leaving his kitchen. He asks, "Your ex was Black, right?" As Shumpei responds affirmatively, our conversation shifts to Taro's dating experiences. Taro begins by saying, "My ex [Alex] is Black. We are still friends. He understands what it means to be a (gay) man of color [in White gay America]. Even though he is not Asian, he never dismisses my feelings of marginalization because he also experiences race and racism every day."

In this reflexive moment, I reconsider the intercultural potentiality of resistance and social change through the lens of my own queer color-to-color engagements. I argue that Asian Americans and Black/African Americans are visibly marked as racial Others. Delgado and Stefancic (2012) remind us that "the dominant society racializes different minority groups at different times" (p. 9). In the present context, the hegemonic formation of racial hierarchy casts Asian Americans as the *model minority* over other racial/ethnic minority groups. Mainstream discourses frame Asian/Americans as hardworking, uncomplaining, successful, and honorary Whites. As Sun (2007) further explains, "The model minority stereotype takes attention off the [W]hite majority by pitting Asian Americans against African Americans" (p. 22). The model minority discursive formation reproduces interracial tensions, competitions, and/or resentments among racial/ethnic minorities (Washington, 2012). However, the intercultural potentiality of queer Asian–Black relationality complicates the hegemonic racial distribution of power. I argue that the materiality of non-White bodies has cultivated the shared meanings of queer intercultural connections between my previous Black/African American partners and me. They have never dismissed my feelings of marginalization when I shared the racialized, gendered, (homo) sexualized, and classed nuances of my everyday intercultural encounters. As Alexander (2005) emphasized, "Our [Black queer] bodies are always already racially historicized, sexualized, physicalized, and demonized" (p. 250). In this historical and ideological context, I continue to interrogate my aesthetic forms of desire for coolness. The potentiality of queer Asian–Black rationality can provide a site of intercultural re-imaginings and possibilities for social justice.

Now my thoughts return to my dinner with Yoshi and Takuya on a Tuesday night in July 2013 that I mentioned earlier. Takuya expresses that "in reality, it is difficult to find a Black man who is husband material. I met many Black men who are discreet. When I was young, I enjoyed hanging out with them." So I question his definition of *men who are discreet*. Takuya instantly replies, "They are on the down low" (DL). Haven't you met them?" I reply, "Of course, I have." Takuya continues, "I am now over 40 years old. So I really want to find a long-term relationship with a man who is out, regardless of his race." In this moment, I relate to his feeling of wanting to be in a long-term committed homonormative relationship. At the same time, I question to myself, "Why do I want to desire a man who is out?"

I critique my intercultural adaptation of gay identity emerging from the Western/US paradigm of coming out. As a non-White queer man, I subscribe to the White/Western (homo)normative illusion of same-sex relationship and marriage to measure my transnational gay identity performance. In my previous experiences, most Black men I met did not consent to the White (homo)normative construction of a straight/gay binary. They are actively navigating the complex webs of race, sex/gender, sexuality, and class to make sense of their non-heteronormative sexualities (i.e., McCune, 2008, 2014; Snorton, 2014). At the same time, I paradoxically continue to wish that John, whom I truly fell in love with in New York in the mid-2000s, had adapted the White US middle-class gay lifestyle. John mentioned that he was expected to be tough while growing up in Brooklyn in the late 1970s and 1980s. John also played football while in college in the Northeast in the early 1990s. In this cultural context, he embodied the heteronormative Black hyper-macho masculinity. I reflect that I was attracted to his African American performance of toughness. At the same time, we constantly argued about when and where to publicly go out in Manhattan while in our queer relationship. He did not prefer to frequent historically known gay neighborhoods such as Chelsea and West Village with me or to be publicly seen with me in certain areas because *he was not gay*. By internalizing the homonormative desire for same-sex relationship and marriage, however, I struggled in the relationship. My privileged priority of living in Manhattan was to enjoy my gay life since I desired to perform the Westernization/Americanization of my sexuality and culture. I enjoyed frequenting historically known gay neighborhoods and wanted to be publicly seen with "my boyfriend." In this context of ideological differences, I needed to end my queer relationship with John after a year of dating. At the same time, I feel that I would currently not be single if he had been "out," because I have yet to feel about anyone else the way I felt about him. In this context, my intercultural adaptation of gay identity has paradoxically functioned as my ongoing life obstacle as I navigate my everyday world.

In the conversation about our desire for a long-term relationship, Yoshi continues, "there are of course Black men who are out as gay/bisexual. But I do not know if they think Asians are cool. If they like Asians, they are awkwardly obsessed about Asian people and cultures." I question why Yoshi sees things this way. He replies, "I feel that Asians are seen as 'wanna-be' Whites. Plus, we are viewed as socially awkward. So Asian stereotypes often limit me in dating men whom I am attracted to." In this moment, I consider that I have avoided men of color who expect me to know Japanese anime just because I am Japanese. Growing up, I was not really interested in anime. After moving to the US, I distanced myself from the mainstream consumerism of Japanese anime. I did not want to conform to the socially awkward geek Asian/American stereotype. At the same time, I engaged in the homoerotic stereotypes of an Asian gay man as *total bottom, feminine, and smooth like a woman* in order to be accepted into the White gay normative bar/club culture. However, my personality is not submissive and passive enough to meet the expectation of a "feminine" Asian gay man. Most men of color I have met have simultaneously hoped for a "total package" of Asian gay male performances in me, as they desire the queer narratives of model minority. As Poon (2006) observed, the recent Western commodifications of Asian popular cultural features such as anime, music, food, and fashion cultivate the aesthetic potentiality of desire for Asian gay men. However, I argue that this materiality of Asian gay male beauty takes place in the historical continuum of globalization. Most queer men of color whom I have previously met continue to internalize and reproduce the homoeroticism of Orientalism by consuming the US media commodifications of Asian/Eastern cultures. I call into question the discursive and ideological reproductions of race and racism in the material realities of queer color-to-color relationalities.

Tetsu also talks about his queer interracial dating difficulty when we go to dinner in Midtown East on a Monday night in July 2013. Tetsu says, "I have been here in New York for three years. I have casually dated White Americans, Black/African Americans, and Asian Americans. But I find it difficult to develop relationships with Americans in general." He continues, "They do not really understand social and cultural meanings behind Japanese soap-opera drama and comedy. They do not laugh at the same moments as I do." Tetsu's comment reminds me of another friend, Taro's, nostalgic fantasy about Japan. Since our first encounter in 2010, I have noticed that Taro keeps up with the trends of Japanese popular culture. He knows new actors, singers, and entertainers in Japan whom I do not know about. I occasionally ask him why he is interested in Japanese popular culture. Taro always says, "I have been in the US since I was a 16-year-old. At first, I was trying to become an American. So I followed a lot of US pop culture. But now I am 40 years old. As I am getting older, I miss Japan." As I remember Taro's diasporic story, Tetsu tells me that "[queer] intercultural relationships are difficult."

Tetsu's perspective offers me an additional space to be reflective about my previous involvements in queer Asian–Black relationalities. I have been unable to fully understand the complex and ambiguous nuances of Black queer male cultures. There have been ambivalent, contradictory, and paradoxical tensions of intersectional differences in such queer intercultural spaces. For example, I regret my "bitchy" action when my ex-partner Luis took me to a Black gay club in Brooklyn in the summer of 2008. Before our entrance to the club, I was shocked that there was a body checkpoint for security. So I kept asking Luis, "Why do I need to be searched?" and telling him "I am not comfortable." When Luis bought me my favorite drink, a Cosmopolitan, to ease my tension, I again complained because it came in a plastic cup. As I dreamed of being *fabulous*, I emphasized that my drink had to be in a cocktail glass. Feeling "bitchy," I refused to dance with Luis when they played Ne-Yo's *Because of You*. As I remember the moment, I critique my racialized classist act. I am privileged to perform the US middle-class constructions of gay fabulousness on my Asian body. I must realize that I have been socialized to reproduce the hegemonic distributions of power. I need to recognize how my privileges and disadvantages are simultaneously working to reproduce the contested and contradictory natures of my intersectional performances. As Martin and Nakayama (2010) maintain, "Individuals may be simultaneously privileged and disadvantaged, or privileged in some contexts and disadvantaged in others" (p. 68). Therefore, I continue to challenge my complex and ambiguous internalizations of racism, (hetero)sexism, homophobia, classism, and xenophobia.

Conclusion

In this essay, I have attempted to interrogate, challenge, and problematize my queer intercultural production of desire to bridge between *Asian* and *Black* in the contexts of White gay America. Specifically, I have attempted to explicitly explicate, elaborate, and elucidate my complex and ambiguous nuances of disidentifications with the queer eroticism of Asian–White colonial encounters. I have alternatively located myself in intraqueer Asian–Black (dis)connections to seek potentialities of desire and attraction within the global–local circulations of White gay normativity. The micro- and meso-acts/processes of queer intercultural encounters remain a contested site of reinforcing the larger macroconditions and structures of White/Western imperialist power. Therefore, I argue that the social and performative constructions of race, along with other multiple identity positionings are not the things of past.

With this queer critical race awareness, I would like to problematize my conception of agency. I previously thought that I could reframe gay racial stigmas imposed on my body by celebrating my exaggerated performance of Asian/Japanese male-femininity. However, I have begun to realize that my seemingly celebratory reframing of my Asian/Japanese male-femininity may have been "wishful" thinking. I do not embody and deploy the magical framing of positive thinking to navigate the everyday world. Instead, I struggle with the discursive and material effects of social, cultural, political, and historical constraints in my everyday queer intercultural contacts. My embodied praxis of critiquing hegemonic circulations of power and privilege is negatively (mis)framed under the White capitalistic hetero-/homo-normative institutional surveillance. I cannot easily pass through the US capitalistic hetero-patriarchal maps of power, oppression, and privilege without being labeled as "negative" and/or "the troublemaker." I am ideologically disciplined to become a queer model minority in the post-civil rights movement period. In this context, I feel forever foreign and I feel down. However, I remain committed to calling out the hegemony and imperialism of racism, (hetero)sexism, homophobia, classism, and xenophobia. As a queer intercultural autoethnographer, I risk the readers potentially characterizing me as "negative" and/or a "troublemaker." My philosophy of writing autoethnography is to openly offer thick descriptions of my emotional vulnerability as the performative vehicle in order to conduct social justice work.

I would also like to express my appreciation for Asian gay bars/clubs/events before closing my autoethnography. As I leave an Asian gay night event in Manhattan with Kenny, I see a couple of rice-queens with their Asian men. Looking at them, I first reflect on the fact that the Asian gay bars/clubs/events have been a contested site of fetishism in which rice-queens consume the homoeroticism of Orientalism. Then I view that such racialized fetish spaces have helped to create a sense of community in which Asian American gay/bisexual/queer men gather to become acquainted with each other and their intercultural allies. Since I moved to the US, I have utilized the Asian gay bars/clubs/events as a way to socialize with other men. I felt empowered by others desiring me in such relational spaces since Asian American men are not in the center of aesthetics in mainstream gay bars/clubs/events. For that reason, I appreciate that I can imagine the potentiality of Asian diasporic queer world-making through the presence of Asian gay bars/clubs/events.

In conclusion, I hope that we as communication scholars continue to interrogate, challenge, and problematize discursive and ideological functions of White gay normativity in the material conditions of GLBTQ identities and spaces across various national and cultural boundaries. By critiquing global–local circulations of White gay normativity, I believe that we will be able to take a step toward encouraging critical transformations of GLBTQ identities and spaces into being more inclusive than they presently are.

Note

[1] My current affiliation's IRB office granted me approval to represent informants in this essay. My Asian/Japanese transnational cisgendered gay male participants are: Taro (40-year-old), Yoshi (40-year-old), Shumpei (30-year-old), Takuya (40-year-old), and Tetsu (25-year-old).

References

Adams, T.E., & Holman Jones, S. (2008). Autoethnography is queer. In N.K. Denzin, Y.S. Lincoln, & L.T. Smith (Eds.), *Handbook of critical and indigenous methodologies* (pp. 373–390). Thousands Oaks, CA: Sage.

Alexander, B.K. (2005). Embracing the teachable moment: the Black gay body in the classroom as embodied text. In E.P. Johnson & M.G. Henderson (Eds.), *Black queer studies: A critical anthology* (pp. 249–265). Durham, NC: Duke University Press.

Alexander, B.K. (2008). Queer(y)ing the postcolonial through the West(ern). In N.K. Denzin, Y.S. Lincoln, & L.T. Smith (Eds.), *Handbook of critical and indigenous methodologies* (pp. 101–133). Thousands Oaks, CA: Sage.

Alexander, B.K. (2012). *The performative sustainability of race: Reflections on Black culture and the politics of identity*. New York, NY: Peter Lang.

Ayres, T. (1999). China doll—the experience of being a gay Chinese Australian. In P.A. Jackson & G. Sullivan (Eds.), *Multicultural queer: Australian narratives* (pp. 87–97). New York, NY: Harrington Park Press.

Boylorn, R.M., & Orbe, M.P. (Eds.) (2014). *Critical autoethnography: Intersecting cultural identities in everyday life*. Walnut Creek, CA: Left Coast Press.

Browning, F. (1994). *The culture of desire: Paradox and perversity in gay lives today*. New York, NY: Vintage Books.

Buckland, F. (2002). *Impossible dance: Club culture and queer world-making*. Middletown, CT: Wesleyan University Press.

Calafell, B.M. (2009). "She ain't no diva!": Reflections on in/hospitable guests/hosts, reciprocity, and desire. *Liminalities; A Journal of Performance Studies, 5*(5). http://liminalities.net/5-4/diva.pdf

Calafell, B.M. (2012). Monstrous femininity: Constructions of women of color in the academy. *Journal of Communication Inquiry, 36*(2), 111–130.

Calafell, B.M., & Moreman, S.T. (2010). Iterative hesitancies and Latinidad: The reverberances of raciality. In T.K. Nakayama & R.T. Halualani (Eds.), *The handbook of critical intercultural communication* (pp. 400–416). Chichester, UK: Wiley-Blackwell.

Carbado, D.W. (2005). Privilege. In E.P. Johnson & M.G. Henderson (Eds.), *Black queer studies: A critical anthology* (pp. 190–212). Durham, NC: Duke University Press.

Chávez, K.R. (2013). Pushing boundaries: Queer intercultural communication. *Journal of International and Intercultural Communication, 6*(2), 83–95.

Cohen, C.J. (1997). Punks, bulldaggers, and welfare queens: The real radical potential of queer politics? *GLQ: A Journal of Lesbian and Gay Studies, 3*(4), 437–465.

Condry, I. (2006). *Hip-hop Japan: Rap and the paths of cultural globalization*. Durham, NC: Duke University Press.

Cornyetz, N. (1994). Fetished Blackness: Hip hop and racial desire in contemporary Japan. *Social Text, 41*, 113–140.

Decena, C.U. (2008). Tacit subjects. *GLQ: A Journal of Lesbian and Gay Studies, 14*(2–3), 339–359.

Delgado, R., & Stefancic, J. (2012). *Critical race theory: An introduction* (2nd ed.). New York, NY: New York University Press.

Eguchi, S. (2011). Cross-national identity transformation: Becoming a gay "Asian American" man. *Sexuality & Culture, 15*(1), 19–40.

Eng, D.L. (2010). *The feeling of kinship: Queer liberalism and the racialization of intimacy.* Durham, NC: Duke University Press.

Ferguson, R.A. (2004). *Aberrations in black: Toward a queer of color critique.* Minneapolis, MN: University of Minnesota Press.

Fung, R. (2005). Looking for my penis: The eroticized Asian in gay video porn. In R. Guins & O.Z. Cruz (Eds), *Popular culture: A reader* (pp. 338–348). London, UK: Sage.

Griffin, R.A. (2012). I AM an angry woman: Black feminist autoethnography, voice, and resistance. *Women's Studies in Communication, 35*(2), 138–157.

Han, C-S. (2006). Geisha of a different kind: Gay Asian men and the gendering of sexual identity. *Sexuality & Culture, 10*(3), 3–28.

Han, C-S. (2008). No fats, femmes, or Asians: The utility of critical race theory in examining the role of gay stock stories in the marginalization of gay Asian men. *Contemporary Justice Review, 11*(1) 11–22.

Han, C-S. (2009a). Asian girls are prettier: Gendered presentations as stigma management among gay Asian men. *Symbolic Interaction, 32*(2), 106–122.

Han, C-S. (2009b). Introduction to the special issue on GLBTQ of color. *Journal of Gay and Lesbian Social Services, 21* (2–3), 109–114.

Holling, M.A. (2006). El simpatico boxer: Underpinning Chicano masculinity with a rhetoric of familia in resurrection blvd. *Western Journal of Communication, 70* (2), 91–114.

Iwabuchi, K. (2002). *Recentering globalization: Popular culture and Japanese transnationalism.* London, UK: Duke University Press.

Johnson, E.P. (2001). "Quare" studies or (almost) everything I know about queer studies I learned from my grandmother. *Text and Performance Quarterly, 21*(1), 1–25.

Kinefichi, E. (2008). From authenticity to geographies: Unpacking Japaneseness in the construction of Nikkeijin identity. *International and Intercultural Communication Annual, 31*, 91–118.

Koshiro, Y. (2003). Beyond an alliance of color: The African American impact on modern Japan. *Positions: East Asian Cultures Critique, 11*(1), 183–215.

Lee, W. (2003). Kuaering queer theory: My autocritography and a race-conscious womanist, transnational turn. In G.A. Yep, K.E. Lovaas & J.P. Elia (Eds.), *Queer theory and communication: From disciplining queers to queering the discipline(s)* (pp. 147–170). Binghamton, NY: Harrington Park Press.

Lim, E-G. (2014). *Brown boys and rice queens: Spellbinding performances in the Asias.* New York, NY: New York University Press.

Martin, J.N., & Nakayama, T.K. (2010). Intercultural communication and dialectics revisited. In T.K. Nakayama & R.T. Halualani (Eds.), *The handbook of critical intercultural communication* (pp. 59–83). Chichester, UK: Wiley-Blackwell.

McCune Jr., J.Q. (2008). Out in the club: The down low, hip-hop, and the architexture of Black masculinity. *Text and Performance Quarterly, 28*(3), 298–314.

McCune Jr. J.Q. (2014). *Sexual discretion: Black masculinity and the politics of passing.* Chicago: University of Chicago Press.

Moon, D.A., & Nakayama, T.K. (2005). Strategic social identities and judgements: A murder in Appalachia. *Howard Journal of Communications, 16* (1), 87–107.

Moreman, S.T., & McIntosh, D.M. (2010). Brown scriptings and rescriptings: A critical performance ethnography of Latina drag queens. *Communication and Cultural/Critical Studies, 7*(2), 115–135.

Morris, D.Z. (2013). The sakura of madness: Japan's nationalist hip hop and the parallax of globalized identity politics. *Communication, Culture, & Critique, 6*(3), 459–480.

Muñoz, J.E. (1999). *Disidentifications: Queers of color and the performance of politics.* Minneapolis, MN: University of Minnesota Press.

Muñoz, J.E. (2009). *Cruising utopia: The then and there of queer futurity.* New York, NY: New York University Press.

Nakayama, T.K. (2012). Dis/orienting identities: Asian Americans, history, and intercultural communication. In A. Gonzalez, M. Houston, & V. Chen (Eds.), *Our voices: Essays in culture, essay, and communication* (5th ed., pp. 20–25). New York, NY: Oxford University Press.

Nero, C.I. (2005). Why are gay ghettos white? In E.P. Johnson & M.G. Henderson (Eds.), *Black queer studies: A critical anthology* (pp. 228–245). Durham, NC: Duke University Press.

Okihiro, G.Y. (1994). *Margins and mainstreams: Asians in American history and culture*. Seattle, WA: University of Washington Press.

Phua, V.C. (2007). Contesting and maintaining hegemonic masculinities: Gay Asian American men in mate selection. *Sex Roles, 57*, 909–918.

Poon, M.K-L. (2006). The discourse of oppression in contemporary gay Asian diasporal literature: liberation or limitation? *Sexuality & Culture, 10*(3), 29–58.

Poon, M.K-L., & Ho, P.T-T. (2008) Negotiating social stigma among gay Asian men. *Sexualities, 11*(1/2), 245–268.

Ross, M.B. (2005). Beyond the closet as a raceless paradigm. In E.P. Johnson & M.G. Henderson (Eds.), *Black queer studies: a critical anthology* (pp. 161–189). Durham, NC: Duke University Press.

Snorton, C.R. (2014). *Nobody is supposed to know: Black sexuality on the down low*. Minneapolis, MN: University of Minnesota Press.

Spry, T. (2001). Preforming autoethnography: An embodied methodological praxis. *Qualitative Inquiry, 7*, 706–732.

Suganuma, K. (2012). *Contact moments: The politics of intercultural desire in Japanese male-queer cultures*. Hong Kong: Hong Kong University Press.

Sun, W. (2007). *Minority invisibility: An Asian American experience*. Lanham, MD: University Press of America.

Washington, M. (2012). Interracial intimacy: Hegemonic construction of Asian American and Black relationships on TV medical dramas. *Howard Journal of Communications, 23*, 253–271

Yep, G.A. (2010). Toward the de-subjugation of racially marked knowledges in communication. *Southern Communication Journal, 75*, 171–175.

Yep, G.A. (2013). Queering/quaring/kauering/crippin'/transing "other bodies" in intercultural communication. *Journal of International and Intercultural Communication, 6*(2), 118–126.

Yep, G.A., & Lescure, R. (2014). Kuareing "home" in Ang Lee's the *Wedding Banquet*. In E. Patton & M. Choi (Eds.), *Home sweet home: Perspectives on housework and modern relationships* (pp. 167–182). Lanham, MD: Rowman & Littlefield.

The Construction of Brownness: Latino/a and South Asian Bloggers' Responses to SB 1070

Anjana Mudambi

The vernacular discourses of Latino/a and South Asian American bloggers in the context of SB 1070, legislation recently passed in Arizona, illustrate how their shared experiences of discrimination (re-)articulate "brownness" as a complex racial formation aligned with constructions of "illegal" immigrants. Bloggers' differentiation of their subjective experiences of alien citizenship and racialized belonging from white or black citizenship problematizes the rigidity of their "middling" positionality within the U.S. racial structure, encouraging a more contextualized approach. I consider the bloggers' varied constructions of brownness, its distinctive positionality within racial structures, and their contestations of the discourses that racialize brown identities.

In 2010, Arizona passed SB 1070, immigration legislation that criminalized unlawful presence and permitted police to request identification from anyone whom they reasonably suspected of such unlawful presence. Its defenders claimed that it targeted "illegal" immigrants without reference to race; naming race as a target of SB 1070 therefore became a resistant strategy. However, this strategy has often entailed an assumption that SB 1070 interpellated only the Latino/a community, which does not recognize the complexity of how the issue of immigration racializes brownness across ethnocultural communities. Cisneros (2012) asserts in his analysis of the law that it "codifies ... the Mexican-Latina/o-brown-illegal-immigrant-body as a source of fear, anxiety, and even hatred" (p. 139). In describing this body, he brings together a number of identity factors that, he argues, are defined in their negative relation to the white, middle-class, male citizen-subject. These factors might be commonly associated with a particularly classed Mexican body, but they speak to SB 1070's reliance on a broader discourse of brownness that racializes across multiple ethnocultural groups, which is surprisingly yet to be explored (see Lugo-Lugo & Bloodsworth-Lugo, 2010). This understanding complicates the construction of race in ways that create a better understanding of the contextualized nature of racial formations and structures in the United States.

Scholars have remarked upon the unique marginalization of brownness as simultaneously ignored for its place beyond the black/white racial binary and highlighted for its perceived threat (Delgado, 2009; Lugo-Lugo & Bloodsworth-Lugo, 2010; Silva, 2010). To conceptualize brownness, I turn to Omi and Winant's (1994) classic notion of a racial formation as a "sociohistorical process by which racial categories are created, inhabited, transformed, and destroyed" (p. 55), which demonstrates the sociohistorically contingent processes that connect race to social organizational structures, including difference, inequalities, and racialized identity. The concept of racial formations makes clear that although brownness ostensibly operates as a visible marker—often equated with a South Asian (see Prashad, 2000; see also Frost, 2010; Sundar, 2008) or Latino/a (Amaya, 2007a; Delgado, 2009) ethnic identity whose skin color may be describable as "brown"—the phenotypes of members of such ethnic groups vary widely, indicating the necessity for alternative explanations for such racial classification (Amaya, 2007b; Semati, 2010).

SB 1070 locates undocumented immigrants—as well as those whose racialization discursively links them—in varying but nonetheless marginalized positions, making it important to hear the voices of "browns," by which I refer to those interpellated by the legislation. However, existing scholarship focuses on how brownness "is defined (knowledge) and disciplined (power)" (Sharma, 2010, p. 187) externally rather than exploring either the identifications constructed by those defined by it or the possibilities for brownness to operate as "a space of belonging, empowerment, or resistance" (Sharma, p. 187). Vernacular discourse offers an important approach for expanding this research. Recent scholarship on immigration has focused on the specific responses of the objects of immigration discourses—immigrants to the United States—as subjects through the critique of vernacular discourse, which examines the daily interactions and discourse from within oppressed or marginalized communities (Hasian & Delgado, 1998; Holling, 2006; Ono & Sloop, 1995, 2002). As Ono and Sloop (1995) clearly state and other scholarship (Anguiano & Chávez, 2011; Córdova, 2011; Ono & Sloop, 2002) has demonstrated, vernacular discourse is not necessarily always positive or counterhegemonic; it does, however, help construct "more fully articulated cultural space[s]. ... [that] allows us to see exactly how such [subject] positions may in fact work against the political project to discover enabling subjectivities" (Ono & Sloop, 1995, p. 25).

Communication studies as a discipline has recently developed a significant body of Latino/a vernacular studies (Enck-Wanzer, 2011; Hasian & Delgado, 1998; Holling, 2006; Holling & Calafell, 2011; Ono & Sloop, 2002) and, to a lesser degree, South

Asian American studies (Durham, 2001, 2004; Gajjala, 2006; Hegde, 1996; Silva, 2010), but it has not substantively looked across their shared experiences. By examining blogs written by members of both communities in response to SB 1070, I explore how bloggers, while contesting and challenging this legislation, use vernacular rhetorics to respond to and rearticulate its construction of brownness.

In the sections that follow, I first review how scholarship regarding the U.S. racial structure has reinforced the notion of a traditional black/white binary that does not adequately address brownness. I then demonstrate how racialized constructions of brownness constitute a racial formation imbued with flexibility; its signification as foreign and threatening has aligned it with constructions of "illegal" immigrants, raising the importance of examining brownness in the specific context of SB 1070. Finally, after a brief review of my methodology, I present my analysis of the blog posts to elucidate how the discourses rearticulate brownness and to analyze strategies that bloggers use to contest the racialization that they experience in the context of SB 1070.

Brownness and the Black/White Binary

The notion of a black/white binary, defined as "the conception that race in America consists, either exclusively or primarily, of only two constituent racial groups, the Black and the White" (Perea, 1997, p. 1219), has historically dominated studies of race in the United States. While the relationship between blacks and whites has been crucial to understanding the structuring of race in the United States (Martínez, 1993), scholars have also highlighted the shortcomings of such an exclusive approach, including, among others, the minimization of differential forms of racism experienced by varying groups of color (Alcoff, 2006; Martínez, 1993; Perea, 1997; Thangaraj, 2012). Although scholarship has responded with such developments as LatCrit studies (Delgado & Stefancic, 2000) and, though not as unified, work that focuses on the experiences of Asian Americans (Das Gupta, 2006; Prashad, 2000; Silva, 2010; Wu, 2003), to name a few, each of these subsets of literature remains focused on its own ethnocultural category individually, with little conversation across their shared experiences or in relation to the larger racial structure as a whole. The black/white binary limits such conversation by simplistically implying that "if a group is not economically and politically located at or near the bottom of the society, which the black/white paradigm associates exclusively with 'blackness,' then such a group is assumed to have achieved 'whiteness'" (Alcoff, 2006, p. 257).

Bonilla-Silva's (2004) three-tiered racial structure, which combines different communities of color into each of three categories—Whites, Honorary Whites, and Collective Blacks—based on a combination of racial identity and empirical data reflecting shared experiences, offers a more nuanced view of racial hierarchy in the United States. Although he maintains some degree of mobility between these categories, the overall structure reconstructs what Alcoff (2006) refers to as "a continuum of color" (p. 257), a racial structure premised on whiteness at the top and blackness at the bottom, with other racial groups falling somewhere between and approaching whiteness. Bonilla-Silva's structure suggests and facilitates the claim by other scholars that "it is the polarity between whiteness and blackness ... that gives intermediate racial groupings (i.e., in-between people; 'ethnic' whites; not-quite-whites; honorary whites; 'brown,' 'yellow,' and 'red people'; etc.) their meaning" (Deliovsky & Kitossa, 2013, p. 165). This contention assumes that the structure is based in a singular form of racism against which all racial groups can be compared (Alcoff, 2006). It also supports antagonisms between racial groups, primarily discord between black groups and Asians/Latino/as; latter groups persist with anti-black racism, while blacks suspect them of simply being on a trajectory towards assimilating and becoming white (Bonilla-Silva, 2004; Perea, 1997; Prashad, 2000).

By exploring constructions of brownness, this study illustrates how the interrelationship between and across racial categories within the U.S. racial structure is not constant but dependent on contextual factors and historical contingencies. This theoretical foundation draws on scholarship illustrating that identifications are shifting and unstable (Hall, 1993) and emerge in relation to and intersect with political agendas (Collier, 2005; Drzewiecka, 2002). In the next section, I demonstrate how brownness shapes a recent racial formation cutting across ethnocultural groups, i.e., Latino/as and South Asians, through a process of historically contingent racialization in conjunction with contemporary immigration discourse.

Brownness and "Illegal" Immigration in the United States

Alcoff (2006) describes racialization as "universalizing negative value across a group that is demarcated on the basis of visible features or essentializing their cultural characteristics as static" (p. 261). In this sense, "brownness," as both a phenotypical and cultural aspect, "is employed broadly, if not often overtly, to mark deviance" (Silva, 2010, p. 172). "Brown" bodies are constructed as a foreign and menacing Other against which the normalized white body must be protected (Calvente, 2011; Cisneros, 2012). It has been a particularly predominant construction in the post-9/11 context (Burman, 2010; Semati, 2010; Sharma, 2010), which has seen not only a reproduction of immigration discourses that position immigrants as foreign threats to the nation but also an increased preponderance of hate crimes against Sikhs and Muslims (Sacirbey, 2012), among others. Consequently, brownness as a racial formation spans across Latino/as, South Asians, Muslims/Middle Easterners/Arabs, and even queers (Amaya, 2007b; Semati, 2010; Silva, 2010). The association of brownness with the "Other" instead of with a particular ethnocultural identity aligns with a cultural racism (Bonilla-Silva, 2009) that attributes political moves "to differences in culture, tradition, and religion [but are] informed by the logic of differentialist racism" (Semati, 2010, p 266). The threat of brownness is therefore not inherent or fixed in the brown body but is imbued with flexibility because it gets constructed in the context of specific issues such as war, terrorism, Islamophobia, and, notably, immigration.

The threat narrative is one such context that associates brownness with constructions of undocumented immigrants by "posit[ing] that Latinos are. ... part of an invading force from south of the border that is bent on reconquering land that was formerly theirs (the U.S. Southwest) and destroying the American way of life" (Chávez, 2008, p. 2). The dominant discourse of illegal immigration naturalizes the "illegality" and consequent immorality of undocumented immigrants as an essence of their characters (Flores, 2003; Ngai, 2004; Sandoval, 2008). Such naturalization is another strategic attempt to erase racism from the discourse by claiming that selections are ostensibly made without regard to race, discursively rendering race inconsequential (Bonilla-Silva, 2009; Flores, Moon, & Nakayama, 2006; Halualani, 2011; Holling, 2011; Omi & Winant, 1994). Despite the omission of naming race, race has never actually been absent from the discourse of illegal immigration (Holling, 2011). Connections persist between illegal immigration and Mexicans who "came to signify illegal alien and, potentially, every Mexican/American became a walking target. Both whites and Mexicans knew that brown bodies were suspect and foreign" (Flores, 2003, p. 379). Hence, Mexican bodies were always already racialized as brown, offering a concrete delineation of this racial formation.

However, as a racial formation, brownness offers a certain flexibility as well around issues of immigration and citizenship. While most undocumented immigrants come from Mexico and other Latin American nations (Chávez, 2008), the reality of undocumented immigration in the United States belies the dominant image of the Mexican surreptitiously crossing the Rio Grande. Many undocumented immigrants originally come through legal provisions from Mexico and other nonbordering countries and then overstay their visas (Berg, 2009). As such, neither the fact that not all undocumented immigrants are Mexican, or even Latino/a, nor the connection drawn between Mexican/Latino/a immigration and illegal immigration should be ignored (Cisneros, 2012). Rather, both statements coexist paradoxically, emphasizing the flexibility of brownness to seamlessly fuse with constructions of undocumented immigrants to construct the brown immigrant as an external threat to the nation-state. According to Dick (2011),

> The conflation between "illegal alien" and "Mexican" is symbolically loaded with phenotypic stereotypes: the idea that "Mexicans" look a certain way—they are dark-skinned, small in stature, possess "indigenous" features such as broad noses, and so on—and so can be visually identified. (p. E37)

Brownness therefore functions to "[mark] a purposeful pattern of articulating perceived threats to the security of the national imaginary as originating from racialized (that is, 'othered') bodies and spaces" (Lugo-Lugo & Bloodsworth-Lugo, 2010, p. 237). The easy slippage from brown to Latino/a to Mexican to "illegal" constructs "a new coherence of racialized discourse, deployed broadly by cultural and political producers" (Silva, 2010, p. 172; see also Potter, 2014) that can be used more freely than an overt discourse that names race. Consequently, across "brown" immigrant communities, members can legally become U.S. citizens, and their children can be born in the United States as citizens in consonance with neoliberal "race-neutral" policies; and yet they remain subject to the racialization by which "brown" immigrants straddle worlds of non-citizens, aliens, alien citizens, and forever foreigners (Camacho, 2008; Chávez, 2009; Ngai, 2004).

SB 1070, by targeting anyone who "looks illegal," draws upon this discourse of brownness "as an initiative to protect Arizona from the crime, drugs, and violence purportedly brought on by undocumented immigration" (Cisneros, 2012, p. 140), thereby marking certain bodies as a threat to national security. Exploring how those interpellated by SB 1070's targeting of brownness re-articulate this identity may provide insight into the complexities of the construction of brownness as a racial formation.

Methodology

Howard (2008a, 2008b) suggests that new forms of participatory media provide new avenues for vernacular expression. Blogs are often written by people not necessarily connected to particular institutions, allowing naturalistic texts that reach widespread Internet audiences without institutional interference, creating an arena of public discourse in which audiences can interact directly with the bloggers (Howard, 2008b). I used the *Google Blogs* search engine to locate blogs about SB 1070 that were not published on websites of institutionally produced media, such as mainstream newspapers. I employed a "virtual" snowball sampling strategy to locate texts linked to each other. I considered all blog posts and comments published up to four months following the passage of SB 1070, after which further responses appeared either repetitive or less directly responsive to the discursive event. To maximize the representation of the overall blog discourse available online over time, within a single blog site, I selected one main post (and its accompanying comments) per blogger.

Ten blog posts were ultimately used in this study; a summary of all blogs is provided in Table 1. This search resulted in a selection of eight blogs written by Latino/as and two by South Asian Americans. Three bloggers identified themselves as undocumented, two Latino/as and one South Asian. Blogger identities were confirmed by reading a combination of their screen names, personal details revealed in their blogs or comments, and linguistic cues. However, absolute confirmation was not possible, as is largely true regardless of methodology. This anonymity offered both advantages and limitations to the analysis. Although it necessitated my judgment in terms of which posts or comments to "count" and contributed to a decontextualization of the texts offered as evidence, it also presented the possible advantage of relatively uncensored and candid engagement with civic and political discourse, including the performance of marginalized identities that may be constrained or even silenced in more mainstream and/or embodied contexts. Therefore, the lack of confirmation is secondary to the analysis of what the discourse constructs (Hookway, 2008).

Each blog site was a personal platform created and maintained by the blogger, many of whom are relatively educated with technological access and skill, with varying degrees of emphasis on personal and political issues; comments in response to them were limited, leading to greater focus on the main blog posts. There were two

Table 1 List of Blog Posts in Response to SB 1070

Number	Blog title	Blogger	Blog site	Original post date
1	"Arizona"	Somfolnalco	Documenting Me	April 20, 2010
2	"SB 1070 National Day of Action"	Prerna Lal	Change.org	May 29, 2010
3	"SB 1070 and Arizona"	El Random Hero	Just a Random Hero	April 14, 2010
4	"What does an illegal alien look like?"	Di	My life as an alien	May 15, 2010
5	"Do you look like an 'illegal immigrant'?"	Latino Politics Blogger	Latino Politics Blog	April 14, 2010
6	"SB 1070: Racial Politics and the Boycott"	Manuél	Maneegee	April 29, 2010
7	"TERRORIST ATTACK!"	Lou	Maneegee	April 23, 2010
8	"Why I stopped blogging regularly"	Manuél	Maneegee	July 21, 2010
9	"How knowledgeable are we about immigration issues?"	Gregory Tejeda	Southchicagoan	April 30, 2010
10	"Arizona's new immigration law affects us all"	Vivek	Sepia Mutiny	May 24, 2010

exceptions. The first was Latino Politics Blog (T5), a platform "where la raza dishes about political leadership and contemporary issues," and which is managed by four bloggers who offer brief biographies but do not identify themselves individually when they post. This post was followed by significant comments and debate, including by some who are "accused" of not being Latino/a; but the posters are unidentifiable beyond their screen names and any self-disclosures that they make. The other exception was Sepia Mutiny (T10), a platform created and maintained by a group of South Asians in the United States for the same diasporic audience.[1] One webpage provides some personal information about many of the bloggers and regular contributors, who clearly identify their posts and comments. The specific post analyzed here was written by Vivek, a regular contributor to the site, and was followed by extensive comments from a wide range of followers expressing a variety of viewpoints that were drawn upon for analysis. By analyzing this range of blogs and comments, I explore the varied ways that bloggers rearticulate brownness as a racial formation, how this formation relates to the larger racial structure, and how bloggers contest the racialization of brownness.

Constructions of Brownness

Brownness as a Racial Formation

In their responses to SB 1070, many bloggers explicitly use the identifier "brown." However, three different explanations of brownness can be found amongst them. First, although SB 1070 ostensibly targets undocumented immigrants living in

Arizona, some bloggers use language that loosely creates identification between brownness and a broader Latino/a community. Manuél (T8), who identifies himself as "Xicano," uses the Spanish word "gente" for "people" to signify his identification with that community:

> The salt in the wound is watching poll after poll show sizeable majorities of the populace agree that brown-skinned gente should bend over and take the violation of our civil and human rights with a smile on our faces. We should "do our part" by accepting racial profiling, the oppression of our culture, and the militarization of our ancestral homeland.

He constructs "brown" in relation to the skin color of a people with a shared "ancestral homeland," suggesting common cultural heritage. In his blog post, he also outlines specific racial and cultural characteristics, such as "our skin color, our accents, our language." In addition, he highlights practices of state racism, such as oppression and racial profiling, as a reference to the racialization that they experience. Therefore, those affected by SB 1070 include Latino/as and Chicano/as who belong to a larger "brown" community.

This construction of brownness changes upon considering the participation of bloggers from the South Asian blog Sepia Mutiny. Vivek (T10), for example, relates a personal experience in Arizona shortly following his high school graduation 10 years earlier. A white friend was permitted to remain in the car while he and a Latina friend were asked by police for identification:

> And although the law states explicitly that no official may "consider race, color, or national origin" when they implement the policy, is that how it's really going to go down every time, given that in this case the two brown kids got pulled out of the car but the white kid didn't?

Similar to Manuél, Vivek defines brownness as encompassing both skin color and pursuant negative treatment; "the two brown kids," in contrast to the white friend, were targeted by the police because of the way in which their brown skin was always already defined. However, he does not imply a shared cultural heritage between them, focusing instead on the shared experience of racialized treatment across different cultural backgrounds based on similar visual markers.

The third construction of brownness involves its disassociation altogether from one's ethnic background. Somfolnalco (T1), an undocumented immigrant who came to the United States at age seven and had since earned a college degree that he could not use, writes, "The bill essentially makes Arizona an apartheid state, where it will be ok for police to ask a brown 'illegal' looking man or woman for their papers." He clearly refers to brownness as an embodied marker directly connected to the presumption of illegality. Although these three bloggers use the same racial signifier of "brown," they present divergent constructions and understandings of brownness in terms of the extent to which they associate it with specific cultural groups as well as to which cultural groups. At the same time, all three appear to identify brownness as a visual marker of otherness that, both in general and specifically as a result of SB 1070, subjects them to oppression, profiling, and/or questioning by the state.

While these variations in the constructions of brownness can be seen throughout the blogs, many bloggers write about how SB 1070 will operationalize this experience of racialization. Chicano future tense (T5) asserts in his comment supporting the main post that, "racial profiling will become acceptable SOP in Arizona." Somfolnalco (T1) states, "The bill essentially makes Arizona an apartheid state." Manuél (T6) states, "Our skin color, our accents, our language are all suspect to an oppressive federal system that SB1070 expands unjustly." These statements all contest the way that SB 1070 racializes belonging by legitimating the harassment of or discrimination against "browns" and demonstrate that, as brown subjects, bloggers perceive material effects of their racialization.

Such effects extend to their experiences of citizenship. DevP (T10), in response to Vivek, refers to this experience as that of a "second-class citizen:"

> The fact is that if I'm driving with White Friend Paul over the AZ border, one of us needs to make sure his papers are in order to avoid police harassment, while the other one of us is fine. I don't think being treated like a second-class citizen is acceptable.

He contrasts his experience of citizenship with that of a white friend; though legally they may have the same status, DevP feels that his is of a lesser quality. Chicano future tense (T5) contends, "In their mindset if you are non-white you could be an 'illegal alien' as they like to say." Whiteness is presumed to signify citizenship in and of itself; brownness signifies otherness and "illegality" and therefore requires external evidence of citizenship.

Moreover, this racialization of citizenship also has implications for assumptions made about one's character. Di (T4), a naturalized citizen who often writes in her blog against "illegal" immigrants, still challenges the law, stating,

> This new law says that police can stop anybody and ask them to prove that they are here legally if the have the 'suspicion' that they are here illegally. What would make you suspicious that somebody is here illegally by just looking at them? Do you think they are going to stop a white, all-american looking man or woman? really?[2]

While criticizing the law's conflation of illegality with the visual marker of brownness, she highlights that white citizenship is not just phenotypical but also "all-american," a descriptor that aligns with Chávez's (2010) notion of "good" citizenship as "personally responsible, financially stable people who work hard to achieve the American Dream" (p. 142). This attribute of "good" citizenship becomes an important factor in bloggers' simultaneous identification with and contestation of their brown racialization, as I will discuss below.

Bloggers therefore construct their citizenship as inchoate, different from those who are "real" citizens (i.e., white) and indicative of what Ngai (2004) terms alien citizenship, "persons who are American citizens ... but who are presumed to be foreign by the mainstream of American culture and, at times, by the state" (p. 2). Within immigrant communities, immigrants can legally become U.S. citizens and their children can be born as U.S. citizens, and yet they remain subject to cultural denial and marginalization. As Mexican American Citizen (T5) posts in a comment,

What has me the most concerned is my rights as a Mexican –American… Since this bill has been signed, I feel when I walk aboutof my house, all eyes are now on me. I feel as though people now have some small right to question my citizenship.

Mexican American Citizen suggests that the racialization of brownness is more than just the experience of state racism; SB 1070 entitles "all eyes" to view him with suspicion of deviance. This statement elucidates how unrelenting this experience of brownness is in public places. Bloggers' subject positions are defined by their racial unassimilability, wherein even a position of legal citizenship is never complete, always subject to mistrust.

Brownness and the Racial Structure

In this section, I look at how bloggers articulate their identities in relation to the larger racial structure. The emergence of a "brown" identification aligns with their distinction from non-brown Americans. El Random Hero (T3), another undocumented blogger who has been in the United States since childhood, writes,

> People are angry and full of rage for problems happening to them and those around them. It's not their fault because they're hard working Americans who pay taxes and follow the laws, grill hot dogs on fourth of July and eat apple pie right ?

"They" indicates dominant white Americans who, because of "their" status as "Americans," are "entitled" to be angry about the situation, distinct from people like himself. Manuél (T6) writes, "Watching the debate unfold across this country, the reaction I've had most commonly is: 'Wow. How very white of you,'" implying an ideological perspective amongst white Americans that is distinct from those within the blogging community. Manuél and El Random Hero are both identifying a mainstream to which they do not belong, but they also demonstrate varying types of differentiation. El Random Hero uses sarcasm to criticize the distinction, highlighting it as a consequence of contextualized racialization, as discussed in the previous section. Manuél, on the other hand, claims and embraces the differentiation as an indication of superior "brown" perspectives. Bloggers seem to vacillate between these two approaches, possibly as a way of making sense of their position in relation to whiteness.

This differentiation from other groups often constructs complex hierarchies. In the previous section, bloggers' differentiation of their citizenship from white citizenship constructed a lower positionality of brownness within this hierarchy. In addition, because many bloggers speak from a position of being viewed as potentially "illegal" and deportable, they also differentiate themselves from and position themselves lower than blacks. As Gregory Tejeda (T9) responds to SB 1070, he describes his perception of a shift in the U.S. racial structure that can be roughly traced to a post-9/11-context, implying its unstable and contextualized nature that has altered the status of blacks and Latino/as: "U.S. residents as a whole see Latinos as the most-discriminated ethnic or racial group in this country, compared with almost a decade earlier when African-American people were the ones that fell into that category." Although Tejeda, a freelance writer who focuses on "Hispanic" issues, refers specifically to "Latinos," this general idea of differentiating between the discrimination experienced by brownness and blackness appears across several of the bloggers. Razib (T10), a regular contributor to Sepia Mutiny, explains in one of his comments:

> [B]lack americans aren't assumed to be non-natives. one reason richard reid, a black briton (or mixed to be precise) was outside of profile. so if you're a dark skinned south asian shave your head and pretend you're black (at least if you're a dude).

He explicitly describes how "illegal" immigration is NOT connected with black people. Razib's comment complicates the typical notion of colorism found within many communities of color in which both phenotypical and cultural identification with whiteness is deemed superior to blackness, creating a hierarchical color spectrum often ranging from "fair" to "dark" (Bonilla-Silva, 2009; Collins, 2005; Parameswaran & Cardoza, 2009). In this context, however, Razib demonstrates the advantage of performing a black identity, constructing a brown subject position subordinate to both whites *and* blacks, who can be and typically are read as "citizens."

Razib (T10) also provides some indication of differential levels within the category of brownness that complicates the racial hierarchy even more. He further explains:

> it depends on what we look like, right? some of us look like black people with straighter hair. some of us look like mediterranean people. most of us look like the darker skinned mexicans (yes, i know this may not be accurate to brown people, but i'm speaking from the perspective of a law enforcement official who may not be schooled in ethnic distinctions).

Because brownness spans across multiple nationalities and ethnicities, the level of suspicion to which one is subject then depends upon yet another level of intersecting hierarchical categorization that privileges certain nationalities over others, for instance, "Mediterranean people" over "Mexicans." When Sameer (T10) writes in a comment, "By illegal immigrant they mean Mexican, and any brown person who they mistake for Mexican," he draws upon the slippery discourse whereby Mexican is assumed to mean "illegal" to distinguish between a generalized phenotypically brown identity and a specific brown identity that is racialized as "Mexican." Razib and Sameer seem to argue that the bottom end of the color spectrum is a "Mexican brownness," where moving towards whiteness, blackness, or other brownness is preferable to brownness that is racialized as Mexican and therefore "illegal." This challenges Deliovsky and Kitossa's (2013) claim that moving away from blackness necessarily denotes greater privilege.

In addition to race and nationality, Latino Politics Blogger (T5) points to aspects of class and culture when he asks,

> Does that mean someone who speaks Spanish most of the time could trigger this 'reasonable suspicion'? Or is it someone who has a Piolin sticker on his car? Could someone with darker skin dressed in blue collar worker clothes be an illegal immigrant?

These intersections further construct hierarchical relationships amongst "brown" bodies. Latino Politics Blogger draws upon traditional notions of colorism that associate darker skin with lower socioeconomic class, which also aligns with dominant notions of "illegality." Speaking Spanish or having a Piolín sticker also become cultural cues to people's reading of one's brownness. The positionality of brownness, therefore, within this hierarchal structure is not fixed but dependent on intersecting factors that influence how bodies are read racially, underscoring the power of others to interpret and ascribe a brown person's identity. This is precisely the effect of racialization, through which an identity is ascribed regardless of the subjective experiences and histories of an individual. This ambiguity also means that "brown" people have some choice in how they perform their "brown" identities in order to effect particular readings, a point eloquently discussed by Amaya (2007b). Razib's comments spoke to the possibility of "passing" as black, which, interestingly, none of the Latino/a bloggers raised.

Unlike the Latino bloggers, who mostly seemed to agree upon their racialization by SB 1070, the South Asian bloggers revealed a somewhat contentious debate regarding the implications of SB 1070 for them. Another commenter, Tenzing (T10), for example, simply ignores his/her interpellation by SB 1070, writing, "Illegalsmexicans make a mexico of all of America." This reproduces dominant assumptions that SB 1070 only targets "illegal" immigrants and that all "illegal" immigrants are Mexicans who merit such treatment. However, other bloggers refute this perspective. Vivek (T10), in his original post, asks, "Do cosmopolitan American Brownz think that they won't be 'lawfully stopped' by 'reasonably suspicious' police officers? Because it happened to Maggie and me, immigrant kids from Mexico and Madras." Darth Paul (T10), applauding Vivek for his post, asserts, "AZ has a serious problem with nonwhite folk. Desis are not immune or capable of whiting out into the background." He challenges those South Asians who want to pass as white specifically because of limitations of their racial phenotype. While comments such as these by South Asian bloggers entail an implicit call for allying with Latino/as because of their shared experiences, the divergent views amongst the South Asians reflect their differential hierarchical status in comparison to Latino/as.

Contesting the Racialization of Brownness

Thus far, this paper has examined how the bloggers responding to SB 1070 construct brownness as a racialized category, with internal variations, composed of both visual markers (brown skin) and associations with threat, otherness, and "illegality." However, a key aspect of the critique of vernacular discourse is the exploration of how the discourse operates in a counterhegemonic manner, if at all (Ono & Sloop, 1995). Bloggers seem to contest their brown racialization in three main ways. First, some bloggers directly contest negative essentialized racializations. Lou (T7), a guest blogger on Manuél's blog site, relies on a combination of family values and civic responsibility to challenge the threat narrative: "And as for Mexican Immigrants TERRORIZING ARIZONANS? Talk to an everyday Arizonan! Working their job, going to school, invested in their community—I'd bet it would be hard to find one that has been TERRORIZED by a Mexican Immigrant." He rebuts the notion that Mexicans either pose any kind of threat or that an "everyday Arizonan" (i.e., white) has actually experienced the threat that is imputed to "browns."

Lou (T7) writes about his grandparents:

> They came to this country for freedom. For the opportunity to work hard, raise a family and have security. I am so fortunate to be a piece of this immigrant legacy and part of this vast family. We are part of something bigger than ourselves and hope that the same opportunity afforded to our family will continue to be afforded to others. BROWN OR OTHERWISE!

He reproduces a dominant narrative of the United States as a racially neutral "nation of immigrants" (Hayden, 2010; Streich, 2009) pursuing the American Dream to demonstrate how his grandparents, and himself as part of that legacy, belong within the larger U.S. American story. He illustrates how "browns" can be "good" citizens (Chávez, 2010) engaged in family, hard work, and the pursuit of freedom, drawing upon broader U.S. American values in order to call for greater inclusivity and a sense of belonging. In the following hypothetical scenario, Mexican American Citizen (T5) demonstrates how SB 1070 can negatively affect such "good" citizens:

> What if I were on my way in to work with a 9am appointment driving through rush hour traffic and I was going to make it just in time to my appointment but now I get pulled over by state enforcement because they felt they had reasonable suspicion. All I'm carrying with me is my insurance, registration, and drivers license just like every other American citizen driving on the road at that time. What if my drivers license is not considered a reasonable amount of proof? What if I'm taken into custody until my identity is verified? At this point, I've now missed my appointment and my job could be in jeopardy or in some instances, I could be let go from my job. So, now I'm unemployed I can no longer provide for my family the way I need to provide for them. Is it still a small price to pay? I'm American just like you. Just because my pigmentation is a little different that yours, does that mean I have to pay that small price and not you?

According to Mexican American Citizen, being stopped owing to suspicion of one's citizenship can have significant implications for one's livelihood. He demonstrates how SB 1070 can prevent "browns" from performing the "good" citizenship that it accuses them of defying, creating a Catch-22. He contests his racialization with calls for his inclusion within the American citizenry, arguing that he is "American, just like you" with the same rights and opportunities as "white" citizens. This strategy illustrates that bloggers' own subjective identifications straddle a world of both belonging and exclusion.

Gregory Tejeda (T9) contrasts the mobilization of the community with the ignorance and inaction of mainstream Americans:

> IT MAKES ME wonder if Latinos have a better understanding than the population at-large of the divisions between our differing types of government and the importance of maintaining those divisions, and if part of the solution to our nation's problems is to have more Latinos in positions of authority. We certainly couldn't do any worse than the political knuckleheads currently in charge.

"We" constructs a positive representation of the population as a more capable community, while "our" also identifies with the larger US population. The brown community better espouses "American" values and ideals than those claiming greater authenticity to the identification of "American." As Dickinson (2002) explains, people's movement creates a space and imbues it with symbolic meaning. Therefore, by referencing their contributions and their activism towards social change, bloggers challenge their positioning as a racialized other and instead position themselves as engaging in a form of cultural citizenship (Rosaldo, 1997) that constructs the space they inhabit.

A second approach is to broaden what "illegality," one of the racialized associations with brownness, encompasses. As Di (T4) writes,

> I have met people that told me that they came legally but overstayed, meaning they were now illegals, from Russia, Romania, Belgium, I don't know what happened to them, if they went back or not, but the where all white, most of the blond, they would never get stopped on "suspicion" of being illegal.

Just as Di presents the possibility of undocumented status being held by a white body, throughout the posts, other bloggers elucidate how "illegal immigrants" can range from Chinese to African to Russian. Although these comments attempt to disarticulate immigration and race altogether, by specifically naming race, they contest the race-neutrality of SB 1070, demonstrating how the law is merely a "cover" or "proxy" for racism and xenophobia targeted at the "brown menace."

> The biggest issue that most people (myself included) is what constitutes reasonable suspicion. If it's the colour of your skin, as Vivek pointed out, it is a big problem—as the guy with the dark skin could just as easily be a U.S. citizen/resident as the guy with white skin could have been a tourist that overstayed his visa. It is just like airport security in the US post-9/11—all those "random" searches in the name of security were not so random, after all. (ak, A10)

In this comment, ak, responding directly to a previous commenter's dismissal of the new requirement to carry identification, argues that the requirement is based on a fallible racial logic because suspicion, or "illegality," is not a dimension of race. When he challenges claims of race-neutrality by questioning the randomness of the application of laws, he relates the dominant discourse around SB 1070 to other instances of post-9/11 profiling and harassment of brown bodies, thereby reinforcing the contextuality of brownness in relation to loosely connected sociopolitical issues and events (Lugo-Lugo & Bloodsworth-Lugo, 2010).

A third related strategy, then, is to shift the associations of otherness and threat away from brown bodies. Bloggers seek to present an inverted structure in which they position racists as the outside threat:

> A terrorist invasion is upon us!!!!! The illegals are coming. Taking our jobs, using up our resources, TERRORIZING our children. Yes I'm talking about the terrorist invasion in Arizona-by racists who have made Arizona a dirty, ethnocentric, xenophobic place to be. A state RICH in history and beauty, is now being subjected to the ugliest attack on civil rights since the 1960s.

Lou (T7) constructs "us" as the citizen—with jobs, resources, and children—as the basis of the nation-state that needs protection from the threat. The same idea is constructed in a photograph from the 2010 National Day of Action (T2), in which a protester holds a poster that depicts Joe Arpaio donning a Ku Klux Klan outfit and labels him as a terrorist. It repositions the relationship between "browns" and certain white "Americans" through an argument that otherness is not about race but about ideological values and beliefs.

Discussion and Conclusion

Through the analysis of vernacular discourse, this study illustrates the complex ways in which bloggers articulate and contest brownness. Although Latino/a and South Asian American bloggers place varied emphases on phenotypic and cultural features as defining "brownness," their discourses demonstrate a shared experience of state oppression and suspicion effected through their racialization. This analysis also illuminates complex strategies for challenging this racialization. To an extent, it reconfirms the notion that vernacular rhetoric does not always translate into counterhegemonic discourses. Bloggers' contestations of the negative racialization of "brown" often result in strategies of "normative belonging" (Chávez, 2010, p. 139) to distance themselves from negative representations of "illegality." Manuel's (T8) remark "that brown-skinned gente should bend over and take" the oppression reproduces an antigay rhetoric. At the same time, by shifting the definition of otherness away from race towards adherence to certain values, albeit based in dominant ideologies, they strategically try to redefine the conversation and demonstrate that citizenship, whether legal or cultural, is not a factor of race.

Bloggers' emphasis on their racialized experiences illustrates how brownness, as a racial formation crossing particular ethnic groups, is reinfused with legitimacy in the specific context of immigration and SB 1070. Many South Asian bloggers were interpellated by legislation that ostensibly targeted the Latino/a community of Arizona. In this context, the model minority discourse, which typically distinguishes South Asians from and privileges them over Latino/as (Prashad, 2000), more or less recedes as their constructed brownness minimizes the difference between these two groups. The racial profiling and state oppression that Latino/a and South Asian American bloggers describe instead highlight their shared or overlapping experiences as "victims of 'nativist' arguments" (Alcoff, 2006, p. 248). The vernacular construction of this formation exemplifies Prashad's (2000) statement,

> Commitment and identification are truly important if we are to fashion a politics at a disjuncture from the way we are used by white supremacy as well as against the types of state policies that continue to exploit the population. (p. 193)

However, any sense of community or coalition constituted in this discourse is admittedly a loose one. The discourses also demonstrate the variations in these experiences brought about by intersectionalities and hierarchies *within* categories of brownness, leading simultaneously to differential experiences. Although South Asian bloggers engage in conversations amongst themselves wherein many encourage others to cease trying to align themselves with whiteness and instead understand the similarities of their experiences with other "brown" cultural groups, this conversation implicitly invokes their model minority positioning. The Latino bloggers, while acknowledging the implications of brownness for other cultural groups to varying degrees, never specifically acknowledge or extend their discussions to South Asians. Ultimately, the South Asian and Latino/a bloggers, despite discussing their shared or overlapping experiences, have yet to discuss them *with each other*. The epistemic privileging of essentialized racial and ethnic identities is not an easy one to challenge, as indicated by those bloggers who maintain a highly ethnocultural construction of brownness. As Prashad (2000) writes, "The tragedy of experiential or identity politics, in its narrow sense, is that it pushes a person or group not toward identification with the struggles of others but toward an exclusive concern with the identity of oneself and one's group" (p. 193). At the same time, this study indicates that such blogs as these could be an ideal site for such conversations to occur.

Lastly, this study contributes to an enhanced understanding of racial structures in the United States. Bloggers' differentiation of their subjective experiences of alien citizenship and racialized belonging from white or black citizenship problematizes the rigidity of their "middling" positionality within the U.S. racial structure, encouraging a more contextualized approach. Identities cannot be fixed within a hierarchy as they are constantly shifting based on diasporic movements and the interactions that occur therein as well as the political and material structures that "delimit and frame the formation/dissolution of diasporic communities [and] their identities (and claims to a nation)" (Drzewiecka & Halualani, 2002, p. 342; Drzewiecka & Steyn, 2012; Halualani, 2008). Therefore, hierarchical structures based in black/white binaries— or even continuums of color that place "browns" in the middle—are incomplete, simplistic, and essentialized frameworks for capturing the complexities of people's racialized experiences. This study highlights the unique forms of discrimination and policing that "browns" experience on the basis of assumed citizenship that have material implications for their lived experiences in the United States. Understanding this contextuality is particularly crucial for complicating the black/white binary constructively without dismissing or negating other forms of oppression faced by black Americans.

This study theorizes the construction of brownness, which, like other racial formations, is not a unified collective identity based in ethnocultural similarities but one that emerges across the shared experiences of cultural groups in specific contexts, in this case, SB 1070. It has important implications for studying racialized belonging and citizenship in the United States as well as for the study of diverse ethnocultural communities that experience browning in the context of immigration discourses. This study of brownness therefore demonstrates the need to reconsider and adapt frameworks for renewed understandings of racial formations and racial structures, as well as some of the challenges of doing so.

Notes

[1] This blog site was ended as of May 2012.
[2] The discursive norms of weblogs minimize the importance of proofreading for grammatical precision, including capitalization, punctuation, and spelling. Therefore, I did not change the texts to suit scholarly norms of grammar, nor have I identified any such instances using the indicator "[sic]." All direct quotes have been directly cut and pasted from the blog texts in order to preserve their integrity.

References

Alcoff, L.M. (2006). *Visible identities: Race, gender, and the self.* New York, NY: Oxford University Press.
Amaya, H. (2007a). Amores perros and racialised masculinities in contemporary Mexico. *New Cinemas: Journal of Contemporary Film, 5*(3), 201–216. doi:10.1386/ncin.5.3.201/1
Amaya, H. (2007b). Performing acculturation: Rewriting the Latina/o immigrant self. *Text and Performance Quarterly, 27*(3), 194–212.
Anguiano, C.A., & Chávez, K.R. (2011). DREAMers' discourse: Young Latino/a immigrants and the naturalization of the American Dream. In M.A. Holling & B.M. Calafell (Eds.), *Latino/a discourses in vernacular spaces: Somos de una voz* (pp. 81–99). Lanham, MD: Lexington Books.
Berg, J.A. (2009). White public opinion toward undocumented immigrants: Threat and interpersonal environment. *Sociological Perspectives, 52*(1), 39–58.
Bonilla-Silva, E. (2004). From biracial to tri-racial: Towards a new system of racial stratification in the USA. *Ethnic and Racial Studies, 27*(6), 931–950.
Bonilla-Silva, E. (2009). *Racism without racists: Color-blind racism and the persistence of racial inequality in America.* Lanham, MD: Rowman & Littlefield.
Burman, J. (2010). Suspects in the city: Browning the 'not-quite' Canadian citizen. *Cultural Studies, 24*(2), 200–213.
Calvente, L.B.Y. (2011). "This is one line you won't have to worry about crossing": Crossing borders and becoming. In M.A. Holling & B.M. Calafell (Eds.), *Latino/a discourses in vernacular spaces: Somos de una voz* (pp. 185–201). Lanham, MD: Lexington Books.
Camacho, A.S. (2008). *Migrant imaginaries: Latino cultural politics in the U.S.–Mexico borderlands.* New York, NY: New York University Press.
Chávez, K.R. (2009). Exploring the defeat of Arizona's marriage amendment and the specter of the immigrant as queer. *Southern Communication Journal, 74*(3), 314–324.
Chávez, K.R. (2010). Border (in)securities: Normative and differential belonging in LGBTQ and immigrant rights discourse. *Communication & Critical/Cultural Studies, 7*(2), 136–155.
Chávez, L. (2008). *The Latino threat: Constructing immigrants, citizens, and the nation.* Palo Alto, CA: Stanford University Press.
Cisneros, J.D. (2012). Looking "illegal": Affect, rhetoric, and performativity in Arizona's Senate Bill 1070. In D.R. DeChaine (Ed.), *Border rhetorics: Citizenship and identity on the US-Mexico frontier* (pp. 133–150). Tuscaloosa, AL: University of Alabama Press.
Collier, M.J. (2005). Theorizing cultural identifications: Critical updates and continuing evolution. In W.B. Gudykunst (Ed.), *Theorizing about intercultural communication* (pp. 235–256). Thousand Oaks, CA: Sage.
Collins, P.H. (2005). *Black sexual politics: African Americans, gender, and the new racism.* New York, NY: Routledge.
Córdova, N.I. (2011). Nuestro Himno as heterotopic mimicry: On the ambivalences of a Latin@ voicing. In M.A. Holling & B.M. Calafell (Eds.), *Latino/a discourses in vernacular spaces: Somos de una voz* (pp. 101–22). Lanham, MD: Lexington Books.
Das Gupta, M. (2006). *Unruly immigrants: Rights, activism, and transnational South Asian politics in the United States.* Durham, NC: Duke University Press.
Delgado, F. (2009). Reflections on being/performing Latino identity in the academy. *Text and Performance Quarterly, 29*(2), 149–164

Delgado, R., & Stefancic, J. (2000). Latino/a critical ("latcrit") legal studies: Review essay. *Aztlán: A Journal of Chicano Studies, 25*(2), 161-189.

Deliovsky, K., & Kitossa, T. (2013). Beyond black and white: When going beyond may take us out of bounds. *Journal of Black Studies, 44*(2), 158-181.

Dick, H.P. (2011). Making immigrants illegal in small-town USA. *Journal of Linguistic Anthropology, 21*(S1), E35-E55.

Dickinson, G. (2002). Joe's rhetoric: Finding authenticity at Starbucks. *Rhetoric Society Quarterly, 32*(4), 5-27. Retrieved from http://www.jstor.org

Drzewiecka, J.A. (2002). Reinventing and contesting identities in constitutive discourses: Between diaspora and its others. *Communication Quarterly, 50*(1), 1-23.

Drzewiecka, J.A., & Halualani, R.T. (2002). The structural-cultural dialectic of diasporic politics. *Communication Theory, 12*(3): 340-366.

Drzewiecka, J.A., & Steyn, M. (2012). Racial immigrant incorporation: Material-symbolic articulation of identities. *Journal of International and Intercultural Communication, 5*(1), 1-19.

Durham, M.G. (2001). Displaced persons: Symbols of South Asian femininity and the returned gaze in U.S. media culture. *Communication Theory, 11*(2), 201-217.

Durham, M.G. (2004). Constructing the "new ethnicities": Media, sexuality, and diaspora identity in the lives of South Asian immigrant girls. *Critical Studies in Media Communication, 21*(2), 140-161.

Enck-Wanzer, D. (2011). Race, coloniality, and geo-body politics: *The Garden* as Latin@ vernacular discourse. *Environmental Communication, 5*(3), 363-371.

Flores, L.A. (2003). Constructing rhetorical borders: Peons, illegal aliens, and competing narratives of immigration. *Critical Studies in Media Communication, 20*(4), 362-387.

Flores, L.A., Moon, D.G., & Nakayama, T.K. (2006). Dynamic rhetorics of race: California's racial privacy initiative and the shifting grounds of racial politics. *Communication and Critical/Cultural Studies, 3*(3), 181-201.

Frost, H. (2010). Being "brown" in a Canadian suburb. *Journal of Immigrant & Refugee Studies, 8*(2), 212-232.

Gajjala, R. (2006). Consuming/producing/inhabiting South-Asian digital diasporas. *New Media & Society, 8*(2), 179-185.

Hall, S. (1993). Cultural identity and diaspora. *Colonial discourse and postcolonial theory: A reader*.

Halualani, R.T. (2011). Abstracting and de-racializing diversity: The articulation of diversity in the post-race era. In M.G. Lacy & K.A. Ono (Eds.), *Critical rhetorics of race* (pp. 247-264). New York, NY: New York University Press.

Halualani, R.T. (2008). "Where exactly is the pacific?": Global migrations, diasporic movements, and intercultural communication. *Journal of International and Intercultural Communication, 1*(1), 3-22.

Hasian Jr., M., & Delgado, F. (1998). The trials and tribulations of racialized critical rhetorical theory: Understanding the rhetorical ambiguities of Proposition 187. *Communication Theory, 8*(3), 245-270.

Hayden, B. (2010). Impeach the traitors: Citizenship, sovereignty and nation in immigration control activism in the United States. *Social Semiotics, 20*(2), 155-174.

Hegde, R. (1996). Narratives of silence: Rethinking gender, agency, and power from the communication experiences of battered women in South India. *Communication Studies, 47*(4), 303-317.

Holling, M.A. (2006). Forming oppositional social concord to California's Proposition 187 and squelching social discord in the vernacular space of CHICLE. *Communication and Critical/Cultural Studies, 3*(3), 202-222.

Holling, M.A. (2011). Patrolling national identity, masking white supremacy: The minuteman project. In M.G. Lacy & K.A. Ono (Eds.), *Critical rhetorics of race* (pp. 98-116). New York, NY: New York University Press.

Holling, M.A., & Calafell, B.M. (2011). *Latino/a discourses in vernacular spaces: Somos de una voz.* Lanham, MD: Lexington Books.

Hookway, N. (2008). "Entering the blogosphere": Some strategies for using blogs in social research. *Qualitative Research, 8*(1), 91-113.

Howard, R.G. (2008a). Electronic hybridity: The persistent processes of the vernacular web. *Journal of American Folklore, 121,* 192–218.

Howard, R.G. (2008b). The vernacular web of participatory media. *Critical Studies in Media Communication, 25*(5), 490–513.

Lugo-Lugo, C.R., & Bloodsworth-Lugo, M.K. (2010). 475° from September 11: Citizenship, immigration, same-sex marriage, and the browning of terror. *Cultural Studies, 24*(2), 234–255.

Martínez, E. (1993). Beyond black/white: The racisms of our time, *Social Justice, 20*(1/2), 22–34.

Ngai, M. (2004). *Impossible subjects: Illegal aliens and the making of modern America.* Princeton, NJ: Princeton University Press.

Omi, M., & Winant, H. (1994). *Racial formation in the United States: From the 1960s to the 1990s.* New York, NY: Routledge.

Ono, K.A., & Sloop, J.M. (1995). The critique of vernacular discourse. *Communication Monographs, 62*(1), 19–46.

Ono, K.A., & Sloop, J.M. (2002). *Shifting borders: Rhetoric, immigration, and California's Proposition 187.* Philadelphia, PA: Temple University Press.

Parameswaran, R., & Cardoza, K. (2009). Melanin on the margins: Advertising and the cultural politics of fair/light/white beauty in India. *Journalism & Communication Monographs, 11*(3), 213–274.

Perea, J.F. (1997). The black/white binary paradigm of race: The 'normal science' of American racial thought. *California Law Review, 85,* 1213–1258.

Potter, J.E. (2014). Brown-skinned outlaws: An ideographic analysis of "illegal(s)." *Communication, Culture, & Critique, 7*(2), 228–245.

Prashad, V. (2000). *The karma of brown folk.* Minneapolis, MN: University of Minnesota Press.

Rosaldo, R. (1997). Cultural citizenship, inequality, and multiculturalism. In W.V. Flores & R. Benmayor (Eds.), *Latino cultural citizenship* (pp. 27–38). Boston, MA: Beacon Press.

Sacirbey, O. (2012, 17 August). Muslims take special precautions for Eid Ul-Fitr. *Huffington Post.* Retrieved from http://www.huffingtonpost.com

Sandoval, Jr., T.F.S. (2008). Disobedient bodies: Racialization, resistance, and the mass (re)articulation of the Mexican immigrant body. *American Behavioral Scientist, 52*(4), 580–597.

Semati, M. (2010). Islamophobia, culture and race in the age of empire. *Cultural Studies, 24*(2), 256–275.

Sharma, S. (2010). Taxi cab publics and the production of brown space after 9/11. *Cultural Studies, 24*(2), 183–199.

Silva, K. (2010). Brown: From identity to identification. *Cultural Studies, 24*(2), 167–182.

Streich, G.W. (2009). Discourses of American national identity: Echoes and lessons from the 1910s–1920s. *Citizenship Studies, 13*(3), 267–287.

Sundar, P. (2008). To "brown it up" or to "bring down the brown": Identity and strategy in second-generation, South Asian-Canadian youth. *Journal of Ethnic & Cultural Diversity in Social Work, 17*(3), 251–278.

Thangaraj, S. (2012). Playing through differences: Black–white racial logic and interrogating South Asian American identity. *Ethnic and Racial Studies, 35*(6), 988–1006.

Wu, F. (2003). *Yellow: Race in America beyond black and white.* New York, NY: Basic Books.

Resisting Whiteness: Mexican American Studies and Rhetorical Struggles for Visibility

Chad M. Nelson

In late 2012, Santino J. Rivera published a collection of Chicana/o literature as a cultural and political response to the closure of Mexican American Studies in the Tucson Unified School District. This essay argues that Rivera's text invites critical interrogation of the whiteness ideologies underlying critiques of MAS in an attempt to make spaces for Chicana/o sensibilities. Such sensibilities, this essay argues, include In Lak'ech *and* mestiza *rhetorics, which emphasize cultural empowerment, identification, spiritual love, and humanization.*

The Tucson Unified School District's (TUSD) Mexican American/Raza Studies program (MAS) is the late harvest of numerous labors including student organizing in the 1960–1970s, Chicana/o[1] grassroots activism, and various class action lawsuits including *Mendoza et al. v. Tucson School District No. 1, et al.* (1978) and *Rosalie Lopez et al. v. Tucson Unified Schools* (1997) (Acuña, 2011; Romero, 2010). Inaugurated in 1998, the MAS department offered courses in literature, mathematics, government, history, and art. Similar to multicultural education in general, these courses aimed for diverse cultural inclusion and educational equity. But unlike dominant forms of multicultural education, MAS teachers achieved their goals through an educational model called Critically Compassionate Intellectualism that combines critical pedagogies, authentic caring of students, and a social justice-oriented curriculum (Cammarota & Romero, 2006). Coupling critical race theory (Delgado & Stefancic, 2001) with critical pedagogy (Freire, 1970/2010), the MAS curriculum centered Chicana/o experiences and knowledge in the educational environment in order to invite students and teachers into dialogic struggles toward critical consciousness of oppressions. This restructuring of the classroom offered "each student the opportunities they need to construct his or her own counterhistory" to "the majoritarian story that legitimizes the Anglo story as the 'American' story" (Romero & Arce, 2011, p. 7). After all, Critically Compassionate Intellectualism was intended to deconstruct systemic injustices in the TUSD, create spaces for previously silenced voices in Tucson, and position all students, especially Latina/o[2] students, for academic success (Cammarota & Romero).

But despite the program's impressive success at closing the achievement gap (Cambium Learning, 2011), the TUSD Governing Board and the state of Arizona belligerently criticized the curriculum and pedagogical model. Tom Horne, the former Arizona Superintendent of Public Instruction (2003–2011) and the current Arizona Attorney General, was the primary critic of MAS. To get a sense of the oft-repeated primary argument against the ethnic studies classes, it is necessary to quote at length from a rather transparent letter Horne distributed to the "Citizens of Tucson":

> I believe people are individuals, not exemplars of racial groups. What is important about people is what they know, what they can do, their ability to appreciate beauty, their character, and not what race into which they are born. They are entitled to be treated that way. It is fundamentally wrong to divide students up according to their racial group, and teach them separately. (T. Horne, personal communication, June 11, 2007)

Following Horne's extensive campaign to shut down MAS, Governor Jan Brewer signed Arizona HB 2281 (2010) into law. Suspiciously parroting the anti-immigrant tone of Arizona SB 1070 (2010), the legislation prohibits courses that "promote the overthrow of the United States government. Promote resentment toward a race or class of people. Are designed primarily for pupils of a particular ethnic group. Advocate ethnic solidarity instead of the treatment of pupils as individuals" (p. 1). Ironically, these texts allege the dangerousness of centering specific racial identities in the classroom while simultaneously minimizing their significance in a student's education. In this supposed "post-racial" moment, individuality is commonly accepted as the elixir for racial inequities (Lacy, 2010). If we somehow treat every person as equal, then racial discrimination will eventually dissipate. Within this colorblind logic, the accusation of racism is racist par excellence in that it violates the fundamental liberal belief in a student's individuality as her only morally legitimate path to academic success. In the absence of racism, multiculturalism and tolerance have emerged as means to celebrate cultural diversity while inadvertently deracializing public discourse and cloaking institutional racism (Flores, Moon, & Nakayama, 2006; Herakova, Jelača, Sibii, & Cooks, 2011).

In this essay, I argue that this twisted post-racial logic underlies and motivates criticisms of TUSD's Mexican American Studies. Colorblind arguments, such as those embedded in Tom Horne's letter and HB 2281, neglect historical positions of white privilege and falsely assume that race can be simply transcended by both whites and non-whites (Crenshaw, 1997). This argument is artistically developed in Santino J. Rivera's collection of Chicana/o literature titled, ¡Ban This!: The BSP Anthology of Xican@ Literature (2012). The collection is a piercing political and cultural critique of the dominant racial discourses and inequitable experiences of Chicana/os in the TUSD. Explicating the present mechanics of racism, Rivera's selections collectively function to expose how xenophobic positions toward Chicana/os are maintained by whiteness. Whiteness ideologically functions to erect and protect discursive and material forms of white privilege (Crenshaw). Because whiteness has become naturalized and seemingly universalized, it is often perceived as the norm by which all "others" are to understand themselves (Nakayama & Krizek, 1995). Of course, whiteness is tricky to delineate owing to its ever adaptable and historically contingent qualities (Frankenberg, 1993). Nonetheless, invisibility does not lighten its effects. Whiteness has been strategically used to marginalize the lived experiences of "others" (Morrison, 1992), further capitalist exploitation (Roediger, 1991), and justify violent racial wars (Baldwin, 2011). It becomes the task of the critical rhetorician to illuminate the historically contingent constructs that promote its socially privileged position (Nakayama & Krizek, 1995).

One of the many pressing questions posed by the study of whiteness is how to interrupt the interpretation of its normative power. Whiteness scholars in Communication Studies have offered several strategies including conversation between whites and non-whites (Simpson, 2008; Warren & Hytten, 2004), critical self-reflexivity (Crenshaw, 1997; Nakayama & Krizek, 1995), intersectionality (Moon & Flores, 2000), and critiques of embodied performances of whiteness (Cooks, 2003; Warren, 2001). Drawing from Rivera's literary collection, this essay offers an additional critical strategy, namely, positioning Chicana/o identities as a resource of intervention into the invisibility of whiteness. Rhetoricians have well documented how Latina/os have articulated their identities through cultural forms such as music (Pineda, 2009), murals (LaWare, 1998), and theater (Holling & Calafell, 2007). Performances such as these are intended to resist, at least in part, hegemonic discourses, empower spaces for alternative cultural narratives, and draw critical attention to the discriminatory political and economic contexts in which co-cultural communities live. For Calafell (2007), embracing a Chicana feminist perspective in a space of overwhelming whiteness places her "experience as a woman of color at the center, allowing me to see myself not as a victim or someone with no history but as a strong woman with an illustrious but silenced history" (p. 14). Centering previously marginalized identities in curricula and pedagogies presents viable opportunities for both critical engagement with whiteness and empowerment of co-cultural communities, as Calafell and TUSD student experiences testify.

Following suit, this essay positions co-cultural consciousness, and particularly the Chicana/o sensibilities and experiences voiced in Rivera's literary collection, as integral to the whiteness studies project. Certainly self-reflexivity of whiteness and privileged practices is crucial for working against white privilege (Jackson, Shin, & Hilson, 2000), but self-reflexivity alone risks becoming a post-racial echo chamber wherein white norms and privileges are reinforced and amplified. John Warren (2001) voiced a similar concern, which he described as "an unreflective immersion in the politics of whiteness" (p. 101). Apprehension over self-reflexivity begs a critical impetus to set reflexivity into motion and to ensure it achieves its anti-racist pursuits, and according to Rivera's collection, Chicana/o sensibilities and experiences function as such impetuses to expose the hegemonic constructions of whiteness and to locate potentialities for Chicana/o empowerment in Tucson. Critiques of whiteness through the lens of Chicana/o sensibilities and experiences extend similar co-cultural critiques of whiteness (Griffin & Calafell, 2011; Jackson et al., 2000). However, I am not suggesting that a redefinition of Chicana/o identities alone is able to improve material conditions for Chicana/os in Tucson or to undermine altogether the discursive and material aspects of whiteness circulating in the TUSD. But rather, as Enck-Wanzer (2011) models, rhetorical critics must view performances of cultural empowerment as negotiated within historical colonialisms as well as the economic and political constraints on that particular community. Out of such work, a nuanced depiction emerges of the ways in which identities in a community contribute to opportunities for political agency that are themselves shaped by dominant interests.

With that being said, the Chicana/o identities read in ¡Ban This! (2012) constitute compelling challenges to the assumption of a "post-racial" society, exposing its representations to be elaborate, persuasive constructs upheld (in)visibly by whiteness. To expose this facade in the TUSD, I employ the tools of critical rhetoric. As McKerrow (1989) argues, "the initial task of a critical rhetoric is one of re-creation—constructing an argument that identifies the integration of power and knowledge and delineates the role of power/knowledge in structuring social practices" (p. 102). Out of this re-creation of the arguments embedded in Rivera's literary selections emerge two rhetorical strategies for interrupting and working against white privilege. Deeply rooted in Chicana/o sensibilities, these rhetorical strategies are referred to in this essay as *In Lak'ech* and *mestiza* rhetorics. The collection suggests that these humanizing rhetorics are at the true center of MAS, and as such, they are intended to empower audiences to challenge embedded whiteness in Tucson.

In writing this rhetorical critique, I first briefly survey the history of Chicana/o educational experiences and the literatures pertaining to Chicana/o identities and resistant literature. I then interpret how Rivera's collection invites critiques of whiteness before explaining how the text empowers Chicana/o sensibilities of *In Lak'ech* and *mestiza* rhetorics.

Historical Background: Chicana/o Educational Experiences

Chicana/o schooling in the U.S. Southwest cannot be understood apart from the historical contexts of Spanish colonialism, Americanization programs, and resistance against these hegemonic forces (MacDonald & Monkman, 2005). That is, the schooling of Chicana/os is situated within the "broader Latina/o collective experience of oppression within the U.S. racial classification system" (Hidalgo, 2005, p. 378). The dominance of core American cultural values in schooling, including individualism and achievement orientation, has historically alienated Chicana/os from their communal identities (Bernal, 2006). Whether it was "Mexican schools" acculturating Latina/os for perceived cultural and linguistic deficiencies after the Mexican–American War, immigrant education designed to produce cheap labor during the twentieth century, or persistently under-resourced and segregated schooling, Latina/o experiences in the U.S. education system have been marked by xenophobia and inequity (Gonzalez, 1990/2013; Spring, 2013).

In the 1960s, addressing these inequitable and culturally exclusive education policies and practices were among the foremost civil rights issues for Chicana/o communities. Before 1960, Mexican American struggles for educational equity centered on overcoming segregation with litigation and were primarily carried out by adults; however, post-1960 Chicana/o involvement in education reform was driven by mass student mobilization and direct action in schools (San Miguel, 2013). Students, teachers, and community activists strategically used strikes, walkouts, boycotts, and demonstrations against English-only and Anglo-centric structures and curricula (Gutiérrez, 2011). For instance, in 1968, thousands of Chicana/o high school students walked out of East Los Angeles public schools to challenge discrimination, cultural exclusion, English-only rules, poor school conditions, and lack of Chicana/o teachers and administrative staff (San Miguel). Additional strategies for addressing educational inequity included increasing Chicana/o school board representation, advocating bilingual and bicultural education, improving Chicana/o student achievement, implementing pluralism, including Mexican American content in the classroom, and attempting to address community poverty (San Miguel).

In the late 1960s, similar struggles for educational justice took place in Tucson. Community organizers, parents, and students participated in a series of school walkouts. The goal simply stated: Chicana/o voices and experiences should be included in the classroom. In spite of these demonstrations, discrimination against Latino/as, African Americans, and Native Americans remained deeply entrenched in the school district. It was not until a series of court rulings that the situation began to change. In June 1978, the court ordered the district to desegregate, and in compliance with the ruling, the parties drew up a comprehensive desegregation plan that added phonetics programs for Chicano/a first graders and a bilingual Standard English as a Second Language program for co-cultural students (Brousseau, 1993). Despite considerable white opposition within the district, Tucson community advocacy led to the inclusion of courses for Native Americans, Mexican Americans, African Americans, and Asian students in 1998 (Brousseau; Romero & Arce, 2011). In 2009, the TUSD filed a petition and was granted an end to federal court oversight of its desecration plans. But, in 2011, the U.S. Court of Appeals for the Ninth Circuit reversed that court's decision and ordered continued oversight of the district's plans to achieve unitary status.

Ch(X)icana/o Identities: Struggles for Empowerment

The identities of the Chicana/os at the center of these struggles for educational equity emerged out of what Anzaldúa (1999) calls *"una herida abierta"* (p. 25) of oppression and illegitimacy. With the signing of the Treaty of Guadalupe Hidalgo (1848), the US–Mexico border crossed those who were once living in Mexico. In these colonized territories lived the "prohibited," "forbidden," and "transgressors" alongside those considered "legitimate inhabitants" (Anzaldúá, p. 25). This crisis of home, and the racism and exploitation that accompanied it, forced most Mexicans to assimilate into Mexican Americans. But the 1950–1970s generation refused to assimilate and constituted an identity that was neither Mexican nor Anglo (García, 1997). Within a context of political and economic marginalization and racial injustice, the assertiveness of their Indigenous, Mexican, and Spanish identities brought about a culture-affirming national consciousness among people who called themselves "Chicano" (Alurista, 1981). In the 1960s, "Chicano" united a heterogeneous population around a common culture and language, and out of this cultural nationalism, a resistance movement emerged to seek equity and social justice for Mexican Americans (Alurista; Hammerback & Jensen, 1994). Vital to the success of this Chicano Movement was the Mexican and Indigenous symbols used to critique dominant racialized ideologies, empower political action, and establish a sense of cultural empowerment among Chicana/os (Delgado, 1998).

Rightly, several scholars have critiqued Chicanismo as harboring masculine biases and gender inequities (Garcia; 1989; Holling, 2006a). Rhetorical critiques of the intersection of Chicana/o identities with gender, sexuality, and class continue to multiply (Calafell, 2007; Holling, 2006b). Additionally, in response to the exceeding complexity and heterogeneity of oppression under neoliberal polices, Xicana/o identities have sprouted (Rios, 2008). "Xicana/o" hails from the Nahuatl spelling of "Chicana/o" and symbolizes a desire to draw from Indigenous cultural roots to locate symbols and strategies for resistance to colonization (Baca, 2008). Extending beyond Mexican Americans to include Central and South Americans, the Xicana/o identity highlights unity and justice as guiding moral principles, represents a willingness to critique other Xicana/os, and incorporates a multidimensional approach to address issues faced by all Xicana/os, including immigration and language barriers (Rios; Urrieta, 2004).

Chicana/o Literature: A Project of Self-Assertion and Resistance

From the 1960 to the 1970s, most Chicano literature embodied the cultural nationalism of the Chicano Movement (Alurista, 1981). Chicana/o authors strategically imported cultural nationalism into their novels and poetry to voice their social alienation and to claim a sense of self for a forgotten and abhorred people (Eysturoy & Gurpegui, 1990). Literary works such as *The Autobiography of a Brown Buffalo* (1972) and *Memories of the Alhambra* (1977) describe characters searching for identity among Spanish, Mexican, and Indigenous roots. Novels such as *... y no se lo* *tragó la tierra* (1971) and the work of Rolando Hinojosa highlight the brutal conditions of Chicana/o farm workers and the politico-economic systems that maintain oppressive Anglo-Chicana/o power relationships (Eysturoy & Gurpegui). Within the Chicano Movement, these literary works spurred a critical consciousness of dispossession and displacement (Pèrez-Torres, 1995). In this context, concientization implies more than mere awareness. It simultaneously requires emancipatory change. As Freire (1970/2010) writes, dialogic struggles with the contradictions of their social and political realities empower the oppressed to take action against dominant structures and false representations of co-cultural communities. Likewise Chicano literature in this historical period functioned as a space wherein Chicana/os could dialogically engage in a critical process of becoming "authors of their realities and self-determine their roles in society" (Berta-Ávila, 2003, p. 128). For instance, cultural myths such as the Nahuatl homeland of Aztlán were used in Chicano narratives including "The Ballad of Gregorio Cortez" to critique Anglo power structures in the U.S. Southwest and to carve out a land for the disinherited to call home (Rodriguez, 2000). This self-assertion of Chicana/o values and political interests in the form of Mexican and Indigenous literary archetypes, bilingual conversational styles, cultural folklore, and Chicana/o imagery also countered popular Anglo representations of Mexican Americans as lazy, criminal, and ignorant (Alurista).

In response to this literary era, Chicana literature emerged as a critique of the patriarchy and stereotypical maternal roles for women in Chicanismo (Eysturoy & Gurpegui, 1990). Whereas Chicanismo was narrowly focused on cultural survival, Chicana feminists also argued for critiques of sexism in Chicana/o communities (Garcia, 1989). In Chicana literature, this critique took the form of opposition to patriarchal institutions, a reinterpretation of Chicana cultural archetypes, and an emphasis on distinctive female experiences (Sandoval, 2008). Several Chicana authors centered the *mestiza* identity in their writing in an attempt to resist both Chicanismo and Anglo stereotypes of Chicanas (Anzaldúa, 1999; Delgadillo, 2011). This *mestiza* trope draws from the inclusive hybrid identity of Chicanas as a means to locate interrelationships between Anglos and Chicana/os as well as to address racism, sexism, and classism (Pèrez-Torres, 1995). Similar to earlier Chicana prose, Ana Castillo's (1994) *Massacre of the Dreamers: Essays on Xicanisma* is an example of both a Chicana feminist critique of traditional gender roles and use of the *mestiza* trope to critique other dominant dualities. She calls this consciousness, Xicanisma: "Xicanisma is an ever-present consciousness of our interdependence specifically rooted in our culture and history. ... It is yielding; never resistant to change, one based on wholeness not dualisms" (Castillo, 1994, p. 226). Drawing from, but not limited to the Chicana experience, Xicanisma empowers a subversive politics that opposes individualism and other capitalistic values (Schoeffel, 2008). Read through Xicanisma and Chicana/o resistance literatures, we begin to see the subversive nature of TUSD's Mexican American Studies and Rivera's collection of Chicana/o literature, and with this in mind, I now turn to the rhetorical text.

¡Ban This!: Making Whiteness Visible in Tucson

Published by his independent publication company, Broken Sword Publications, Santino J. Rivera's collection includes selections of poetry, short stories, nonfiction, and excerpts from larger novels. The book is divided into 40 short sections. Each section is devoted to a single author, and typically includes a brief biography of the author followed by one or more of her works. These selections vary from a poem about breakfast tacos to Rodolfo Acuña's defense of TUSD's Mexican American Studies program.

Taken as a whole, Rivera's collection rhetorically serves to expose the whiteness tropes underlying critiques of MAS. One way in which the collection does this is by interrupting the perceived normativity of whiteness by which all "others" are judged. In her poem, "Finding a Voice," Adrianna Simone describes her childhood experiences in the U.S. education system:

> When I was young, I had no voice./ I tried to speak, but no one understood me./ I spent fourteen long years in speech therapy./ I knew I was different, and I was tormented for it./ I needed to learn perfect English/ if I wanted to "fit in." (p. 293)

In this state of "loneliness" separated "from potential friends and the family who loved me," she desperately attempted to learn English by reading "European" books (p. 294). "I started with *their* tradition, *their* norm./ What I discovered was my culture, my history./ Always there, sitting on the bookshelves,/ if a bit hidden behind other crap" (p. 295). Simone is disclosing the pain associated with the cultural deficit ideology in education (Apple, 2006). This ideology shares the basic suppositions as colonialism in that both assume the superiority of the colonizer, implicitly constituting the other as inferior (Beck & Allexsaht-Snider, 2001). Pushing the argument further, it seems that cultural deficiency also exemplifies the paradoxical "violent normativity" of whiteness (Shome, 2000, p. 367). For those occupying the position of whiteness, English-only instruction and Western knowledge are the unacknowledged, and often unconscious, norms in the classroom. In the style of Toni Morrison (1992), Simone's poem attempts to convey through anecdotes of isolation and abandonment that knowledge claims and linguistic forms are not ideologically innocent. Their existence as "standards" is legitimized through violent suppression of other "facts" and cultural voices in the classroom, particularly in the TUSD.

In fact, Simone confronts the TUSD School Board asking, "Who are you to say what/ the facts are?/ Have you experienced this/ racism and prejudice?/ Your privilege and/ 'colorblindness'/ just perpetuates/ the same raping of our culture that has been forced on us/ for decades" (pp. 292–293). "Facts," in the closing of MAS, signify what Frankenberg (1993) calls the privileging of a normative racial group. In 2006, Dolores Huerta gave a speech at Tucson High Magnet School in which she told students "Republicans hate Latinos." In response, Tom Horne sent his deputy, Margaret Dugan to address the students. "When she began speaking, some students stood, turned their backs and lifted clenched fists in the air. ... Some walked out" (Ceasar, 2011, para. 14). Hailing symbols from the 1960–1970s Chicano Movement, clenched fists and walkouts symbolize Chicana/o consciousness raising and resistance to the political status-quo. Responding to this threatening cultural self-assertion, Horne wrote a letter listing reasons for closing MAS. He concludes the letter with, "I can use my pulpit to bring out the facts" (p. 7). When whiteness norms are exposed and critiqued by the voicing of racial grievances, race privileged bully pulpits appeal to the colorblind objectivity of "facts" to squash the threat. This rhetorical tactic is attractive to those in similar positions of whiteness because the appeal functions as a defense of "*realpolitik* waged against pernicious forms of identitarian distraction" (Giroux, 2010, p. 83). In this context, the supposedly amoral cultural deficit ideology buttresses the violent normativity of whiteness in the face of threatening divisiveness that follows from centering other cultural identities in the classroom.

Like "Finding a Voice," other poems in Rivera's collection decry the normative violence of whiteness that alienates Chicana/o students from their own cultural sensibilities. For instance, in "Lament," Andrea Serrano recalls, "Opening my US history book in the 11th grade/ and not finding a single person who looked like me/ felt like a slap in the face/ reminded me I am invisible/ almost made me lose all hope" (p. 83). In "Of Codices and Culture," Santino J. Rivera describes the paradoxical positionality of Chicana/os who "bleed to death/ from wounds/ opened by extreme/ prejudice/ and the censorship/ of an invisible people/ who walk the lines/ between a pejorative/ and a falsehood/ *still* lost in a world/ of confusion, scorn/ and manipulation" (p. 126). The MAS classes were designed to heal said wounds caused by cultural deficit ideologies through strategies of cultural empowerment. Incorporating Latina/o cultural knowledge and values as well as bilingual education into curricula is important for Latina/o academic success (Garcia, 2001). But as with the lackluster success of the Chicano Movement, so too the elimination of MAS courses reestablishes a colorblind equality that paradoxically denies the importance of other cultures while hiding one's own privileged racial standpoint. This rhetorical strategy parallels what Nakayama and Krizek (1995) identify as whiteness's ability to "transcend" race while maintaining demeaning racial categories for others. Although the strategy purports equality, colorblindness actually works to justify "contemporary racial inequality and thus help maintain 'systemic white privilege'" (Rothenberg, 2007, p. 132).

This is the essentializing function of whiteness, and it also appears in Frank Mundo's "How I Became a Mexican." Mundo reflects on how he became "Mexican" while playing basketball in California. He describes the haphazard method used to select teams as "a variation on the old shirts-and-skins theme, they called it Whites versus Mexicans, and it was pretty simple. Everyone with brown skin was on one team, and everyone with white skin was on the other" (pp. 1–2). Mundo's problem with these practices: "it's not like I even had a choice what to call myself" (p. 4). Remaining colorless, whiteness forces cultural others into its own ideologically fashioned racialized categories (Crenshaw, 1997), and in the process, Chicana/os are stripped of their complex identities and essentialized to their skin color. In "What's a Mexican 'Supposed' to Look Like?," Sara Calderón gets to the violent crux of this racist essentializing: "Every time someone denies who I am, it's more than just a stereotype; it's insistence that who I am is not valuable" (p. 80). Robbed of identity,

Chicana/os become empty signifiers that can be raced and dehumanized by those in positions of power. As Roberto Rodriguez attests, Chicana/os in the TUSD are "at best ... mongrels, undeserving of full human rights. The survival of this narrative is dependent upon the process of de-indigenization and de-humanization" (p. 19). The privilege of naming divides and objectifies Chicana/os. Erasing Chicana/o histories, banning Chicana/o knowledge, and restricting Chicana/o culture to mere celebration, the TUSD Governing Board has delegitimized each Chicana/o's Indigenous and Mexican heritages and divided the Chicana from her cultural self. This does not mean that Chicana/os lack agency. As Rivera's literary collection and the former existence of MAS attests, Chicana/o voices have been successful engaging and challenging racism in the public sphere. But those engagements are often met with objectification strategies, and it is through this objectification of Chicana/os that whiteness is able to maintain its privileged position in Tucson.

In addition to the violent normativity of whiteness, Rivera's collection reveals a second rhetorical strategy of whiteness in Tucson. To sustain the privileged social status of whiteness, mythic narratives of "America" and fear escalation tactics permit nativism and obscure systemic racism in Arizona, and particularly in Tucson. In Rivera's collection, Roberto Rodriguez writes that Arizona HB 2281 and SB 1070 "seek to maintain the narrative of conquest, an archetype dictating that the deaths of some 5,000 primarily Indigenous Mexicans and Central Americans in the Arizona/Sonora desert in the past dozen years mean little in this clash" (p. 18). This "Manifest Insanity" (p. 17) narrative has maintained the discursive conditions for racist attitudes toward Chicana/os in Arizona, and Rivera's collection implicates whiteness. Satirically, Luis Urrea's poem, "Arizona Lamentation," unmasks how whiteness uses mythic constructions of an "American" homeland to legitimize white claims to the land and to repress accusations of racism. Urrea opens the poem describing a pre-European invaded homeland as "always Odin's garden,/ a clean white place" (p. 20). Odin's garden is a reference to both Norse mythology and the Garden of Eden in the Christian tradition. Furthermore, "white" is equated with "clean," implying that whiteness is without racial features. Without color, whiteness can arrange racial and social hierarchies incognito (Nakayama & Krizek, 1995). But then Urrea goes on to describe what tragically happened to Odin's garden:

> No Mexican was ever born/ in our land./ Then their envy, their racial hatred/ made us build a border fence/ to protect our children./ But they kept coming/. ... We had family values, we had clean sidewalks./ Then these strangers came./ These mudmen./ They invaded our dream/ and colored it. (p. 20–21).

Urrea's themes of erasure and flipping illustrate how whiteness functions to erase and flip cultural histories allowing other mythical constructions of homeland to sprout. Such mythical constructions of "America" function to inversely position Chicana/os as "invaders." Perhaps this topsy-turvy, slight-of-hand rhetorical strategy of whiteness is better exemplified in Urrea's short poem, "Definition": "*Illegal Alien, adj. / n./* A term by which/ an invading colonial force/ vilifies/ indigenous cultures/ by identifying them as/ an invading colonial force" (p. 40). Utilizing Burke's (1969) master trope of irony, Urrea invites his readers to critique the privileged positionalities that not only reinforce a mythic "America," but are also used like "pulpits" to justify nativism toward Chicana/os, the impure invaders of "Odin's garden."

Michelle Holling (2011) argues that these mythic conceptions of "America" are propped up by white privilege and racial oppression. Implicating whiteness in racial oppression, Rodriguez similarly writes that underlying HB 2281 and SB 1070 is a systemic "attempt to maintain, amid the 'browning' of the nation, the myth of America as the pristine home God promised to English-speaking, white, Anglo-Saxon Protestants" (p. 17). This passage is reminiscent of Roediger's (1991) argument that white fear emerged as means for white workers to distance themselves from black workers and to maintain their own political and economic interests in light of the development of wage labor. Several deeply personal narratives in Rivera's collection testify to the ways in which white fears over losing their "homeland" have justified material racial oppression of Chicana/os. For example, in his poem, "Never Forget," Rivera lists his evidence, including small pox infected blankets, 1492, crack cocaine, and Operation Wetback. He concludes the poem with an urgent call: "never forget the white-washers/ never forget the book banners/ never forget the silencers/ never forget them/ never forget their inhumanity" (p. 121). Utilizing a rhetorical strategy of chronological shifting through discriminatory events, his poem undermines claims that racial oppression is restricted to the past and brings to light historical and present examples of Chicana/o suffering. In her poem, "¡Ban This!," Odilia Rodriguez builds on Rivera's argument suggesting that white fears of Chicana/o claims to the U. S. Southwest justify attempts at silencing Chicana/o histories and voices. "Aztlán/ the place you fear/ we might want to reclaim ~ /our ancestral home, occupied/ by you /by you/ who erase truths/ that can not be silenced/ by boxing up or burning books" (p. 307). Instead of abandoning her cultural markers, Rodriguez claims terms such as "Aztlán" from Chicana/o resistance literature in an attempt to illuminate the irony of white claims to the ancestral home of Chicana/os. Furthermore, Rodriguez's poem redresses dominant interpretations of Aztlán as "promoting the overthrow of the United States government," and instead suggests that the nativism voiced in Arizona HB 2281 continues both the political disenfranchisement and material agony that have been a part of Chicana/o experiences in Arizona since 1848. Like the MAS classes themselves, the authors in Rivera's collection strive to overcome whiteness's deflection strategies to expose historical and present institutional injustices and the whiteness tropes that sustain racial bigotry.

To summarize, Rivera's collection of Chicana/o literature rhetorically makes visible the veiled whiteness tropes that lurk in critiques of MAS classes. It carries out this task by interrupting the violent, dehumanizing project of whiteness and exposing white fears and mythical constructions of "America" as constructs that hide and justify systemic racism and prejudiced treatment of Chicana/os in Tucson.

Mestiza and *In Lak'ech Rhetorics*: Making Spaces for Chicana/os

Hidden and demeaned by white privilege, Chicana/o sensibilities are offered in Rivera's literary collection as an empowering resource of hope and intervention for Chicana/os in Tucson. One such sensibility in Rivera's text is *mestiza* rhetoric. Gloria Anzaldúa (1999) describes the *mestiza* as containing diverse subjectivities forming a hybrid identity of one who lives in conflict torn between opposing Mexican, American, Indigenous, and Spanish cultural values in an Anglo-dominated world. To simply survive requires a *mestiza* "to be an Indian in a Mexican culture, to be Mexican from an Anglo point of view" by operating "in a pluralistic mode" (p. 79). Hence, the *mestiza* understands her own cultural identities as flexible and continually negotiated within her socially situated positionalities.

Rivera's collection explores how these *mestiza* rhetorical tropes initiate a problematizing of racial categories in Tucson. For instance, in "How I Became Mexican," Mundo refuses the "or" of Hispanic or Latino or White and identifies instead with liminal characters. He describes this liminality as "the mucky residue on the rim of the melting pot, and my very existence is repulsive and horrifying because I represent the future" (p. 5). His new identity represents a future that is "necessarily ambiguous mixed-raced American human, void of classification, stereotypes and, by extension, pride" (p. 5). In contrast to the celebratory superficiality of multi-culturalism, centering the *mestiza* identity in anti-racist curricula and pedagogies is, as Mundo claims, often perceived as horrifying, repulsive, and even "illegal." But within this space of offensiveness, *mestiza* positionalities have the rhetorical capacity to absorb cultural contradictions, ambiguities, and white fear to produce something hopeful. That something hopeful is the undermining of the racial binaries and categories created and curated by white privilege. Similar to the Xicanisma ideology, the *mestiza* trope in Rivera's collection, and particularly in Mundo's piece, refuses to be racially classified while embracing the distinction of being Chicana/o (Castillo, 1994). In other words, centering the *mestiza* in the classroom is a strategy for resisting racial classification and claiming the right to name one's self. This radically undermines Horne's assertion that "it is fundamentally wrong to divide students up according to their racial group." For example, the *mestiza* positionality, embodied in the liminal figure, composes a holistic subjectivity that relies on self-conceptions *and* others for definition. As Elenes (2000) puts it in her reading of Anzaldúa, Castillo, and Lucas, "Chicanas have constructed a multiple and contradictory subject that reflects the discontinuities and heterogeneity of the Chicana/o community" (p. 110). Therefore, the self can only be known in relation to the experiences and ambiguities of the Chicana/o community, of which she is a part. Collapsing the dualism of individualism–collectivism, the Chicana/o identity, as represented in *mestiza* tropes, is intimately tied into the pluralistic experiences of historical and present Chicana/o communities. Hence, curricula and pedagogies similar to TUSD's Mexican American Studies allow opportunities for Chicana/o students to dialogically discover their identities and means for empowerment in an Anglo-dominated world.

Milo Alvarez incorporates this interrelation into his poem, "The Trail of Quisqueya." "I will do right by my ancestors by,/ Keeping this Fire burning,/ And their Knowledge sacred./ Because it is the only hope either one of us got./ And you will correct the wrongs of your people/ by seeking the humanity that your grandfather destroyed" (pp. 244–245). This *mestiza* positionally shines light on the varied experiences of anguish and abandonment that is part of Chicana/o experiences and represented in the poems of Cuevas, Gomez, and Urrea. Additionally, the poetry of Lopez and Martinez highlights the economic struggles of Chicana/o families in the borderlands. These admittedly uncomfortable stories forefront Chicana/o experiences on their own terms, and as such, they reveal the complex humanity of Chicana/os and provide opportunities for resistance to white stereotypes of Chicana/os, both in and out of the classroom.

The second means of Chicana/o empowerment offered in Rivera's literary collection is *In Lak'ech*. Before their termination, each MAS class started with the same phrase. The phrase means "You are my other me. If I do harm to you, I do harm to myself. If I love and respect you, I love and respect myself." This phrase encapsulates the Mayan philosophy of *In Lak'ech*. Arnoldo Vento describes *In Lak'ech* as, "the principle of love and respect for your fellow human being. It humanizes humankind by eliminating the ego. It unites as opposed to disuniting; it humanizes as opposed to dehumanization and fragmentation. It is the ultimate principle of spiritual love" (Rodriguez, 2011, p. 7). In Rivera's collection, Roberto Rodriguez argues that *In Lak'ech* is related to another concept called *Panche Be*, which means "'to seek the root of the truth' or 'to find the truth in the roots'" (p. 16). Rodriguez explains that these complementary ways of living are rooted in the maize culture of Indigenous peoples. In addition to affirming the Indigenous roots of Chicana/os, these Maya-Nahua concepts create a basis for a revolutionary spiritual love. Coupled with *Panche Be*, we get the sense that *In Lak'ech* is not a passive love, but rather one that motivates toward unity and political action in pursuit of social justice. In "Finding a Voice," Adrianna Simone describes Chicana/o narratives of suffering as "stories of adversity and hope bound up in the ugliness of history and a willingness to believe in the changing effects of love" (p. 295). Responding to the banning of books in the TUSD, Odilia Rodriguez writes, "words live we remember them, our love, our stories ~ history, cannot be erased not banned" (pp. 307–308). Grounded in Chicana/o suffering and hope, this revolutionary spiritual love hails Anzaldúá's concept of spiritual activism (Keating, 2008). "Spiritual activism is spirituality for social change, spirituality that posts a relational worldview and uses this holistic worldview to transform one's self and one's worlds" (Keating, p. 54). Keating identifies three aspects of spiritual activism: self-reflection must be reciprocity related to political action; the process of spiritual activism, like the *mestiza* identity, is filled with ambiguity; and pain/violence are to be expected. Spiritual activism as an act of love, rooted in Chicana/o sensibilities is positioned for rectifying the inhumanity created by whiteness. As Rodriguez writes in Rivera's collection, *In Lak'ech* constitutes "the essence of who we are or who we can be;

human beings connected to each other, to all of life and creation. Part of creation; not outside of it" (p. 16).

This rhetorical appeal to the connectedness of humanity embedded in the Mayan philosophy of *In Lak'ech* is a basis both for organizing identification among diverse peoples and for motivating toward social justice. For instance, Andrea Serrano writes in "Lament" that even though she is not from Arizona, "Arizona's influence/ spills over to New Mexico/ boils over to Texas/ seeps into Birmingham/ where four little girls/ were martyred on September 15, 1963/ because they were defenseless/ because their lives were deemed worthless/ because they were Black" (p. 84). In his poem, "The Ballad of Troy Davis," Rivera identifies with those that are unjustly sentenced to death: "I am Troy Davis and I *am* a man/ just like countless others who held signs/ and marched/ and said the same thing/ until they died with a glimmer of hope/ in their eyes/ and cold doubt in their still hearts" (p. 115). Emanating from Maya-Nahua-specific language, *In Lak'ech* invites all peoples to identify with the paradoxical human reality of suffering and hope that we each experience, but is more pronounced in the experiences of co-cultural communities. So, identification then invites both critical reflexivity and social change.

This *In Lak'ech* understanding of identification and spiritual love is at the heart of TUSD's Mexican American Studies. As part of an independent audit of MAS courses, Cambium Learning (2011) conducted a series of focus groups with various stakeholders to determine the program's educational effectiveness. According to the report, one elementary student "spoke of the Tezcatlipocas, and how that instruction teaches them to love themselves and respect other people" (p. 105). In the high school focus groups:

> Several students spoke of En Lak'Ech [sic], saying they have learned to respect people of all cultures by seeing them as an extension of themselves. Students say this is the philosophy is what [sic] propels them into their community involvement. They look outside of their own lives and want to learn about other people, how they feel, what their issues are, and do something about it. (p. 106)

The interplay of *mestiza* and *In Lak'ech* rhetorics to resist whiteness can be heard in MAS student testimonies about the program. For instance, one student voiced that the courses helped her gain "so much confidence. ... I have learned so much about myself that now I can talk and use my voice to inform people" (Bodfield, 2008, para. 50). In an education system that focuses "on winning at all costs, a ruthless competitiveness, hedonism, the cult of individualism" (Giroux, 2003, p.185), centering *mestiza* and *In Lak'ech* rhetorics undermines neoliberal education policies and radically flips the classroom into a space for practicing cultural empowerment, critical reflexivity, and social justice pedagogies.

Conclusion: A Brief Reflection on Counterstorytelling

In Tucson, the conditions for dialogue on whiteness and race seem bleak. But the voices of TUSD's Chicana/o students persistently point us toward hope in the midst of desperation, and Chicana/o literature plays a vital role in their counterstorytelling

(Yosso, 2006). Counterstorytelling is the intentional sharing of co-cultural stories and experiences to promote both critical consciousness of oppression from the perspectives of the marginalized and resistance to racism by restoring the humanity of the oppressed (Yosso). In a state that aggressively harasses Chicana/o communities, counterstorytelling in the form of Chicana/o literary activism contains the humanizing rhetorical impetus crucial to challenging and interrupting dominant racial logics in Tucson.

Counterstorytelling may also provide an ethical framework for critical race rhetoric projects. As a white rhetorical critic, what should be my position toward whiteness texts? For Warren (2003), the only ethical position was to deconstruct the whiteness in his own locality while being ever-conscious of his implication in white privilege and desire to see that privilege diminished. Linda Alcoff (1998) suggests that critics can and should speak for co-cultural others only to the degree that they are consistently attentive to issues of motives, context and speaker location, representation, responsibility, accountability, and affects of our criticism. For her, it is essential that the critic of whiteness be guided by the ethical *raison d'être* that she ends her essay: "Will it enable the empowerment of oppressed peoples?" (p. 31). Ultimately, it is not the critic that makes such determinations, but rather her readers and "oppressed peoples," themselves. Implicated in this ethic is also the critic's responsibility "to create wherever possible the conditions for dialogue and the practice of speaking with and to rather than speaking for others" (Alcoff, p. 23). Centering co-cultural communities in criticism of whiteness texts not only encourages critic sensitivity to the counterstories of racially marginalized communities, but also creates the necessary conditions to engage the dialogic relationships between whiteness and co-cultural experiences with the intent of taking action against oppressive structures and representations. Perhaps it is through this social justice ethic that white critics can set out to understand and work against whiteness from the perspective of co-cultural communities; however imperfectly.

Notes

[1] Throughout the essay, I follow the lead of TUSD's Mexican American Studies by using the "Chicana/o" identity marker to indicate the complex histories, cultural knowledge, experiences, and identities of Mexican Americans. The use of "a/o" is the author's conscious effort to forefront continuing struggles over gender inclusivity and equity.

[2] When using this pan-ethnic identifier, I am ever attentive to "the (real or assumed) commonalities and differences attached to the sign 'Latina/o'" (Holling & Calafell, 2011, p. xvi).

References

Acosta, O.Z. (1972). *The Autobiography of a Brown Buffalo*. San Francisco: Straight Arrow Books.
Acuña, R.F. (2011). *The making of Chicana/o Studies: In the trenches of academe*. New Brunswick, NJ: Rutgers University Press.
Alcoff, L.M. (1998). What should white people do? *Hypatia, 13*(3), 6–26.
Alurista (1981). Cultural nationalism and Xicano literature during the decade of 1965–1975. *MELUS, 8*(2), 22–34.

Anzaldúa, G. (1999). *Borderlands/la frontera*. San Francisco, CA: Aunt Lute Books.
Apple, M. (2006). Understanding and interrupting neoliberalism and neoconservatism in education. *Pedagogies: An International Journal, 1*(1), 21–26.
Arizona House Bill 2281 (2010). Arizona Revised Statutes A.R.S. §15–112. 15–701.
Arizona Senate Bill 1070 (2010). Arizona Revised Statutes A.R.S. §11–1051.
Baca, D. (2008). *Mestz@ scripts, digital migrations, and the territories of writing*. Basingstoke, UK: Palgrave Macmillan.
Baldwin, J. (2011). An open letter to my sister Angela Y. Davis. In R. Kenan (Ed.), *The cross of redemption: Uncollected writings* (pp. 254–260). New York, NY: Vintage Books.
Beck, S.A.L., & Allexsaht-Snider, M. (2001). Recent language minority education policy in Georgia: Appropriation, assimilation, and americanization. In S. Wortham, E.G. Murillo, Jr., & E.T. Hamann (Eds.), *Education in the new Latino diaspora: Policy and the politics of identity* (pp. 37–66). Westport, CT: Greenwood Publishing Group.
Bernal, D.D. (2006). Learning and living pedagogies of the home: The Mestiza consciousness of Chicana students. In D.D. Bernal, C.A. Elenes, F.E. Godinez, & S. Villenas (Eds.), *Chicana/Latina education in everyday life: Feminista perspectives on pedagogy and epistemology* (pp. 113–132). Albany, NY: State University of New York.
Berta-Ávila, M. (2003). The process of conscientization: Xicanas/Xicanos experiences in claiming authentic voice. *Journal of Hispanic Higher Education, 2*(2), 117–128.
Bodfield, R. (2008, May). TUSD's Raza unit survives under fire. *Arizona Daily Star*. Retrieved from http://azstarnet.com/news/local/education/precollegiate/article_4cc80569-97a1-5571-bafc-77fe70185173.html
Brousseau, G.C. (1993). *Bridging three centuries: The history of Tucson school district, 1867–1993*. Retrieved from http://www.tusd.k12.az.us/CONTENTS/distinfo/history/history93.asp
Burke, K. (1969). *A rhetoric of motives*. Berkeley, CA: University of California Press.
Calafell, B.M. (2007). *Latina/o communication studies: Theorizing performance*. New York, NY: Peter Lang.
Cambium Learning (2011). Curriculum audit of the Mexican American Studies Department Tucson Unified School District. Retrieved from http://www.tucsonweekly.com/images/blogimages/2011/06/16/1308282079-az_masd_audit_final_1_.pdf
Cammarota, J., & Romero, A. (2006). A critically compassionate intellectualism for Latina/o students: Raising voices above the silencing in our schools. *Multicultural Education, 14*(2), 16–23.
Candelaria, J. (1977). *Memories of the Alhambra*. Tempe, AZ: Bilingual Review Press.
Castillo, A. (1994). *Massacre of the dreamers: Essays on Xicanisma*. New York, NY: Plume.
Ceasar, S. (2011, November 20). Arizona educators clash over Mexican American studies. Retrieved from http://articles.latimes.com/2011/nov/20/nation/la-na-ethnic-studies-20111120
Cooks, L. (2003). Pedagogy, performance and positionality: Teaching about whiteness in interracial communication. *Communication Education, 52*, 245–257.
Crenshaw, C. (1997). Resisting whiteness' rhetorical silence. *Western Journal of Communication, 61*, 253–278.
Delgado, F.P. (1998). Chicano ideology revisited: Rap music and the (re)articulation of Chicanismo. *Western Journal of Communication, 62*, 95–113.
Delgado, R., & Stefancic, J. (2001). *Critical race theory: An introduction*. New York, NY: New York University Press.
Delgadillo, T. (2011). *Spiritual Mestizaje: Religion, gender, race, and nation in contemporary Chicana narrative*. Durham, NC: Duke University Press.
Elenes, C.A. (2000). Chicana feminist narratives and the politics of the self. *Frontiers: A Journal of Women Studies, 21*(3), 105–123.
Enck-Wanzer, D. (2011). Tropicalizing East Harlem: Rhetorical agency, cultural citizenship, and Nuyorican cultural production. *Communication Theory, 21*(4), 344–367.
Eysturoy, A.O., & Gurpegui, J.A. (1990). Chicano literature: Introduction and bibliography. *American Studies International, 28*(1), 48–82.
Flores, L.A., Moon, D.G., & Nakayama, T.K. (2006). Dynamic rhetorics of race: California's racial privacy initiative and the shifting grounds of racial politics. *Communication and Critical/Cultural Studies, 3*(3), 181–201.

Frankenberg, R. (1993). *White women, race matters: The social construction of whiteness.* Minneapolis, MN: University of Minnesota Press.
Freire, P. (2010). *Pedagogy of the oppressed* (M.B. Ramos, Trans.). New York, NY: The Continuum International Publishing Group. (Original work published 1970)
Garcia, A.M. (1989). The development of Chicana feminist discourse, 1970-1980. *Gender and Society, 3*(2), 217-238.
Garcia, E.E. (2001). *Hispanic education in the United States.* Lanham, MD: Rowman & Littlefield.
García, I.M. (1997). *Chicanismo: The forging of a militant ethos among Mexican Americans.* Tucson, AZ: University of Arizona Press.
Giroux, H. A. (2003). Spectacles of race and pedagogies of denial: Anti-black racist pedagogy under the reign of neoliberalism. *Communication Education, 52,* 191-211.
Giroux, S.S. (2010). *Between race and reason: Violence, intellectual responsibility, and the university to come.* Stanford: Stanford University Press.
Griffin, R.A., & Calafell, B.M. (2011). Control, discipline, and punish: Black masculinity and (in)visible whiteness in the NBA. In M.G. Lacy & K.A. Ono (Eds.), *Critical rhetorics of race* (pp. 117-138). New York, NY: New York University.
Gonzalez, G.G. (1990/2013). *Chicano education in the era of segregation.* Denton, TX: University of North Texas Press.
Gutiérrez, J.A. (2011). The Chicano Movement: Paths to power. *Social Studies, 102*(1), 25-32.
Hammerback, J.C., & Jensen, R.J. (1994). Ethnic heritage as rhetorical legacy: The plan of Delano. *Quarterly Journal of Speech, 80,* 53-70.
Herakova, L.L., Jelača, D., Sibii, R., & Cooks, L. (2011). Voicing silence and imagining citizenship: Dialogues about race and whiteness in a "postracial" era. *Communication Studies, 62*(4), 372-388.
Hidalgo, N.M. (2005). Latino/a families' epistemology. In P. Pedraza & M. Rivera (Eds.), *Latino Education: An Agenda for Community Action Research* (pp. 375-402). Mahwah, NJ: Lawrence Erlbaum Associates.
Holling, M.A. (2006a). El simpático boxer: Underpinning Chicano masculinity with a rhetoric of *familia* in Resurrection Blvd. *Western Journal of Communication, 70*(2), 91-114.
Holling, M.A. (2006b). The critical consciousness of Chicana and Latina students: Negotiating identity amid sociocultural beliefs and ideology. In D.D. Bernal, C.A. Elenes, F.E. Godinez, & S. Villenas (Eds.), *Chicana/Latina education in everyday life: Feminista perspectives on pedagogy and epistemology* (pp. 81-94). Albany, NY: State University of New York Press.
Holling, M.A. (2011). Patrolling national identity, masking white supremacy: The minuteman project. In M.G. Lacy & K.A. Ono (Eds.), *Critical rhetorics of race* (pp. 98-116). New York, NY: New York University Press.
Holling, M.A., & Calafell, B.M. (2007). Identities on stage and staging identities: ChicanoBrujo performances as emancipatory practices. *Text and Performance Quarterly, 27*(1), 58-83.
Holling, M.A., & Calafell, B.M. (2011). Introduction. In M.A. Holling & B.M. Calafell (Eds.), *Latina/o discourse in vernacular spaces: Somos de Una Voz?* (pp. xv-xxv). Lanham, MD: Lexington Books.
Jackson, R.L., Shin, C.I., & Hilson, K.B. (2000). The meaning of whiteness: Critical implications of communicating and negotiating race. *World Communication, 29,* 69-86.
Keating, A. (2008). "I'm a citizen of the university": Gloria Anzaldúa's spiritual activism as catalyst for social change. *Feminist Studies, 34*(1/2), 53-69.
Lacy, M.G. (2010). White innocence myths in citizen discourse, the Progressive Era (1974-1988). *The Howard Journal of Communications, 21,* 20-39.
LaWare, M.R. (1998). Encountering visions of Aztlan: Arguments for ethnic pride, community activism and cultural revitalization in Chicano murals. *Argumentation and Advocacy, 34,* 140-153.
MacDonald, V.M., & Monkman, K. (2005). Setting the context: Historical perspectives on Latino/a education. In P. Pedraza & M. Rivera (Eds.), *Latino Education: An Agenda for Community Action Research* (pp. 47-74). Mahwah, NJ: Lawrence Erlbaum Associates.
McKerrow, R.E. (1989). Critical rhetoric: Theory and praxis. *Communication Monographs, 56,* 91-111.
Moon, D., & Flores, L.A. (2000). Antiracism and the abolition of whiteness: Rhetorical strategies of domination among "race traitors." *Communication Studies, 51*(2), 97-115.

Morrison, T. (1992). *Playing in the dark: Whiteness and the literary imagination.* New York, NY: Random House.
Nakayama, T.K., & Krizek, R.L. (1995). Whiteness: A strategic rhetoric. *Quarterly Journal of Speech, 81,* 291–309.
Pèrez-Torres, R. (1995). *Movements in Chicano poetry: Against myths, against margins.* New York, NY: Cambridge University Press.
Pineda, R.D. (2009). Will they see me coming? Do they know I'm running? Los lobos and the performance of mestiza identity through journey. *Text and Performance Quarterly, 29*(2), 183–200.
Rios, F. (2008). From Chicano/a to Xicana/o: Critical activist teaching revisited. *Multicultural Education, 15*(4), 2–9.
Rivera, S. (Ed.) (2012). *Ban This: The BSP Anthology of Xican@ Literature.* Saint Augustine, FL: Broken Sword Publications.
Rivera, T. (1971). *...y no se lo tragó la tierra [...and the earth did not devour him].* Berkeley, CA: Quinto Sol.
Rodriguez, R.C. (2011). Tucson's Maiz-based curriculum: MAS-TUSD profundo. Retrieved from http://indigenouscultures.org/nakumjournal/tucsons-maiz-based-curriculum-mas-tusd-profundo
Rodriguez, R.E. (2000). Chicana/o fiction from resistance to contestation: The role of creation in Ana Castillo's *So Far from God, MELUS, 25*(2), 63–82.
Roediger, D.R. (1991). *The wages of whiteness: Race and the making of the American working class.* New York, NY: Verso.
Romero, A.F., & Arce, S. (2011). Saving the lives, the culture and the history of our children: Telling the truth in Arizona's cultural war. *Regeneracion, 2*(1), 4–11.
Romero, A.F. (2010). At war with the state in order to save lives of our children: The battle to save ethnic studies in Arizona. *Black Scholar, 40*(4), 7–15.
Rothenberg, P.S. (2007). *Race, class, and gender in the United States* (7th ed.). New York, NY: Worth Publishers.
San Miguel, G., Jr. (2013). *Chicana/o struggles for education: Activism in the community.* Houston, TX: University of Houston.
Sandoval, A.M. (2008). *Toward a Latina feminism of the Americas: Repression & resistance in Chicana & Mexicana literature.* Austin, TX: University of Texas Press.
Schoeffel, M.A. (2008). *Maternal conditions: Reading Kingsolver, Castillo, Erdrich, and Ozeki.* New York, NY: Peter Lang.
Shome, R. (2000). Outing whiteness. *Critical Studies in Media Communication, 17*(3), 366–371.
Simpson, J.L. (2008). The color-blind double bind: Whiteness and the (im)possibility of dialogue. *Communication Theory, 18,* 139–159.
Spring, J. (2013). *Corporatism, social control, and cultural domination in education: From the radical right to globalization.* New York, NY: Routledge.
Treaty of Guadalupe Hidalgo, the Mexican Republic and the United States of America (1848, February 2). Retrieved from http://avalon.law.yale.edu/19th_century/guadhida.asp
Urrieta, L. (2004). Chicana/o activism and education: An introduction to the Special Issue. *High School Journal, 87*(4), 1–9.
Warren, J.T. (2001). Doing whiteness: On the performative dimensions of race in the classroom. *Communication Education, 50*(2), 91–108.
Warren, J.T. (2003). *Performing Purity: Whiteness, Pedagogy, and the Reconstitution of Power.* New York: Peter Lang.
Warren, J.T., & Hytten, K. (2004). The faces of whiteness: Pitfalls and the critical democrat. *Communication Education, 53*(4), 321–339.
Yosso, T.J. (2006). *Critical race counterstories along the Chicana/Chicano educational pipeline.* New York, NY: Routledge.

Our Foreign President Barack Obama: The Racial Logics of Birther Discourses

Vincent N. Pham

This essay centers race in taking serious an often-dismissed movement, the Birthers, who question Barack Obama's citizenship and deem him as an illegitimate president. Through a historical and relational lens, I argue that the Birther rhetoric of constitutional protection relies on racial logics used in previous discourses about foreignness to delineate acceptable citizenship for the presidency and mark Obama as untrustworthy. By analyzing the Birthers.org website and two Birther movement-associated media figures, Orly Taitz and Donald Trump, Birther discourses manipulate rationality, reinforce a White racial state, and activate anxieties over an increasingly multi-racial and global society.

From 2008 to 2012, a fringe group associated with the Tea Party known as the Birthers questioned the legitimacy of Barack Obama's presidency. By claiming Obama's birth certificate was falsified and thus not a "natural-born citizen," the Birthers asserted that Obama was constitutionally ineligible to be the president and akin to a foreigner usurping the White House. The conservative *National Review Online* circulated Birther discourses to mainstream news consumers, fueling rumors that Obama's illegitimacy could be "theoretically possible, if not plausible" (Geraghty, 2008, para. 11). As a result, Birther discourse took hold.[1] By the summer of 2009, an early August national poll conducted by Public Policy Polling firm found that 24% of Americans thought that Obama was not born in the United States, and 14% were unsure (Jensen, 2009).

On April 27, 2011, compelled by the longstanding Birther rumors and desire to dispel challenges about his birthplace, President Barack Obama obtained and released his long-form birth certificate, which clearly illustrated his birthplace (see Figure 1; "Indeed, born in the U.S.A.," 2011).[2] In an interview with Oprah Winfrey, President Obama shared his reasons for taking two and a half years to release his long-form birth certificate (Zia, 2012). He stated that he "didn't take it [the rumors regarding his birth place] very seriously" and dismissed the rumors as a "silly thing" that would eventually disappear (Zia, 2012).[3] President Obama hoped the release of his long-form birth certificate would refocus the country's attention on more pressing issues instead of being distracted by what he described as "sideshows and carnival barkers" (Zia, 2012). After the release of the long-form birth certificate, the Tea Party and

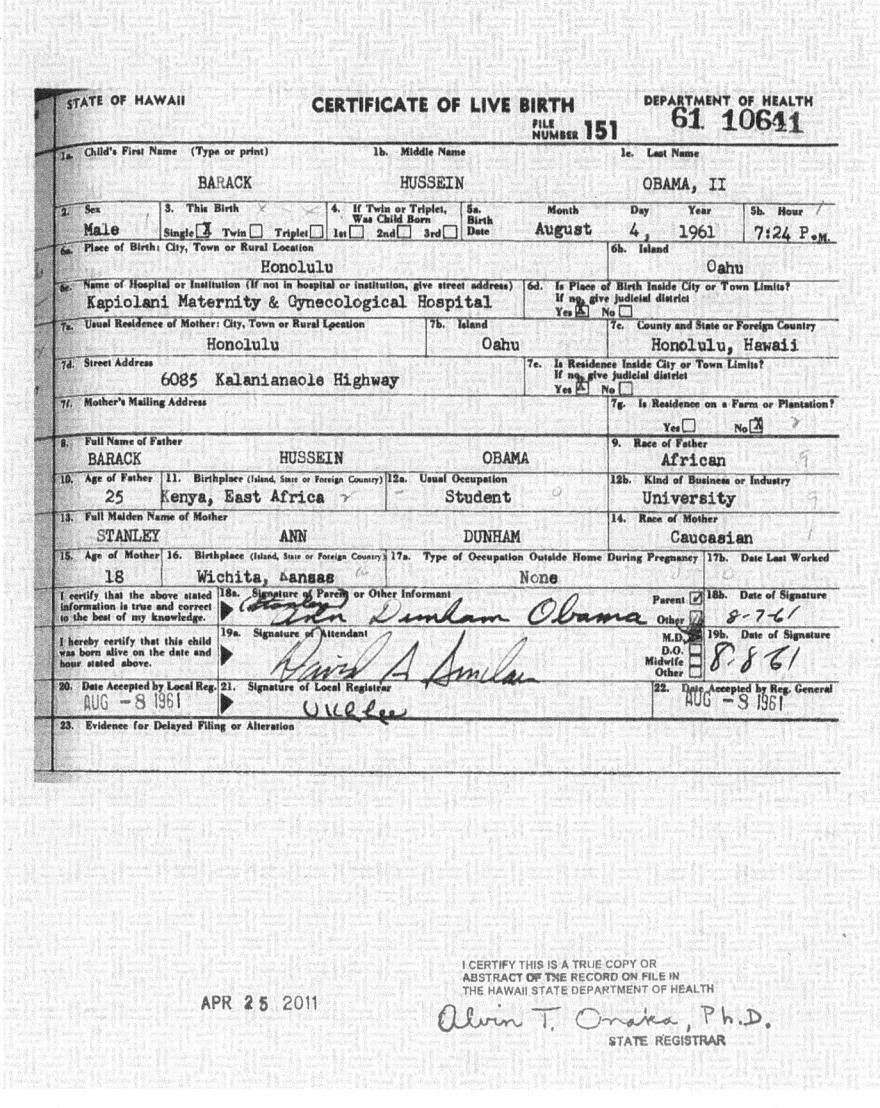

Figure 1 Long-Form Birth Certificate. From the White House Website (Pfeiffer, 2011).

Republican political parities distanced themselves from the Birther movement. As a result, the Birther movement eventually lost momentum and mainstream credibility.

Birther discourses have largely receded to the background. Even during the height of the Birther movement, the mainstream polity ignored the Birthers, dismissed their conspiratorial claims, and marked them as a racist, irrational, and ignorant fringe group with little credibility (Deis, 2010; Hughey, 2012; "Indeed, born in the U.S.A.," 2011; Miller, 2009; Pitts, 2011; Younge, 2009). However, conservative icons—notably Arizona Maricopa County Sheriff Joe Arpaio (Associated Press, 2012) and businessman Donald Trump—continued to recirculate Birther claims (ABC News, 2013). Birther discourses also resonated with some members of the electorate, displaying xenophobic and racist sentiments (Deis, 2010; Howell, 2012).[4] For example, 2012 Michigan Republican Senate candidate, Pete Hoekstra, proposed a national "Birther" office to confirm the eligibility of presidential candidates to avoid having "this kind of question [of eligibility] for a president of the United States" in the future (Johnson, 2012; Reens, 2012). Even as the Birthers faded from the spotlight, their skepticism about Obama's legitimacy as a U.S.-born citizen and the fear of his foreign affiliations remained. How can scholars account for xenophobic discourses about Obama—ones that cast doubt on his citizenship and question his right to the presidency—that are largely dismissed within mainstream media and culture as ridiculous and conspiratorial?

Despite the marginality of Birther discourses, the fervent promotion of Obama's illegitimacy from 2008 to 2012 created a precedent for demanding proof of eligibility and legitimized the questioning of presidential eligibility based on citizenship—demands and questions that were not present prior to Obama's presidency. In addition, Tea Party and Republican participation in challenging Obama's legitimacy validated Birther fears and concerns over foreign usurpation of the presidential office. Although the Birther movement no longer occupies the mainstream public, the Birther discourse of ineligibility via "natural-born citizenship" planted seeds of doubt about Obama's presidential legitimacy that endure to this day. This essay takes Birther discourse seriously in order to explore the racial logics that remain resonant and that re-inscribe perceived "foreignness" as a racially coded boundary of acceptable citizenship in an increasingly multi-cultural United States and globalizing world.

Although Obama is often considered as solely a Black subject, this essay expands Obama's subjectivity to encompass his multi-racial and global aspects in order to critically address and understand Birther anxieties over race, birthright, and citizenship. African Americans have historically and legally been deemed unfit for citizenship, perhaps most explicitly by the *Dred Scott* case (Molina, 2013). However, contemporary anti-Black discourses have threatened Black citizenship in various ways. Anti-Black discourses have shifted away from threatening *de jure* citizenship—the legal entitlement to citizenship—to allowing Blacks to be included within the United States as "formal citizens" with voting rights and legal protections that prevent discrimination and exclusion from places like diners or universities. Instead, anti-Black discourses become de facto, working primarily through cultural, social, and political practices that threaten Black citizens' *enactment* of their citizenship. So while Blacks may be assumed to be "formal citizens," contemporary anti-Black discourses challenge such rights via literacy laws or strip them of citizenship's rights through practices including but not limited to criminalizing Black bodies, incarceration, and voter identification laws. Thus, Birther discourses about Obama—ones that question his *de jure* citizenship while leaving untouched de facto ways of challenging his citizenship—provide a unique set of challenges since they concurrently mobilize anti-Black and xenophobic discourses. I argue that although anti-Black discourses directly target Blacks, such discourses can also deploy implied logics that signal racial anxieties and provide mechanisms to justify those anxieties vis-à-vis contemporary "post-racial" rhetorical codes. Instead of figuring anti-Blackness as the *only* way to view President Obama, this essay considers how racist discourses utilize racial scripts most commonly associated with Asian Americans and Latin@s. In considering how Birthers cast Obama as "foreign," this essay centers Obama's racialization *relationally*, in conjunction with other marginalized groups and within an already circulating environment of racial discourses embedded in historical and social contexts. This essay argues that Birthers mobilize anti-Black and forever foreigner discourses via yellow peril in a parallel fashion and in concert to create a web of racist discourse that entangles audiences and beckons them to question Obama's presidential eligibility and hence legitimacy.

Drawing on scholarship in critical race studies, Asian American studies, sociology, and rhetorical studies, I argue that the Birthers publicly framed and contested Obama's presidency in racialized and racist ways even as their discourses attempted to mask racism under pretenses of constitutionality and national integrity. This essay situates Birther discourses within histories of national belonging and foreignness and argues that Birther discourses about Obama draw upon racist discourses from the past and present. Furthermore, these discourses deploy a racial logic that is citational, contextual, and deeply embedded in racial scripts that mirror nativist fears over citizenship. Through this logic, Birther discourses move within a larger field of racist discourses that justify implicitly racist claims against Obama under a mask of Constitutional protection and rational skepticism. In return, the discourses reinforce a cultural logic of race as the basis of national belonging, legitimate citizenship, and access to the presidency—all while reinforcing a post-racial discourse that avoids racial signification.

This essay proceeds in three parts. First, I situate Obama within a larger discourse of post-raciality—one that limits Obama's subject positions while using Obama to reinforce ideas of a post-racial society. In doing so, I elucidate how post-racial discourses that evade race paint a limited portrait of Obama's complex racialization. In addition, I explain how the current post-racial context establishes the norms of discourse in which Birthers can avoid explicit racial signifiers in condemning Obama even as their discourses seethe with racial undercurrents. Second, I take up a theoretical frame of racial scripts (Molina, 2013) to analyze how Obama was subjected to racial discourses not commonly associated with contemporary anti-Black discourses and to consider the relationality of racist discourses by applying them to Birther discourses. I analyze Birther texts from the Birthers.org website, self-proclaimed "Queen of the Birthers" Orly Taitz, and business magnate Donald Trump—all which challenge Obama's claim to presidency by casting doubt on his citizenship and formal requirements of presidential eligibility. Finally, I reveal that the "natural-born citizenship" logics of Birther discourses emphasize Obama's inscrutability, condemn the birth certificate's untrustworthy nature, and rely on historical, contextual, and relational understandings of foreignness implicative of yellow peril discourses. Through a seemingly non-Black and non-racial understanding of foreignness, the Birthers justified their efforts to uphold and protect the Constitution from corruption as a non-race based challenge.

Rhetoric of Obama's Post-Raciality

The election of the first Black president unearthed fervent discussions about race and the presidency. The discussions beckoned rhetorical scholars to address how Obama addresses race and communicates racial ideas. Although experts have widely accepted that race is a socially constructed reality that represents a way of living and being in the world (Bonilla-Silva, 2010; Goldberg, 2009), race is treated as a problem and schism dividing U.S. society. Scholars have critically attended to Obama's rhetorical negotiations of racial politics. Obama functioned as a racial unifier through his rhetorical signatures (Frank, 2011), by embodying "unity" via his multi-raciality (Dilliplane, 2012), by his empathic use of double-consciousness (Terrill, 2009), or through his collaborative identity performance that negotiates the idea of an "American people" (Sweet & McCue-Enser, 2010). Obama disavowed race (Isaksen, 2011) or transcended it (Hoerl, 2012; Smith, 2009). He has rhetorically shifted away from race, reuniting and reinvigorating the U.S. public under communitarian values and public engagement (Rowland & Jones, 2007) or the American dream (Rowland, 2011). As these rhetorical scholars have illustrated, Obama's racial discourses communicate a post-racial ideology, contributing to a public perception of a unified post-racist society realized through the election of the first Black president.

However, post-racial ideology problematically attempts to eradicate racial conceptions but not necessarily racism (Goldberg, 2009). It erases the idea that groups of people have visibly distinct traits and behavioral characteristics but not the corresponding structures that maintain inferiority, exclusion, and disenfranchisement for those groups (Goldberg, 2009). It ultimately gives way to "anti-racial commitments at the expense of antiracist effects" (Goldberg, 2009, p. 21). Although seemingly innocuous or even beneficial, post-racial thinking reinforces racism by assuming racism will be eradicated by removing racial conceptions and racial signifiers.

Despite this public perception of a post-racial climate reinforced by the inauguration and rhetoric of the first Black president, there remain extant anti-Black racist discourses. Overtly racist images of Obama as a thug, ape, or terrorist coupled with inferentially racist imagery of Obama as a "white guy's Black friend" circulated the Internet and reinforced post-racial ideology (Joseph, 2011, p. 396). Racist slogans, such as "Put the White back in the White House" or "Don't Re-Nig in 2012," sought to remove Obama and his Blackness from the presidency in order to reinstate a more familiar "White" into the White House in literal and figurative terms (McAlister, 2009; Shepherd, 2012). Conservative groups have long challenged Obama's competency—from questions regarding his experience as a community organizer to his drug use as a college student—in ways that relate to his Blackness (O'Reilly, 2014; Wells, 2014). In short, being a president has not prevented explicit anti-Black discourses from being directed at Obama.

Although some scholarship has been critically attentive to Obama's Blackness and the negotiations around anti-Black discourse, Birther indictments focused on the status of "natural-born citizen" provide a different set of challenges. Such discourses consider Obama broadly marked as foreign even as they avoid addressing his Blackness. I do not want to understate the importance of anti-Black discourse on Obama, as Blacks have had a unique racial formation within the United States—influenced by and subjected to fugitive slave laws, state violence, lynching, Jim Crow laws, and contemporary mass incarceration (Hughey, 2012; Omi & Winant, 2014). Nonetheless, the current post-Civil Rights and mainstream assumption of a post-racial context warrants theoretical lenses that grapple with the complexity of Obama's racialization and discursive construction as a multi-racial, Black, foreign, and global subject. This essay expansively addresses the Birthers' demonization of Obama as foreign by considering his racialization relationally with other marginalized groups and within the historical context of other racial discourses.

Examining racialization relationally and historically is not a novel project. Kim's (1999) racial triangulation and field of racial positions studied how Black, White, and Asian racializations cross paths and influence each other. Kim theorized that these groups are racialized in relation to each other on the axes of insider/outsider in civic belonging and superior/inferior in valorization.[5] Schueller (2009) demanded a relational and historical understanding of race and racism, particularly focused on how imperial structures operate in different racial sites. Molina (2013) approached race and racism historically and relationally in her analysis of Mexican immigration from 1924–1965, during which "the Irish 'become' white and the 'heathen' Asians transformed into model minorities" (pp. 2–3). Molina's (2013) term "racial scripts" attempts to understand how racialization processes extend across time and space and affect racial groups "even when they do not cross paths" (p. 6). Racial scripts endure in cultural representations, institutions, and practices and let us "…see connections between groups and corresponding impact of external forces" (Molina, 2013, p. 7). Approaching race historically and relationally opens up avenues for understanding the pervasiveness of racist discourses throughout U.S. society.

Although a relational approach to race is not new, it acknowledges how Obama (a man who is foremost racialized as Black) is also subject to a variety of other racial discourses. Since Obama is often perceived *only* as Black, other racial discourses are often overlooked. Instead, a relational approach focuses on what Obama *signifies*—a concatenation of racial threats that take into account Obama's multi-raciality and diasporic experience. Racial triangulation reminds us that racialization occurs in multiple dimensions, on various axes, or pertaining to different characteristics (Kim, 1999). Molina's (2013) racial scripts orient us to how racial discourses—anchored in history—reoccur, interact, and work concomitantly to constitute our ideas about racial groups in relation to other racial groups. By examining Birther discourses in racially relational ways, we can understand Birther discourses and analyze purportedly illogical and implicitly racist discourses when they are coded under the guise of citizenship and citizen rights—both of which attempt to avoid issues of race even as they target racialized groups.

Given the Birthers' fear of the foreign, racial scripts regarding Asian Americans are especially pertinent to viewing Obama's racialization relationally. Concerning Asians and Asian Americans, there two dominant and interrelated racial scripts: the "forever foreigner" and "yellow peril." Asian and Asian Americans are often seen as forever foreigners and not as American, regardless of their histories in the United States (Nakayama, 2000; Ono & Pham, 2009). Kim (1999) found that Asian Americans are deemed culturally and racially "immutably foreign and unassimilable" and hence unable to join the body politic (p. 107). Thus, being seen as forever foreigner means that Asians and Asian American allegiances lay not with the United States but with the Asian "homeland." Related to the lack of allegiance is an implicit yellow peril discourse, which frame Whites as "vulnerable, threatened or otherwise in danger" and Asians and Asian Americans as "threatening to take over, invade, or otherwise negatively Asianize the U.S. nation and its society and culture" (Ono & Pham, 2009, p. 25). Although the United States has a long history of yellow peril discourses, more recent "yellow peril" discourse has emerged in contemporary political and popular culture—from the Citizens Against Government Waste's (2010) "Chinese Professor" political advertisement, to Michigan GOP Senate candidate Pete Hoekstra's "Debbie-Spend-It-Now" Super Bowl political advertisement (UpNorthLive, 2012), and to the 2012 remake of 1984 film *Red Dawn* (MOVIES Coming Soon, 2012) that replaced the Soviet invasion of Colorado with North Korean invasion and takeover of the Pacific Northwest. The recent occurrence of anti-Asian sentiment provides relationally relevant racial scripts for understanding the Birther discourses of foreignness and their questioning of Obama's presidential eligibility.

Following the work of McGee (1990), I approach texts as inherently fragmented. I construct a representative sample of Birther discourses through various sites to gain insight into Birther discourses about Obama. In this essay, I examine three sites of Birther discourses. First, I analyze the Birther movement website, Birthers.org, because it functions as a repository for Birther discourses and provides informational resources to circulate that is often dismissed by mainstream media. Second, I analyze an October 13, 2009 interview of Orly Taitz's on the *Joy Behar Show*. Since Orly Taitz is the self-ascribed "Queen of the Birthers," her media appearances as a vocal supporter of the Birther movement and outspoken critic of Obama on many television networks such as CNN, MSNBC, and HLN thrusts the fringe elements of the Birther movement into the mainstream. Finally, I analyze well-known businessman, investor, and reality television personality, Donald Trump's August 11, 2013, interview with Jonathan Karl on ABC's *This Week*. Real estate magnate and reality television host Donald Trump is likely the most recognizable mainstream public persona who does not explicitly identify as a Birther but echoes their concerns.

Two principles guided the selection of these texts: its alignment with Birther identity and its distance from the mainstream political parties. The selected representative sample of texts illustrates how Birthers identify as non-partisan, independent, and civic-minded citizens without lofty political goals. I purposefully avoided Tea Party or other conservative politicians and instead focused on public discourses by non-institutional actors. Although Republican, Libertarian, and Tea Party factions and politicians often align with Birther concerns, their alignment with and use of Birther discourses could be considered suspect or disingenuous for serving their own (re)election purposes. The distance from mainstream political parties reinforces their independence and buttresses the "concerned citizen" aspect of Birtherism. Although Donald Trump might have considered himself a viable political candidate, conservatives did not treat his 2012 election bid seriously but instead treated it as self-congratulatory discourse (Geraghty, 2012; Lowry, 2011; National Review Online Editors, 2011).

In addition, I focus primarily on the written and oral text and avoid the visual texts of the Birthers. The written text of the Birthers.org website and the broadcasted interviews provide the opportunity to see Birther discourses as its public leaders trumpeted the Birther cause across a variety of media. I acknowledge that the Taitz and Trump interviews are edited and mediated outside their control. However, the extended engagement and the dialogic nature of the interviews allowed Taitz and Trump to articulate their logic beyond visual snapshots and sound bytes that might otherwise be captured and circulated in media. A full exploration of the Birthers' visual and embodied discourses is outside the scope of this paper, but this analysis will provide a springboard for future studies.

Finally, these texts serve a role and function for Birthers. The Birther website was founded and Orly Taitz's interview took place at the height of the Birther movement in 2009—both of which highlight the emergence of the Birther discourses in mainstream media. While Taitz's interview is an ephemeral media text, the Birther website maintains the same look with marginal updates to its content as of November 2014.[6] On the other hand, Donald Trump's interview in 2013 came over two years after Obama released his birth certificate, yet Trump still deployed Birther discourses in his interviews. Both the Birther website and Taitz's interview illustrate the fringe aspect of Birther discourses. However, Donald Trump is an influential case—no other public figure in the Birther movement is as recognizable by a national audience.

By analyzing these three fragments as a representative sample of public Birther discourses, I construct a discursive field where Birther rhetoric, undergirded in constitutional protection and race-blindness, emphasizes "eligible citizenship." I illustrate that the Birthers' attempted to delegitimize Obama's presidency without explicit anti-Black racial signifiers while tapping into racial scripts of foreignness that are reminiscent of and parallel with anti-Asian American discourses.

Questioning "Natural Born"

The Birthers.org website articulates arguments without misrepresentation and circulates information that positions Birthers as rational protectors of the United States and its Constitution.[7] According to Birthers.org, the moniker "Birther" has a twofold meaning: the first refers to the issue of presidential eligibility by natural-born citizenship and the second to the mission of upholding a certain interpretation of the Constitution. They name the opposition "O-borters" who seek to abort the Constitution by violating its principles through their support of Obama (Birthers, "About," para. 6). In naming the opposition, the Birthers construct themselves as the defenders of the Constitution explicitly and the protectors of life implicitly, referencing "abort" and abortion through "O-borters" and hence mobilizing a pro-life conservative base to conflate the fight over abortion as similar to the fight over the Constitutional integrity. The website states that Birthers "seek strict adherence to the Constitution of the United States of America," which manifests itself through their interpretation of the Constitution (Birthers, "About," para. 8).[8] The name "Birthers" and the phrase "strict adherence" shift the attention away from race and toward the founding technicalities and intentions of the Constitution. Thus, Birthers present themselves as true patriots who protect the U.S. Constitution from those who seek to violate the Founding Fathers' intentions. I tease out how Birther logics re-interpret the Founding Fathers' intentions through an analysis of the website's "Logical Analysis" and "FAQ" sections and a downloadable "Ineligibility" flyer—all, which outline their rationale and address questions of a doubting audience

One widely accepted intention of the Founding Fathers is that the presidency should be held by a person with citizenship conferred by birthright—either by being born in U.S. territory (*jus soli*) or born to U.S. citizen parents (*jus sanguis*). However, the Birthers extend this premise of birthright citizenship requirement by asserting that the U.S. presidency needs to be occupied by a "natural-born citizen." Developed from their own research and interpretation of the Constitution, Birthers provide a definition of "natural-born citizen" that justifies racist nativism about Obama while attempting to avoid explicit discussions of race. In order to prevent foreigners (in this case, Barack Obama) from taking office, the Birthers shift from "born citizen" and to re-defining "natural-born citizen" as the primary requirement for presidency. In the "Logical Analysis" section of the website, they use a mix of syllogisms, logical matrixes, Euler diagrams, and Venn diagrams to illustrate that "natural-born citizen" belongs to a narrow subset of "born citizens" who are *both* (1) born to two United States citizens and (2) born within the United States (Birthers, "The Logical Analysis..."). These claims highlight the perceived untrustworthiness of Obama's multi-racial heritage and reconfigure his global experiences as threats to the U.S. Constitution. They assert their definition as the one true understanding of a natural-born citizen and redefine acceptable birthright citizenship for the presidency as one that meets both their requirements. In doing so, Birther arguments present a seemingly logical and persuasive conclusion about the importance of their conception of "natural-born citizen" that, while not technically valid for the standards of eligibility, draws on the *topos* of the Founding Fathers' intent and Constitutional integrity.

The Birther approach to "natural-born citizen" springs from the lack of definitional clarity provided by the Constitution. Birther discourses aim to clarify the intent of the Founding Fathers whose aim was to prevent foreigners from gaining foothold and control of the newly created Republic (Birthers, 2009, "Ineligible..."). Birthers marshal evidence, first citing the Law of Nations as the basis for understanding natural-born citizens from the Constitution's Framers' perspective and then a letter sent from John Jay to George Washington, which asserts that the position of Commander in Chief "shall not be given to nor devolve on, any but a natural-born citizen" (Birthers, "The Original Intent…" para. 9). By tracing the roots of the Constitution, these arguments reassert Birther expertise regarding the Constitution and reinforce the never-ending threat of foreigners invading and usurping the Office of the President. Furthermore, the Birthers invoke the Framers and deem that the Office of the President is "too important to trust to anyone but a person who was born to parents who were both U.S. citizens at the time of the child's birth" (as cited in Thomasos, 2012, para. 3). This final assertion about natural-born citizenship centers a specific type of born citizenship—one that requires dual U.S. parental citizenship—as the priority and frames those who disagree as untrustworthy. Utilizing the lack of clarity within the Constitution, these claims and the seemingly logical means by which they are supported—the roots of the Constitution—communicate to its skeptics, but more importantly Birther sympathizers, that the Birthers are rational protectors of the Constitution and the Founding Fathers' intentions.

While Birthers outline their seemingly non-racial logic about natural-born citizenship, they are acutely aware of the criticisms that they are "racist" toward Obama. They do not directly answer the hypothetical question "Are you racists, because Obama is black (*sic*)?" posed in the FAQs section (Birthers, "FAQs"). Rather, they justify targeting Obama, declaring, "the question of Constitutional eligibility transcends color" and shield themselves from racist accusations by proclaiming, "many of our supporters and members are people of different skin color" (Birthers, "FAQs," para. 27–28). Here, their answer distances themselves from explicit anti-Black discourses and racists and instead, emphasizes the Constitutional aspect. Their arguments do not dispute Obama's born citizen status (citizenship by birth on U.S. soil) but rather that he is a "natural-born British subject" owing to his father's British citizenship.[9] Despite no longer having dual citizenship passed from his father, the Birthers focus on the possibility of Obama harboring dual loyalties because of his previously held citizenships in the UK and Kenya. For the Birthers, Obama's birthright and familial associations with foreign countries are the cause for fear.

Yet, a racial logic is hidden underneath the Birthers' defensive comments. Despite the overwhelming majority of Birthers and Tea Partiers being White (Montopoli, 2012), the discourse of having racial minority supporters coupled with the race-neutral Constitutional approach is an act of post-racial rhetoric that attempts to absolve them from being "racist." Birther discourses re-center protecting the Constitution's integrity as justification for questioning Obama's natural-born citizenship. Hence, Birther discourses reinforce a post-racial citizenship, one that ignores the complexities of race and focuses upon the seemingly clear-cut definitions of citizenship put forth by the Constitution. Their rhetoric perpetuates racist discourses against racialized (and hence Othered) bodies even as it actively avoids and omits explicit racial signifiers. Birther rhetoric targets Obama by accentuating his foreignness—primarily through his father's citizenship while alluding to the foreign racialized body in the White House. In doing so, Birther discourses position native birth and parental citizenship as the most important aspects of a presidential candidate and a determinant to protecting the integrity of the Constitution and the Office of the President.[10] The natural-born citizenship discourse serves as a post-racial code about legitimacy and belonging, implying that birthright citizenship is not enough to demonstrate undivided allegiance—familial ties to other nations and a foreign experience forever taints loyalty to the United States.

Inscrutable Subject and Untrustworthy Evidence

Whereas the Birther website exists for those who seek out the information, Taitz's mainstream media interviews exposed Birther discourses to more public audiences—network television viewers or Birthers who are concerned with their representation in the media. On October 13, 2009, Taitz was interviewed on the *Joy Behar Show* on the HLN network. The YouTube video recording of the Behar interview is titled "Orly Taitz gets Joy Behar very nervous about the Obama Eligibility..." (CNIN242, 2009; Taitz, 2009). During the interview, Taitz puts forward a series of arguments in regards to Hawai'i and its policies central to understanding Birthers. Based on her understanding of Hawai'i's policies for issuing birth certificates, she suggests that Obama's birth certificate is not reliable nor is it valid for proving his natural-born citizenship. Taitz asserts that foreign born children of Hawai'ian residents can receive a Hawai'ian birth certificate based off the statement of his/her birth of just one relative and "they can even mail this statement" (CNIN242, 2009). Taitz implies that Obama was born in Kenya and that his mother or grandmother provided a fabricated statement to give Obama U.S. citizenship. However, the White racial identity of Obama's maternal side is absent from Taitz's implicit claim. Rather than focus on Obama's multi-racial identity, she attacks Hawai'i, the site where his multi-racial identity was conceived and formalized. Taitz's claims about the untrustworthiness of Hawai'ian birthright citizenship documents are in line with information found on the Birthers' website. Birthers.org criticizes the Hawai'ian Department of Health Director, Dr. Chiyome Fukino and her statement verifying Obama's birth certificate as being "very carefully crafted" (Birthers, "FAQs," para. 4). It doubts Dr. Fukino's statement, stating it only indicates that Obama's "original birth certificate is on file" and not Obama's birth location (Birthers, "FAQs," para. 4). Both Taitz and the Birthers.org simply do not trust Dr. Chiyome Fukino and Hawai'ian birth records and thus deem the citizenship records unreliable. Moreover, Hawai'i is viewed as a threat to the Constitution and the presidency. Hawai'i is construed as a place where birth certificates can be forged and citizenship records are inherently untrustworthy. For Birthers, Hawai'i is the entry point for Obama and his family to manipulate their way into the White House.

When Behar asks for proof this fabrication happened, Taitz responds with "that's the point. His [Obama's] behavior shows a guilty mind." Thus, Obama has something to hide. He is unscrupulous and untrustworthy. He is forever connected to his supposed homeland of Kenya. In casting doubt on Obama's birth certificate and questioning Hawai'i's policies, she implicates Hawai'i as part of the plan, allowing and accepting such fabrications and keeping open loopholes for establishing citizenship. Taitz's comments suggest that Hawai'i is not a state with equal ability to create citizens but rather a place where birthright citizenship is unreliable and untrustworthy as foreigners retain their foreignness.

Behar cites the non-partisan FactCheck.org as affirmation of Obama's eligibility, only to have Taitz dismiss it because of financial support given to Obama by the FactCheck.org's sponsor, the Annenberg Foundation. When Behar asks why Taitz wants to discredit Obama, Taitz shifts the conversation to a court order document, contending that his citizenship is "a legitimate issue" for the courts. This shift resituates Taitz within the discourse of Constitutional protector and away from personal vendettas, echoing Birther discourses on Birther.org. Behar finally asks, "What religion do you think he [Obama] is?" Taitz replies, "I don't know but it doesn't matter," and launches into a critique against the GOP's positing of rising star Bobby Jindal as a potential presidential candidate. Taitz attempts to evade the issue of race and shield against charges of partisanship by shifting the conversation from a question about Obama's religion to a critique of a South Asian American Republican politician. In their discussion, Taitz quickly asserts that Jindal, born of immigrant parents, is not a natural-born citizen and thus ineligible to become president. However, Taitz is not necessarily concerned with Jindal as his family background, birthplace, and ineligibility are clear—there is no doubt that he is not a natural-born citizen according to Birther requirements whereas everything about Obama's background and eligibility is suspect. In shifting to a conversation about Jindal, Taitz rhetorically aligns Jindal and Obama by juxtaposing Jindal's confirmed lack of natural-born citizenship with questions over Obama's citizenship. Her critique of Jindal attempts to safeguard her against critiques of racism while coupling Jindal and Obama together and racially coding them as foreigners. Jindal is established as a confirmable and trustable assimilated immigrant whereas Obama is an inscrutable foreign subject. Taitz's Birther rhetoric reinforces the notion of an untrustworthy Obama. His deceptiveness via his manipulation of Hawai'ian birthright citizenship policies is evident when positioned against other forthright and verifiable subjects, like Jindal.[11]

Whereas Taitz speaks on behalf of the Birthers from the fringe, Donald Trump acts as a well-known follower of the Birthers and echoes their discourses in the mainstream media. The danger of Trump's espousal of the Birther position is that "Trump's big mouth and bigger stage ... may bring a lot of Birthers out of the closet" (Stein, 2011). Trump asserts himself as the mainstream public figure supportive of the Birther position and states that people have contacted him, pleading "Please don't give up on this issue" (Mann, 2011). On a 2011 episode of the afternoon television chat show *The View*, Trump openly supported an Arizona's Birther-inspired bill that would require candidates to provide proof of U.S. citizenship prior to appearing on the ballot (Castro & Davenport, 2011). Prior to the release of Obama's long-form birth certificate, Trump provided his official Department of Health Birth Certificate to conservative website *Newsmax* (Edwards, 2011) and wrote an editorial for *USA Today*, stating "If there is nothing to hide, come clean" and "many people have the same doubts as I have" (Trump, 2011). These instances in high-profile news media outlets reaffirmed accusations that Obama is remiss in not efficiently providing readily available documents and therefore implicitly guilty.

However, Birther-inspired doubts did not wholly subside after Obama released his long-form birth certificate. A Gallup Poll conducted from May 5 to May 8, 2011, showed that 33% of those polled thought that Obama was probably born (8%) or definitely born (5%) in another country, with an additional 20% stating that they "don't know enough to say" (Morales, 2011). Nearly a quarter of Republicans (23%) and 14% of Independents still believed Obama was definitely or probably born in another country (Morales, 2011). Even the release of the long-form birth certificate demanded by the Birthers was not enough to upend the seeds of doubt they planted. Donald Trump was amongst the most vocal doubters, continuing even two years later after Obama proceeded to "come clean" and released his long-form birth certificate.

On August 11, 2013, Donald Trump appeared in an interview with Jonathan Karl on ABC's *This Week* (ABC News, 2013). In this short four-minute edited interview, Karl questions Trump on his strengths and weaknesses as a potential 2016 candidate and his (one-word) opinions on other GOP candidates. Although Trump sees himself as a strong candidate on account of his business acumen and success, he is surprised when Karl marks him as "not serious" owing to his belief of Birther discourses. Trump responds "Why does this make me not serious? I think that resonated with a lot of people." In defending himself against Karl's dismissal of Birther discourses, Trump re-establishes the widely doubted Birther claims as plausible and their concerns as valid. Karl presses further and inquires if he still questions Obama's birthplace, Trump responds with "I have no idea." Karl alludes to Obama's widely accepted Hawai'ian birthplace after the release of the long-form birth certificate. Yet Trump responds more forcefully, stating, "Well, I don't know. Was that a birth certificate? I don't know. And *you* don't know either. You're a smart guy and *you* don't know." Utilizing a rhetoric of ignorance, Trump's defense casts doubt upon Dr. Fukino and Hawai'i's system while aligning Karl with Trump on the same side of "not knowing" the validity of Obama's long-form birth certificate. Trump quickly changes the topic to the threat of China, stating "But my issue is economic. Our country is being ripped apart by China...." Although Karl's question did not address issues of race, Trump's answer conflates race and nationality with foreign threat. Trump's rhetoric of doubt concerning Obama's legitimizing documents relocates Trump's primary concern to the economic destruction by the hands of China and other foreign countries. By shifting the discussion from foreignness of Obama to the threat of China, Trump's answer associates Obama with China even as it attempts to distance itself from attacks on his credibility owing to his association with Birther discourses. Trump places Obama as a foreign illegitimate president immediately prior to positioning China as an impending threat, allowing audiences to form a causal relation between Obama's legitimacy to the (economic) decline of the country. Thus, Obama's illegitimate presidency parallels the threat of China.

Karl further presses Trump about any doubts he might have regarding the birth certificate issue, only to have Trump interrupt and redirect the burden of confirming eligibility back, stating "…you [Karl] can't be pretty sure. You have to be 100% sure." Karl states, "I'm a 100% sure," only to have Trump quickly dismiss his assurance with, "I don't think you are." Karl asks about Ted Cruz's eligibility, after which Trump states, "It'll be ironed out … that's his [Ted Cruz] thing." Trump's interview with Karl parallels Taitz's interview with Behar, where both Taitz and Trump jettison questions about their knowledge by turning to Asian figures—Taitz turns to Jindal whereas Trump turns to China as a foreign economic threat. Yet, Trump's engagement with and circulation of Birther discourses differs from Taitz's and those found on the Birthers.org. Taitz and the Birthers.org primarily utilized affirmative arguments to indict Obama; Trump's support of Birther beliefs came from a rhetoric of objective doubt. That is, the U.S. polity does not absolutely know since we were not present to observe Obama's birth. Trump's replies rely on an appeal to ignorance where it is always up to the accused to provide evidence for the accusers' benefit and (impassable) standard. Even as Karl brings up Republican Senator Ted Cruz's possibility of being a non-natural-born citizen, Trump simply tells Karl that "you'll have to ask him that (if Cruz was born in Canada)." In doing so, Trump recasts himself as the skeptical outsider interested in the truth, simply asking the difficult and controversial questions, whereas the mainstream liberal media is uninterested in criticizing Obama.

Trump normalizes Birther rhetoric despite Karl's various attempts to stigmatize Birther discourses by associating Birther ideas with compromised credibility. In addition, Trump furthers acceptance of Birther discourses through his own embodiment. For example, his expertise as a businessman confers legitimacy upon his warnings of the Chinese (and hence foreign) threat. Trump's doubt regarding Obama's birth certificate elevates him above the political fray and into a rational and logical skeptic of Obama's citizenship. And the logic goes: since Trump is a successful and smart man who believes that Obama's eligibility is still unproven, then the Birther discourse is not as "crazy" or irrational as depicted by the mainstream (i.e., liberal) media.

Xenophobic Constitutional Protection

At its core, Birther discourses deploy a rhetoric of natural-born citizenship and inscrutability to defend the Constitution against foreigners. Couched within post-racial discourses, Birthers mask their racial logics by recasting its goals and purposes as ones that uphold the trustworthiness of systems and procedures that, to Birthers, have been compromised by foreign bodies. In the case of Obama, his questionable and unverifiable background is a threat to the Constitution. It is this logic—a technical one that is seemingly devoid of race yet relies on racist and nativist notions of citizenship—that resonates in the political and public sphere despite certified documentation that confirms Obama's eligibility.[12] This resonance occurs, in part, because the xenophobia present in Birther discourses mirrors the longstanding fear of immigrants, whose presence in the United States would introduce "cultural elements … that would destroy the American national character" (Dorsey & Harlow, 2003, p. 60). Although early twentieth-century xenophobic discourse included southern and eastern European "races" or nationalities, current iterations of xenophobia are focused on Latin@s. This is particularly evident in the anti-immigration opposition to transporting Central American migrant children/refugees fleeing violence. The anti-immigration activists rationalize their opposition by citing a disregard of U.S. immigration law, the threat of overwhelming U.S. schools with a "flood" of these children, and a wish that "America would be America again because it's not" (Martinez & Yan, 2014). The fear of foreign bodies via immigrants is a longstanding U.S. practice.

Yet, the Birther rhetoric of xenophobia comes tinged with fears of foreign domination and invasion through intelligent, unscrupulous, and deceptive means, drawing upon and running parallel to the discourses of yellow peril and forever foreigner. Forever foreigner discourses assume that Asians and Asian Americans will forever be seen as foreigners with allegiances to their Asian "homeland" whereas yellow peril assumes that the United States is vulnerable to or threatened by an Asian invasion, whether it is impending or already present. Yet, yellow peril and forever foreigner discourses work in concert and "shifts public understanding and discussion of Asians and Asian Americans as yellow peril whether or not it ... exists" (Ono & Pham, 2009, p. 43). For example, Japanese American internment acted upon both forever foreigner and yellow peril discourses to provide the (il)logical grounds for internment by asserting that U.S. citizens of Japanese descent maintained loyalty to the Japanese emperor and that their presence compromised the war effort. In 1999, another instance of the convergence of these discourses happened with Los Alamos nuclear scientist, Wen Ho Lee. Accusations couched in yellow peril and forever foreigner discourses, Lee, a Taiwanese-born, U.S. educated, a husband, and father of two children, was wrongly accused of stealing and giving nuclear secrets to the People's Republic of China (Lee & Zia, 2001).[13] The recent rise of the Tea Party also brought fears of rising economic stability and wealth within Asian countries, which they perceived was at the expense of the United States. Thus, Asians and Asian Americans are the foreigners that threaten the United States, its values, and its economic system, despite whether or not any of it is true; the truth is irrelevant when it comes to yellow peril and xenophobia. In the case of Obama, Birther xenophobia relied on the construction of President Obama as a promiscuous global citizen whose United States' "natural-born citizenship" is suspect, whose diasporic identity is inassimilable, and whose presence inevitably threatens the United States in how he changes the political, economic, social, and racial terrain of the United States, much like yellow peril's threat of a negative Asian influence.

The Birther rhetoric of xenophobia comes tinged with fears of foreign domination and invasion through intelligent, unscrupulous, and deceptive means, drawing upon and running parallel to the discourses of yellow peril and forever foreigner. Although the mainstream public noted that the idea of Obama as foreign was racist or ridiculous (Hughey, 2012; Pitts, 2011), the discourses of natural-born citizenship, inscrutable subjectivity, and untrustworthiness resonated with Birthers and Birther sympathizers and are familiar racial scripts for Asians and Asian Americans. Molina (2013) suggests that the familiarity of these racial scripts generates credibility, "making ideas about race that might otherwise be considered outrageous or flagrantly racist seem normal" or even racist ideas as "common sense" (p. 140). Thus, it is possible and plausible that a foreigner falsified documents and tampered with evidence in order to gain citizenship, even if it is the President Obama. The Birther discourses operate through what Ono describes as the "rhetoric of rationality" that draws on "paranoia" and the nation as a "vulnerable masculine body fearful of masculine penetration" and links those two ideas with irrational skepticism and (un) critical thinking (Ono, 2001, p. 82). Couched in the rationality of Constitutional interpretation and fear of foreign invasion, Birther discourses denaturalize Obama, strip him of citizenship, and construct him as an internal threat to the Constitution, the United States, and the very fabric of the U.S. polity.[14]

This internal threat is a racialized one that articulates untrustworthy or suspicious behavior as an essential characteristic of anyone with foreign ties or simply foreign experiences. Obama is configured as a forever foreigner, ripe with perilous potential. Obama's birth certificate and citizenship are irrelevant to the Birthers; his racialized and foreign body is a threat to the Constitution and the only branch that can decide his legitimacy is the Supreme Court. Obama is not seen as a legitimate President but one who has infiltrated the presidency and subsequently puts the nation in peril. Birther rhetoric framed Obama as a foreign threat to the Constitution, and it is up to the (predominantly White) Birthers to protect the Constitution and the body politic.

Despite contrary evidence, Birthers continued to assert that Obama is disloyal, defies the Constitution, and invalidates governmental authority through the presence of his foreign body. Birthers claim that Obama's previously held citizenships in the UK and Kenya are signs of his multiple allegiances to other countries instead of a sole allegiance to the United States. They interpret Obama's association with Kenya, his experience in Indonesia, his Hawai'ian birth, and his lack of (as they define) "natural-born citizenship" as inherent characteristics of disloyalty. The general public sees these Birther logics as irrational since such discourses are not typically targeted at African Americans. Those unfamiliar with the yellow peril and forever foreigner discourses typically intended for Asian Americans may not recognize this discursive move by the Birthers and identify them as "crazy" while, in fact, these racial scripts have been effective in questioning the very presence of Asian Americans in the United States and are now being mobilized to question Obama's legitimacy.

Conclusion: Fear of a Post-Racial Society

Given the acceptance of post-racial and multi-cultural ideology in society, the audacity of Birther discourses—in its prima facie irrationality and ignorance—reinserted a discourse of fear of a foreign usurpation of the highest office. It drew upon post-racial thinking and complicated logics to reconfigure and re-inscribe racist discourses across racial groups. In centering the relationality of race, this essay argues that Birther discourses draw upon the racial scripts of pre-existing anti-Asian discourses to question the legitimacy of President Obama. In doing so, Birthers complicate the field of racist action by enacting racist discourses through the guise of protecting the Constitution—an act that is seen as post-racial, color-blind, and non-partisan. Yet besides Obama, from whom does the Constitution need protection? Per their rhetoric, the Constitution needs protection from the "foreigner," one who threatens the U.S. polity from within and gains access to the presidency through unconstitutional means—primarily non-natural-born citizenship status.

For Birthers, Obama is disloyal, violates the Constitution, and jeopardizes the future of the United States. Yet Obama is a product of the multi-racial "paradise" of Hawai'i (Obama, 2010; Okamura, 2011; Rah, 2008; Yang, 2008). Hawai'i represents the threat of a "post-racial paradise" where multi-racial and global communities thrive without the racial baggage of the mainland. If Hawai'i is a post-racial and multi-cultural paradise, then the Birthers' discourses reveal the fear of such a society and its effect on U.S. political integrity. Whereas Hawai'i could be read as the multi-cultural and post-racial future (Kelleher, 2012; Niesse, 2008), Birther discourses have positioned Hawai'i and its policies as a weak link in maintaining the integrity of citizenship afforded by the U.S. Constitution, an unreliable portal through which foreign entities can infiltrate the U.S. polity. Birther discourses imply that Hawai'ian law, which allows for citizenship to be declared, renders the whole state's populace suspect. Thus, Hawai'i is an example of what happens when the United States becomes multi-cultural and global: our Constitution is threatened, our borders become diffuse, and formerly acceptable forms of citizenship are unreliable markers of "loyalty."

I argue that the Birthers racialized Obama using post-racial discourses and drawing from previously established racial scripts. This illustrates that Birther discourses possess a powerful internal logic that inadvertently draws on pre-existing racial discourses typically levied against Asians and Asian Americans, circulating anti-Blackness and yellow peril in parallel fashion in order to re-inscribe contemporary White supremacist attitudes. It is obvious that Birther discourses attempt to maintain White ideology; however, it is more insidious in that it also reinforces a racial state where viable state power is legitimized through seemingly undeniable claims to natural-born citizenship. Birther discourses re-inscribe political power and access to the presidency by essentializing loyalty, legitimacy, and allegiance through the rhetoric and logic of the "natural-born" citizen, untarnished by foreignness. This "natural-born citizen" logic sets a barrier to the presidency for those who are perceived as foreigners—primarily Asian and Latino/a but even Black as demonstrated by Obama. Yet, this can disproportionately affect Asian Americans. From a recent survey of Asian American voters nationwide, 58% were born in another country, and 39% were born in the United States. But more importantly, 69% of the 39% had a least one parent born in another country[15] (Lake, Mermin, & Grover, 2012), thus increasing the possibility that they are not "natural-born citizens" in the eyes of the Birthers. The conditions of their presence within the United States and the Birther discourses concerning natural-born citizenship cast doubt on their ability to be accepted as viable citizen subjects, let alone political leaders. As Howell (2012) mentions, "the Birther narrative is not embraced by a majority of the Americans but its influence is everywhere" (p. 443). While Birther discourses can easily be disregarded as irrational and ignorant, its lingering presence in the public sphere disperses a racist logic that racializes birthright citizenship. It provides the groundwork for future disagreements and entanglements over eligible and legitimate citizens, effectively communicating to racial groups—particularly Asians and Asian Americans but also to others—that although you might have been born in the United States, you will be forever suspect.

Acknowledgments

I would like to thank Dr. Dreama Moon and Dr. Michelle Holling for their guidance through the editing process. Thank you also to Dr. Natalie Fixmer-Oraiz, Dr. Alyssa Samek, Dr. Peter Campbell, Yaejoon Kwon, Talitha Matlin, Laura Stengrim, Dr. Mattea Garcia, and the anonymous reviewers of this article for their insightful comments and helpful suggestions. An earlier version of this paper was presented at the Rhetoric Society of America Bi-ennial conference in 2012. Thank you to the CSUSM's College of Humanities, Arts, Behavioral & Social Sciences Faculty Development grant for travel funds for this research.

Notes

[1] The first rumors regarding Obama's place of birth supposedly arose from disgruntled Hilary Clinton supporters during her 2008 presidential bid (Smith & Tau, 2011). Birther discourses continued despite President Obama releasing a "certification of live birth" document, which is considered legally sufficient evidence of birth in Hawai'i (CNN, 2011).

[2] The non-partisan Annenberg Public Policy Center's FactCheck.org confirmed the validity of President Obama's birth certificate.

[3] The interview was filmed the same day President Obama released the long-form birth certificate but aired afterwards.

[4] Enck-Wanzer (2011) noted that Tea Partiers often expressed nativist and racial anxieties with their discontent. Birther discourses radically extend this anxiety.

[5] Kim (1999) found that valorization was in relation to Blacks and civic ostracism was in relation to Whites.

[6] One major change is that the homepage focuses on Senator Ted Cruz's lack of natural-born citizenship as of November 2014.

[7] WorldNetDaily (www.wnd.com) is also a major website for Birther movement. Its editor, Joseph Farah, produced a documentary, *A Question of Eligibility*, about Obama's citizenship.

[8] Critical Race theorists argue the legal system of the United States is inherently steeped in White supremacy. Thus, taking a strict interpretation of the Constitution would lead to replicating White supremacist institutions and laws. See Bell (1995), Delgado (1989), and Delgado and Stefancic (2001).

[9] According to FactCheck.org, Obama was a citizen of both the United States and United Kingdom at the time of his birth (Miller, 2009). Since Kenya was a colony of Great Britain, his father passed on British citizenship to Obama. After Kenyan independence, Obama's U.K citizenship was converted to Kenyan citizenship, which expired when he turned 23 years old (Miller, 2009).

[10] Birther rhetoric could be characterized as mirroring Red Scare rhetoric that activates fear about Communist spies infiltrating the United States. Although this characterization helps us understand the paranoid aspects of Birther rhetoric, this perspective too readily dismisses its racial logics.

[11] The Birther website similarly rhetorically aligns Obama with his Indonesia born half-sister Maya Soetoro-Ng (Birthers, "FAQs"). Obama and Soetoro-Ng share the same type of document, the Certification of Live Birth. But Soetoro-Ng is confirmed in not having "natural-born citizenship." Hence, if Obama is not disclosing his official birth certificate, it is plausible that he does not have natural-born citizenship.

[12] Although Howell (2012) explained the resonance of the conspiratorial Birther rhetoric as means to express their dissatisfaction and scapegoating, it does not foreground the racial logic of the Birthers and their anxieties.

[13] Lee attributes his treatment to his Chinese background. He was acquitted of all accounts except for retention of national defense information (something as commonplace as not securing information on a flash drive) and was awarded a $1.6 million dollar settlement from the U.S. Government and media institutions as part of a civil suit.

[14] This is similar to the treatment Chinese Americans received during the 1996 Campaign Finance Reform, where accusations of Chinese money from abroad into the U.S. Democratic fund-raising and U.S. policy (Wang, 1998).

[15] This is also in part due to the history of U.S. immigration policies—such as the 1882 Chinese Exclusion Act, the 1908 Gentleman's Agreement, the 1922 Cable Act, the 1924 Johnson-Reed Act, and the 1952 Walter-McCarran Act—that barred the vast majority of Asian immigrants until the latter part of the twentieth century.

References

ABC News. (2013). *Donald trump "this week" interview* [Video file]. Retrieved from http://www.youtube.com/watch?v=FC_wapgQLxw

Associated Press. (2012, March 1). Arizona sheriff unveils Obama birth probe. *USA Today*. Retrieved from http://usatoday30.usatoday.com/news/nation/story/2012-03-01/arizona-sheriff-joe-arpaio-obama-birth-certificate/53318688/1

Bell, D. (1995). Who's afraid of critical race theory? *University of Illinois Law Review, 4*, 893–909.

Birthers. (2009). *Ineligible under Article II of U.S. constitution*. Retrieved from http://birthers.org/misc/TeaPartyFlyer.pdf

Birthers. (n.d.). *About*. Retrieved from http://birthers.org/birthers.html

Birthers. (n.d.). *FAQ's*. Retrieved from http://birthers.org/faqs/FAQ.html

Birthers. (n.d.). *The logical analysis of a natural born citizen and the clear and compelling evidence that Barack Hussein Obama, II is not a natural born citizen*. Retrieved from http://birthers.org/misc/logic.htm

Birthers. (n.d.). *The original intent the natural born citizen*. Retrieved from http://birthers.org/misc/originalintent.htm

Bonilla-Silva, E. (2010). *Racism without racists: Color-blind racism and the persistence of racial inequality in contemporary America* (3rd ed.). Lanham, MD: Rowman & Littlefield.

Castro, C., & Davenport, P. (2011, April 17). Arizona birther bill stirs controversy. *The Bismarck Tribune*, p. 2A.

Citizens Against Government Waste. (2010, October 10). *Chinese professor* [Video file]. Retrieved from https://www.youtube.com/watch?v=OTSQozWP-rM

CNIN242. (2009, October 13). *Orly Taitz gets Joy Behar very nervous about the Obama eligibility case* [Video file]. Retrieved from https://www.youtube.com/watch?x-yt-cl=85027636&x-yt-ts=1422503916&v=xNEEcUVbLh8

CNN. (2011). President Obama's birth certificate. *CNN*. Retrieved from http://www.cnn.com/interactive/2011/04/politics/interactive.obama.birth.certificate/index.html?hpt=c1

Deis, C. (2010, April 7). The tea parties: Built on fear, violence, and race resentment. *Alternet*. Retrieved from http://www.alternet.org/story/146190/the_tea_parties%3A_built_on_fear%2C_violence_and_race_resentment?paging=off

Delgado, R. (1989). Storytelling for oppositionists and others: A plea for narrative. *Michigan Law Review, 87*, 2411–2441.

Delgado, R., & Stefancic, J. (2001). *Critical race theory: An introduction*. New York, NY: New York University.

Dilliplane, S. (2012). Race, rhetoric, and running for president: Unpacking the significance of Barack Obama's "A more perfect union" speech. *Rhetoric & Public Affairs, 12*(1), 127–152.

Dorsey, L.G., & Harlow, R.M. (2003). "We are want Americans pure and simple": Theodore Roosevelt and the myth of Americanism. *Rhetoric & Public Affairs, 6*(1), 55–78. doi:10.1353/rap.2003.0027

Edwards, S. (2011, March 30). Trump's birthplace questioned following Obama comments; Mogul challenged U.S. president's nationality. *Ottawa Citizen*, p. A8.

Enck-Wanzer, D. (2011). Barack Obama, the Tea Party, and the threat of race: On racial neoliberalism and born again racism. *Communication, Culture, and Critique, 4*, 23–30. doi:10.1111/j.1753-9137.2010.01090.x

Frank, D.A. (2011). Obama's rhetorical signature: Cosmopolitan civil religion in the presidential inaugural address, January 20, 2009: Michigan State University Press. *Rhetoric & Public Affairs, 14*, 605–630. doi:10.1353/rap.2011.0044

Geraghty, J. (2008, June 9). Obama could debunk some rumors by releasing his birth certificate. *The Campaign Spot*. Retrieved from http://www.nationalreview.com/campaign-spot/9490/obama-could-debunk-some-rumors-releasing-his-birth-certificate

Geraghty, J. (2012, May 30). Why is Trump bigger news than, say, Jon Corzine? *The Campaign Spot*. Retrieved from http://www.nationalreview.com/campaign-spot/301266/why-trump-bigger-news-say-jon-corzine

Goldberg, D.T. (2009). *The threat of race: Reflections on racial neoliberalism*. Malden, MA: Blackwell.

Hoerl, K. (2012). Selective amnesia and racial transcendence in news coverage of President Obama's inauguration. *Quarterly Journal of Speech, 98*, 178–202. doi:10.1080/00335630.2012.663499

Howell, J. (2012). Not just crazy: An explanation for the resonance of the Birther narrative. *Communication Monographs, 79*, 428–447. doi:10.1080/03637751.2012.723813

Hughey, M.W. (2012). Show me your papers! Obama's birth and the whiteness of belonging. *Qualitative Sociology, 35*, 163–181. doi:10.1007/s11133-012-9224-6

Indeed, born in the U.S.A. (2011). *FactCheck.org: A project of the Annenberg Public Policy Center*. Retrieved from http://www.factcheck.org/2011/04/indeed-born-in-the-u-s-a/

Isaksen, J.L. (2011). Obama's rhetorical shift: Insights for communication studies. *Communication Studies, 62*, 456–471. doi:10.1080/10510974.2011.588082

Jensen, T. (2009, August 19). *A deeper look at the birthers* [Web log comment]. Retrieved from http://publicpolicypolling.blogspot.com/2009/08/deeper-look-at-birthers.html

Johnson, L. (2012, May 30). Pete Hoekstra, senate candidate, proposes office to verify presidential candidates' eligibility. *Huffington Post*. Retrieved from http://www.huffingtonpost.com/2012/05/30/pete-hoekstra-presidential-candidate-eligibility-office_n_1555932.html

Joseph, R.L. (2011). Imagining Obama: Reading overtly and inferentially racist images of our 44th president, 2007–2008. *Communication Studies, 62*, 389–405. doi:10.1080/10510974.2011.588074

Kelleher, T. (2012, January 30). *Could Hawaii be the model for a multiracial and multicultural society?* [Web log post]. Retrieved from http://www.commhive.com/profiles/blogs/could-hawaii-be-the-model-for-a-multiracial-and-multicultural

Kim, C.J. (1999). The racial triangulation of Asian Americans. *Politics Society, 27*(105), 105–138. doi:10.1177/0032329299027001005

Lake, C., Mermin, D., & Grover, S. (2012). *Asian-American survey: Findings from a survey of 700 Asian-American voters nationwide plus 100 each in FL, NV, VA, and IL*. Retrieved from Lake Research Partners website: http://www.lakeresearch.com/news/AAJC/May7SEIUPresentation%20AsianAmericanSurvey.pdf

Lee, W.H., & Zia, H. (2001). *My country versus me*. New York, NY: Hyperion.

Lowry, R. (2011, April 11). *The Trump moment*. Retrieved from http://www.nationalreview.com/articles/264796/trump-moment-rich-lowry

Mann, S. (2011, April 2). Tycoon Trump questions Obama's place of birth. *The Sydney Morning Herald*. Retrieved from http://www.smh.com.au/world/tycoon-trump-questions-obamas-place-of-birth-20110401-1crqg.html

Martinez, M., & Yan, H. (2014, July 3). Showdown: California town turns away buses of detained immigrants. *U.S.* Retrieved from http://www.cnn.com/2014/07/02/us/california-immigrant-transfers/

McAlister, J.F. (2009). ____ Trash in the White House: Michelle Obama, post-racism, and the pre-class politics of style. *Communication & Critical/Cultural Studies, 6*, 311–315. doi:10.1080/14791420903063844

McGee, M.C. (1990). Text, context, and the fragmentation of contemporary culture. *Western Journal of Speech Communication, 54*, 274–289.

Miller, J. (2009, September 3). Obama's Kenyan citizenship. *Ask Factcheck.org*. Retrieved from http://www.factcheck.org/2008/08/obamas-kenyan-citizenship/

Molina, N. (2013). *How race is made in America: Immigration, citizenship, and the historical power of racial scripts*. Berkeley: University of California Press.

Montopoli, B. (2012, December 14). Tea Party supporters: Who they are and what they believe. *CBS News*. Retrieved from http://www.cbsnews.com/news/tea-party-supporters-who-they-are-and-what-they-believe/

Morales, L. (2011, May 13). Obama's birth certificate convinces some, but not all, skeptics. *Gallup*. Retrieved from http://www.gallup.com/poll/147530/obama-birth-certificate-convinces-not-skeptics.aspx

MOVIES Coming Soon. (2012, August 10). *Red Dawn TRAILER (2012) Chris Hemsworth, Josh Hutcherson Movie HD* [Video file]. Retrieved from https://www.youtube.com/watch?v=nGoe7BdGdlg

Nakayama, T. (2000). Dis/orienting identities: Asian Americans, history, and intercultural communication. In A. González, M. Houston, & V. Chen (Eds.), *Our voices: Essays in culture, ethnicity, and communication* (3rd ed., pp. 13–18). Los Angeles, CA: Roxbury.

National Review Online Editors. (2011, December 5). *Trump's sideshow debate*. Retrieved from http://www.nationalreview.com/articles/284857/trump-s-sideshow-debate-editors

Niesse, M. (2008, August 7). Island life in multiracial Hawaii shaped Obama. *USA Today Politics*. Retrieved from http://usatoday30.usatoday.com/news/politics/2008-08-07-1974308754_x.htm

Obama, B. (2010). *Remarks by the president at reception celebrating Asian American and Pacific Islander Heritage Month*. Retrieved August 21, 2012, from http://www.whitehouse.gov/the-press-office/remarks-president-reception-celebrating-asian-american-and-pacific-islander-heritag

Okamura, J. (2011). Barack Obama as the post-racial candidate for a post-racial America: Perspectives from Asian America and Hawai'i. *Patterns of Prejudice, 45*(1–2), 133–153.

Omi, M., & Winant, H. (2014). *Racial formation in the United States* (3rd ed.). New York, NY: Routledge.

Ono, K. (2001, January). *Guilt without evidence: Informal citizenship and the limits of rationality in the case of Wen Ho Lee*. Paper presented at the Proceedings of the Twelfth NCA/AFA Conference on Argumentation, Annadale, VA.

Ono, K.A., & Pham, V.N. (2009). *Asian Americans and the media*. Malden, MA: Polity Press.

O'Reilly, B. (2014, June 24). Were the conservative radio talk show hosts correct? *FOX Nation*. Retrieved from http://nation.foxnews.com/2014/06/24/oreilly-were-conservative-radio-talk-show-hosts-correct

Pfeiffer, D. (2011, April 27). President Obama's long form birth certificate. *The White House Blog* [Web log]. Retrieved from http://www.whitehouse.gov/blog/2011/04/27/president-obamas-long-form-birth-certificate

Pitts, L., Jr. (2011, March 30). Birthers' blather just racism. *Spokesman Review*. Retrieved from http://www.spokesman.com/stories/2011/mar/30/birthers-blather-just-racism/

Rah, S.-C. (2008, May 11). *I am Barack Obama* [Web log post]. Retrieved from http://sojo.net/blogs/2008/11/05/i-am-barack-obama

Reens, N. (2012, May 30). Pete Hoekstra: Establish national "birther" office for presidential candidates. *MLive Michigan*. Retrieved from http://www.mlive.com/news/grand-rapids/index.ssf/2012/05/pete_hoekstra_establish_nation.html

Rowland, R.C. (2011). Barack Obama and the revitalization of public reason. *Rhetoric & Public Affairs, 14*, 693–725.

Rowland, R.C., & Jones, J.M. (2007). Recasting the American dream and American politics: Barack Obama's keynote address to the 2004 democratic national convention. *Quarterly Journal of Speech, 93*, 425–448. doi:10.1080/00335630701593675

Schueller, M.J. (2009). *Locating race: Global sites of post-colonial citizenship*. Albany: SUNY Press.

Shepherd, E. (2012, October 19). *Racism is alive and well: 35 incredibly racist anti-Obama images* [Web log post]. Retrieved from http://www.defshepherd.com/2012/10/racism-is-alive-and-well-35-incredibly.html

Smith, S.M. (2009). Obama's whiteness. *Journal of Visual Culture, 8*(2), 129–133. doi:10.1177/14704129090080020202

Smith, B., & Tau, B. (2011, April 24). Birtherism: Where it all began. *Politico.* Retrieved from http://www.politico.com/news/stories/0411/53563.html

Stein, G. (2011, April 1). Is Donald Trump giving credibility to the birther movement? *South Florida Sun-Sentinel.* Retrieved from http://articles.sun-sentinel.com/2011-04-01/news/sfl-donal-trump-is-the-donald-giving-credibility-to-the-birther-movement-20110401_1_birther-donald-trump-credibility

Sweet, D., & McCue-Enser, M. (2010). Constituting "the people" as rhetorical interruption: Barack Obama and the unfinished hopes of an imperfect people. *Communication Studies, 61,* 602–622. doi:10.1080/10510974.2010.514679

Taitz, O. (2009). *Orly on CNN—Joy Behar Show 10/13/09* [Video file]. Retrieved from http://www.orlytaitzesq.com/?p=4889

Terrill, R.E. (2009). Unity and duality in Barack Obama's *A More Perfect Union. Quarterly Journal of Speech, 95,* 363–386. doi:10.1080/00335630903296192

Thomasos, C. (2012, January 31). *"Birther" debate: Growing movement looks to keep Obama off state Ballots.* Retrieved from http://www.christianpost.com/news/birther-debate-growing-movement-looks-to-keep-obama-off-state-ballots-68140/

Trump, D.J. (2011). Obama, come clean. *USA Today,* p. 8A.

UpNorthLive. (2012, February. 6). *Senate candidate Pete Hoekstra under fire for ad* [Video file]. Retrieved from https://www.youtube.com/watch?v=2-E2IhOc58k

Wang, L.-C. (1998). Race, class, citizenship, and extraterritoriality: Asian Americans and the 1996 campaign finance scandal. *Amerasia Journal, 24*(1), 1–28.

Wells, R. (2014, January 31). *Obama's criminal past revealed.* Retrieved from http://www.americasfreedomfighters.com/2014/01/31/obamas-criminal-past-revealed/

Yang, J. (2008, July 30). Could Obama be the first Asian American president? *San Francisco Gate.* Retrieved from http://www.sfgate.com/entertainment/article/ASIAN-POP-Could-Obama-be-the-first-Asian-2481103.php

Younge, G. (2009, August 3). Why we can't ignore the birthers. *AlterNet.* Retrieved from http://www.alternet.org/story/141730/why_we_can%27t_ignore_the_birthers

Zia, Anjum. [Anjum Zia]. (2012, September 4). *The Oprah Winfrey show Barack Obama and Michelle Obama part1* [Video file]. Retrieved from https://www.youtube.com/watch?v=KaGKrkcoDdY

New Media, Old Racisms: Twitter, Miss America, and Cultural Logics of Race

J. David Cisneros & Thomas K. Nakayama

This article examines the phenomenon of racist speech on social media, focusing on the controversy over racist tweets about the first Indian American Miss America, Nina Davuluri. The essay highlights tensions between "old" and "new" cultural logics about race. Specifically, it explores why such an "old" form of racist discourse, which explicitly imputes racial difference and exclusion, resurfaces on social media in the era of "new" or "color-blind" racism. Our study demonstrates the perseverance of racist discourse, its complementarity with ideologies of post-racialism, and the ways in which social networking technologies shape communication about race, culture, and identity.

When Nina Davuluri was crowned the winner of the 2014 Miss America Pageant, it elicited more attention than usual for two reasons: (1) she became the first Indian American to win the competition and, (2) her victory resulted in an immediate firestorm of racist comments on social media, particularly Twitter. While journalists and pop-culture commentators hailed Davuluri as the "evolving US ideal" and as "an ideal answer to racism" (Hetrick, 2013; Tandon, 2013), Twitter users denounced the ascent of an "Arab" to the position of Miss America, suggested that it was a victory for Al Qaeda, or tweeted stereotypes about Indians (Broderick, 2013). These comments elicited backlash by other Twitter users and extensive commentary by bloggers and news reporters, some of whom maligned the social media users in question as bigoted "rednecks" or "yahoos" (Abcarian, 2013; Le Tellier, 2013).

Scholars have shown that beauty pageants are significant sites for the negotiation of multiple identities (Ahmed-Ghosh, 2003; Banet-Weiser, 1999; Banet-Weiser & Portwood-Stacer, 2006; Dow, 2003; Parameswaran, 2004). But setting aside for the moment the racial, national and gendered dimensions of the Miss America Pageant itself, this particular example is interesting insofar as it represents what has become a fairly persistent and predictable pattern of controversies about racist, sexist, and homophobic speech on social media, including racist comments directed at Black athletes, controversies surrounding the casting of actors of color in popular film and television, and racist tweets following President Obama's victory in the 2012 election (Greenhouse, 2013; Zook, 2012). Controversies surrounding objectionable speech on social media have become both ordinary and extraordinary: ordinary because of their frequency and periodicity but extraordinary because they seem to be a conspicuous exception to a larger cultural reticence to invoke race in what is perceived as a "post-racial" society (Bonilla-Silva, 2010). Although scholars acknowledge this phenomenon, they have yet to examine how and why it might be so prevalent on social media (Bartlett, Reffin, Rumball, & Williamson, 2014; Highfield, Harrington, & Bruns, 2013).

Scholarship on new media, race, and intercultural communication represents a new and evolving area, and most of the attention has been paid to technologies such as websites, discussion forums, blogs, and online news venues, rather than social media. One way scholars have approached digital rhetorics of race is by examining the discourse of specific organizations, community groups, or locales, such as BlackPlanet, white supremacist groups, or local newspapers (Atkinson, Rosati, Berg, Meier, & White, 2013; Brock, 2009, 2012; Brown, 2009; Byrne, 2008; Holling, 2011; Josey, 2010; Loke, 2012, 2013). Other scholars explore the hypermediated, visual and aesthetic dimensions of digital rhetorics of race, including the multimodality of websites, chat, and gaming (Gajjala, 2007; Nakamura, 2008; Zhang, Gajjala, & Watkins, 2012). On the one hand, the Internet has provided a new space for the cultivation of racial intolerance and hate speech, in part, because of the ease of communication and organization online, the possibility for the creation of niche publics, and the anonymity and speed of online communication (Klein, 2012). On the other hand, some online discourses emphasize post-racialism and mobilize diversity and difference in the service of consumer culture (Gajjala, 2007; McEwan & Sobre-Denton, 2011).

This essay analyzes the controversy over tweets following Davuluri's victory in the 2014 Miss America Pageant as a case study of this broader cultural phenomenon of racist discourse in social media. The regular and recurring nature of such controversies over racist, nativist, sexist, or homophobic comments on social media raise questions about the impact that social media have on norms of racial discourse. Thus this essay responds to recent calls to explore the ways in which new media affect intercultural communication as well as how culture affects new media communication (Shuter, 2011, 2012; Smith Pfister & Soliz, 2011).

We argue that the rather episodic social media controversy surrounding Davuluri's victory highlights tensions between "old" and "new" cultural logics about race. We contrast an "old" type of racist expression, which explicitly imputes difference and exclusion/domination based on racial ascription and essentialism, with what scholars variously call "new racism" or "color-blind"[1] racism that departs from explicit appeals to racial essentialism and instead collapses race into culture and denies the significance of race (Omi & Winant, 1994). Our case study explores why such an "old" form of racist discourse resurfaces in the new medium of Twitter and examines how cultural efforts to suppress such racist discourse act in the service of and entrench "new" racism.

The essay unfolds over three sections: (1) a review of literature on racial logics and racial expression and the (racialized) history of the Miss America Pageant, (2) an analysis of the Twitter controversy after Davuluri's crowning as Miss America, and (3) discussion of implications of the study and the importance of bridging studies of social media and intercultural communication with critical studies of race.

The Miss America Pageant and "Old" and "New" Racisms

"Miss America represents the highest ideals. She is a real combination of beauty, grace, and intelligence, artistic and refined. She is a type which the American Girl might well emulate" (quoted in Terrace, 2013, p. 256). So proclaimed Frederick Hickman, President of the Atlantic City Chamber of Commerce, in 1934—a time during which pageant contestants were required to be white. Thus the "highest ideals" that the pageant winner represented, according to Mr. Hickman, were intricately tied to racial nationalism and white supremacy. These historical connections between whiteness and "beauty, grace, and intelligence" are neither new nor unique to the Miss America Pageant.

Racism reflects this form of racial thinking, as an attitude and ideology that implies racial superiority/inferiority. More than that, as George M. Fredrickson (2002) explained, racism "either directly sustains or proposes to establish *a racial order*, a permanent group hierarchy that is believed to reflect the laws of nature or the decrees of God" (p. 6, emphasis in original). Roots of racial thinking extend back to the time of colonialism and the birth of the nation-state, and, in Western culture, to the mid-nineteenth century publication of Arthur de Gobineau's (2011) book, *Essay on the Inequality of the Human Races*. These legacies can be seen in several broad strands that articulated subsequent forms of racism, including white racial superiority, fear that racialized "others" would destroy society, and thus the need to exclude non-whites.

In the United States, this form of racial thinking took shape through a number of "racial projects" (Omi & Winant, 1994, p. 79), particularly the institution of slavery and, later, Jim Crow laws, prohibitions on interracial marriage, and racist/xenophobic immigration laws. The civil rights movement challenged and changed many of the laws that were entrenched by these older forms of racist thinking, as well as the appropriateness of racism in the public sphere (pp. 90–91). Thanks to these changes, or so it is often said, the U.S. could move beyond racism and embrace its true potential for diversity and multiculturalism (Jones & Mukherjee, 2010).

As a result, a "post-racial" or "color-blind" attitude has become the understood expression of anti-racist thinking and has been expressed in a number of debates, including affirmative action and "reverse racism," racialized debates about welfare policy (Omi & Winant, 1994), and, most recently, in pronouncements of a "post-racial" society after President Obama's election (Bonilla-Silva, 2010). In the wake of the supposed successful dismantling of "old racism" in the public sphere, to stand against racial reference, racial identification, and the concept of race ("anti-racialism") has become the apogee of anti-racist politics (Goldberg, 2009, pp. 21–22).

Yet a rhetoric and politics of "color-blindness" allowed for a shift in logics of racism, "remov[ing] from personal thought or public discussion any taint or suggestion" of racism "while legitimating existing social, political, and economic arrangements" of white privilege (Gallagher, 2003, p. 26). This "new" racism involves the purported embrace of individual difference and diversity along with the eschewal of racial identification and/or claims of structural racism (seen as playing the "race card" or reverse racism). This is what makes "color-blindness" so insidious, because it may appear a significant shift from "old" to "new" racism, but the rupture is not so easy. Not only do explicit racist expressions by public figures arise in the public sphere with increasing frequency (a point to which we return below), but, as Jennifer Simpson (2008) observed, "Color blindness [is] an ally to White supremacy" because, "by dismissing the difference in lived experience of White people and people of color as an irrelevant distinction, it upholds and affirms dominant ways of being, knowing, and doing" (p. 142). The rise of this new racism, then, shifts the ground from social structures to the everyday lived experiences of race in contemporary society.

Thus what we are calling "old" racism rests on imputing difference, exclusion, and domination based on biological and cultural essentialism. It is governed by racial categorization, ascriptions of characteristics based on these categories, and attitudes of superiority and/or domination. Such forms of racist discourse can "involve enunciations of racist principles, supposed justifications of differences, advantages, claims to superiority (whether considered 'natural' or 'developed'), and legitimations of racist practices and institutions" (Goldberg, 1993, p. 42). In the era of "new" racism such forms of explicit racist expression are increasingly marginalized and discouraged in the public sphere. "Modern racial ideology does not thrive on the ugliness of the past or on the language and tropes typical of slavery and Jim Crow," wrote Eduardo Bonilla-Silva (2010); "Today most whites justify keeping minorities from having the good things of life with the language of liberalism" (p. 265). Racial classification and hierarchy, which were at once explicit and public forms of racist expression, are no longer sanctioned. Instead, public discourse focuses on meritocracy and individualism, or cultural "deficiency," at the expense of discussions about a system rigged in favor of some groups over others (Flores, Moon, & Nakayama, 2006).

However, regular, public violations of norms of "color-blindness" and "post-racialism" demonstrate the persistence of "old" racism. For example, "racist violations" by white public figures, such as comedian Michael Richards and former Senator Strom Thurmond, often circulate "old school" (Holling, Moon, & Jackson Nevins, 2014, p. 5) racist microaggressions and insults that entrenched white supremacy, and are followed by "racializing apologia" that deploy whiteness to save face and reassert norms of "color-blindness" (p. 21). This demonstrates the dynamic between "new" and "old" logics of racism. The latter is unsanctioned, privatized, and individualized, and when it arises, it is policed and disavowed in favor of a more publicly embraced yet still racialized form of discourse (e.g., "post-racialism"). While new and old racisms are different in their deployment, neither serves to disrupt white supremacy.

These same racial logics are reflected in the history of the Miss America Pageant. The Pageant has long been a part of the project of imagining national identity/citizenship, "a site for both the constitution and the realization of particular utopian fantasies" about liberal individualism, gender, and whiteness (Banet-Weiser, 1999, p. 154), and a spectacle that mobilizes bodies and/or difference to resolve issues of national identity in particular historical moments. For example, the victory of Bess Myerson, the first and only Jewish Miss America, who won the pageant in 1945, was used, according to Banet-Weiser (1999), to further shore up U.S. American democratic pluralism and the melting-pot ideal. After the crowning of Vanessa Williams as the first African American Miss America in 1984, "popular discourses" framed her victory as validation of "America being a 'colorless' society" and a "harmonious, multicolored society" (Banet-Weiser, 1999, p. 132), notwithstanding the significant racism and prejudice that Williams experienced during her tenure as Miss America (including her loss of the title). Thus the pageant has reflected and tracked broader cultural logics of race, including originally embracing racial requirements that associated an "ideal" American womanhood with upper-class whiteness, and later mobilizing difference to validate a race-neutral and purportedly "multicultural" ideal.

It is into this context that we can place the victory of Nina Davuluri, the first Indian American to win the pageant. Davuluri's win was not only seen as a significant event in the history of the Miss America Pageant, but it also generated attention because it caused a substantial amount of racist discourse on Twitter. These "racist violations" (Holling et al., 2014) created an ensuing backlash that attempted to reassert the predominance of "color-blind" norms about race in the public sphere. We are particularly interested in this Twitter controversy as a case study of the ways that social media shape logics of race and racism in "vernacular" expression (see Howard, 2008). The questions we seek to answer are: What kinds of "old school" racist discourses circulate on social media, and why do we witness these sorts of recurring controversies about racist speech on platforms such as Twitter?

We argue that social media such as Twitter create an atmosphere for the expression of "old" racisms and racist discourse because of the enthymematic nature of tweets and the "context collapse" of Twitter (Marwick & boyd, 2011). The controversy over racist Tweets about Davuluri illustrates the ways in which cultures of social media blur the lines between sanctioned and discouraged forms of discourse and present new contexts for the violation of cultural logics of race. Our analysis also suggests that the explosion of racialized discourse online, as well as its policing by other Twitter users and mainstream media, contributed to the project of "new" racism. Thus such moments of explicit racist discourse highlight the ways that "new" and "old" logics of racism coexist in the world of social media.

Miss America, Racist Tweets, and Social Media Cultures

Davuluri, Miss New York, was crowned the 87th Miss America on September 15, 2013 during a nationally televised evening broadcast of the pageant on ABC. Almost immediately, controversy surfaced around a series of objectionable tweets about Davuluri. The controversial comments initially rose to wider attention when they were exposed by several bloggers and media commentators. In particular, a widely shared article on Buzzfeed (a popular content aggregator site) was posted shortly after Davuluri's win (1:33 am on September 16), and collected over a dozen of the tweets (Broderick, 2013). Although one among several other such posts (see note 2), the Buzzfeed article itself became enormously popular and has over 5 million total views and has been shared over 63,000 times on Facebook and over 15,000 times on Twitter. The tweets that objected to Davuluri's victory relied on a number of stereotypes and themes (e.g., biological/cultural essentialism, exclusion, white supremacy) characteristic of "old" forms of racist expression. As a result, the offensive tweets generated almost immediate backlash on Twitter, websites, and blogs, which maligned the original commentators. The explosion of new media discourse—offensive tweets about Davuluri and attacks on the original tweeters—elicited commentary in news media, as reporters and bloggers attempted to make sense of the ideas of race, national identity, and the norms of communication being contested.

In the first part of the analysis, we discuss how the tweets participated in "old" forms of racist expression, reasserting logics of whiteness and racial exclusion in response to Davuluri's victory. The second part of the analysis turns to the question of why Twitter (and social media more broadly) provided a particularly prevalent platform for the publicizing of such forms of racist discourse. In the third and final part of the analysis, we briefly discuss the contestation of these objectionable tweets and the public controversy they created, showing how rebukes of the offending tweeters and efforts to celebrate Davuluri's victory both worked to shore up cultural logics of "new" racism.

Racist Tweets about Miss America

As we read a number of the tweets that attacked the decision to award the crown to Davuluri, we pulled out a number of themes.[2] First, Twitter users claimed that Davuluri should not be Miss America because she is an Arab: (1) "And the Arab wins Miss America. Classic"; (2) "How the fuck does a foreigner win miss America? She is a Arab!#idiots" (Binder, 2013a; Broderick, 2013; Hafiz, 2013). No doubt connected to this understanding of her as an "Arab," other users suggested that Davuluri's win was an insult to the memory of the victims of September 11 and/or was a victory for Al Qaeda: (3) "9/11 was 4 days ago and she gets miss America?"; (4) "@ABC2020 nice slap in the face to the people of 9–11 how pathetic#missamerica"; (5) "Congratulations Al-Qaeda. Our Miss America is one of you" (Binder, 2013a; Broderick, 2013).

Other users were shocked that a woman of Indian descent could be designated as a representative of "America": (6) "I swear I'm not racist but this is America"; (7)

"Asian or indian are you kiddin this is america omg"; (8) "Miss New York is an Indian ... With all do [sic] respect, this is America"; (9) "this is America. Not India" (Binder, 2013a; Broderick, 2013; Hafiz, 2013). Finally, some of the tweets drew upon and circulated stereotypes of Indians and Indian Americans: (10) "Miss America? You mean Miss 7–11"; (11) "Miss America is brought to by their sponsors PF Changs and 7–11"; (12) "miss New York looks like a dot head without a dot"; (13) "I hope the next snake she tries to charm bites the shit out of her" (Binder, 2013b; Broderick, 2013; Hafiz, 2013). At the same time, tweets and Internet memes circulated about another of the finalists, Theresa Vail (Miss Kansas), who attracted media attention because she is a member of the National Guard and an avid archer and hunter. Some Twitter users chalked up the selection of Davuluri over Vail to political correctness or liberal bias. For example: (14) "Man our president nor [sic] our new Miss America isn't even American I'm sorry but Miss Kansas I salute you your [sic] the real American#MissAmerica"; (15) "Darn ... I wish Miss Kansas would've won! Real American woman!!"; (16) "The liberal Miss America judges won't say this—but Miss Kansas lost because she actually represented American values. #missamerica" (Broderick, 2013; Hafiz, 2013; Sultan, 2013; Zara, 2013).[3]

The tweets about Davuluri generated immediate backlash by other Twitter users, who reacted strongly with efforts to publicly shame and attack the offending tweeters. Some responses pointed out the racism in the original tweets and expressed anger, shame, or indignation: (17) "Wow America, you've really embarrassed yourselves now! Racist pieces of crap! #MissAmerica is American, not Muslim or a terrorist. #Idiots"; (18) "A country full of racists. That is America. #MissAmerica"; (19) "This world is so ignorant. #MissAmerica Indian or not had every right to gain the title of MissAmerica. This is why I want to leave America!"; (20) "So Indians and Arabs are the same now? O for sure ... #MissAmerica" (Hafiz, 2013; "Miss America Faces Abuse," 2013). Individual users directed angry and sometimes equally offensive or violent tweets at the original individuals. Greenhouse (2013) documented one such exchange in which a user who posted objectionable tweets about Davuluri was bombarded with sexist and angry tweets in response, and received threats. Outside of Twitter, individuals engaged in the process of shaming those who had posted offensive tweets by collecting them in weblogs and other sites, such as the Public Shaming Tumblr (Binder, 2013a, 2013b; Broderick, 2013; Grumet, 2013; Schlarmann, 2013). Some of the users who were publicly shamed for their comments responded by removing their Twitter accounts (Greenhouse, 2013; "Miss America 2014 Win," 2013; Zara, 2013). The social media world momentarily bled into mainstream news, which covered and dissected the controversy for months.[4]

Many of the offending tweets worked through and circulated dimensions of racist expression characteristic of "old" racism discussed above, such as the imputing of biological and cultural hierarchy based on racial categorization, the use of racial stereotypes, and the construction of "difference, deviance, and threat" (van Dijk, 1987, p. 58). For example, one type of tweet about Davuluri seemed to express affective and emotional outburst: (2) "How the fuck does a foreigner win miss America? She is a Arab!#idiots"; (7) "Asian or indian are you kiddin this is america omg"; (21) "#MissAmerica ummm wtf?! Have we forgotten 9/11?" Tweet 21 perhaps most directly drew on "threat" by invoking 9/11, while tweets 2 and 7 engaged in discourses of racial threat through the problematic of "cultural difference." There, "foreigner," "Arab," and "Asian or indian" were marked as different and thus as sources of implicit or explicit threat to "American." These tweets echoed the racial thinking that excluded racialized others (non-whites) from full participation in society, at best because of their presumed difference and, at worst, because of the threat that they supposedly provided.

The threat seemed especially pronounced in the context of the Miss America Pageant, which according to Banet-Weiser (1999) frames itself as representative of an ideal, feminized national subject. The linguistic and grammatical cues of these tweets (e.g., cursing and exclamation marks) suggest genuine emotional and/or affective reactions. The tweets seemed to express surprise, shock, or anger at Davuluri's victory, as a violation of a particular set of norms about U.S. national identity. These users seemed to react strongly against the elevation of a woman of color and perceived "foreigner" to the position of Miss America [e.g., (2) "How the fuck does a foreigner win miss America? She is a Arab!#idiots"]. In violation of cultural norms against such forms of racist expression, these tweeters did not engage in "color-blind" rhetoric (cf. Bonilla-Silva, 2010) nor did they try to shade their comments to minimize the loss of face stemming from being seen as racist (cf., van Dijk, 1987); rather they explicitly engaged in racialization and exclusionary discourse.

Other tweets seemed to be marked not by emotional outburst but by conscious efforts at self-presentation through humor, for example: (22) "Miss America is a terrorist. Whatever. It's fine"; (23) "Miss America, footlong buffalo chicken on whole wheat. Please and thank you"; and (24) "Miss Arab wins Miss America and the score of the Seattle/SanFran game is 5–0 at the half? What is life?" Like all humor, the tweets served as rhetorical tools of unification and division; Tweets 22 through 24 shared the same themes as those above (e.g., difference, deviance, and threat, stereotypes and prejudice), but in contrast to excessive emotion they demonstrated deliberate understatement (in 22) or calibrated hyperbole and contrast (in 24) as tools of humor. Tweet 23, in particular, used what Simon Weaver (2011) called the "logic of inferiorization," in which "the joke does not exclude the [person of color] from society, but allows him [or her] to stay on condition that he [or she] remains inferior and exploited" (p. 421). The joke/tweet designated Davuluri as the exception to the proper place of South Asians as members of the food service industry (or, as in the case with tweets 10 and 11, as best suited to work in convenience stores). Although working through humor and/or sarcasm, these tweets, too, demonstrated dimensions of deliberately racist expression discussed above. If we contrast these tweets to other forms of racist jokes in "offline" settings, we again see a difference in the forms of racist expression being used on social media. Scholars have found that, when asked to tell a racist joke, individuals attempt to distance themselves from the joke, to attribute the joke to others, or to qualify it so as to minimize being seen as racist and to adhere to a purportedly "post-racial" ideal (Bonilla-Silva, 2010, p. 56). In contrast, in this example of online discourse, users did not immediately qualify the jokes. As with the emotional outbursts, these joke tweets served the role of identification and division, using humor as a rhetorical tool to manage the violation of presumptive cultural norms about whiteness, femininity, and nationalism with Davuluri's victory.

Whether the tweets about Davuluri can be categorized as uses of humor or as forms of emotional self-expression, whether they called Davuluri an Arab, a terrorist, or circulated stereotypes of Indians and Indian Americans, the tweets in question engaged in explicit (a.k.a. "old") forms of racism and racist expression. While the "new" racisms eschew explicit racial appeals or racist discourse, "older" expressions of racisms, such as the tweets discussed above, frequently advocate such expressions of difference, superiority, essentialism, and exclusion. Davuluri was racialized as "Arab" or "brown" and then associated with terrorism, cultural inferiority, and deviance, thereby erasing racial/ethnic, cultural, and geographic differences and racializing Indians, Middle-Easterners, Arabs, and Muslims as "brown" and "terrorist." Davuluri was positioned in relation to "illegal brownness"—a sort of racialized and malleable identification (Silva, 2014). According to Silva (2014), brown is defined as "by default 'un-American'" (p. 139), as "the irrational insurgent on American soil" (p. 134). Thus Davuluri's foreignness was read in relation to both whiteness and brownness.

By racializing Davuluri as brown/foreign and reading this as unworthy of representing "America," the tweets also worked to identify U.S. national identity/culture with the invisible space of whiteness (see Nakayama & Krizek, 1995) and to protect "American" identity from the supposed encroachment of multiculturalism and diversity. Because Miss America is culturally identified as representing a sort of "ideal" gendered, raced, national subject (see Banet-Weiser, 1999), Davuluri's win presumptively violated (and validated) users' particular visions of that national subject. This violation was potentially exacerbated because Davuluri's persona and performance as a candidate—including her "talent" performance (a Bollywood fusion dance) and her platform ("Celebrating Diversity Through Cultural Competence")—explicitly highlighted her racial and cultural difference. In response, Twitter provided the platform to express anxieties about (and to reassert the link between) whiteness, national purity, and national culture that her victory seemed to provoke amongst some users. Contravening the cultural disapproval of "old school" racist expression, the tweets engaged in explicit efforts to reassert the racialized national ideal in response to its violation, rather than in implicit and veiled attempts at recentering whiteness (cf. Zhang et al., 2012).

The tweets created public backlash and controversy, in part because they circulated "old" forms of racism. In response, tweeters and journalists criticized the offending users and implicitly and sometimes explicitly reasserted the norms of "colorblindness" discussed above. Before considering this response, however, we discuss the medium of Twitter (and social media more broadly) in greater detail. Given the short length of tweets (which are limited to 140 characters), they can often be interpreted in a number of ways. Thus it is not clear that the tweets were sincere or that they represent broader attitudes or ideologies among the users in question, let alone amongst the U.S. populace. Yet simply dismissing them out of hand on this count precludes the possibility of making sense of these tweets as a recurring type of online speech. As we noted above, controversies over racist speech on social media such as Twitter, whether about public figures like Miss America and the President of the United States, or about fictional pop-culture characters, have become a recognized and recurring cultural phenomenon (Bartlett et al., 2014; Greenhouse, 2013; Highfield et al., 2013). Thus the next section begins to answer the question of why such forms of racist expression recur on social media platforms such as Twitter.

Racist Tweets and Social Media Cultures

Although the phenomenon of racist comments on social media has not received explicit scholarly attention to date, social media researchers provide insights about some of the cultural dimensions of Twitter that illuminate the contours and recurrence of such controversies. Specifically, the phenomena of "context collapse" and "publicized privacy" associated with social media technologies can help to explain, in part, how objectionable, racist tweets about Davuluri surfaced and created (and continue to create) such widespread controversy.

First, scholars have argued that social media networks are characterized, in greater and lesser degrees, by a phenomenon known as "context collapse" (boyd, 2010; boyd & Ellison, 2007; Vitak, 2012). Context collapse refers to the ways in which many social media platforms collapse social, geographic/spatial, and temporal contexts that are key to understanding and interpreting specific messages. As a microblogging site, Twitter, for example, "flattens multiple audiences" into one (Marwick & boyd, 2011, p. 122) because it does not rely on an exclusive audience/addressee, and it is not tied to a specific community of interest or identity. In other words, "context collapse" means that Twitter is addressed to an invisible and acontextual audience. All tweets can be seen by anyone and can be retweeted by any other user, even when one uses a direct tweet "at" a specific user. At the same time, not all of one's "followers" will necessarily see all of one's tweets, even when one is presumably tweeting "at" or for one's followers.

The audience of one's tweet is invisible and acontextual even when it is specific and contextual, which also produces a problem for the type of "public" that Twitter and other social media create, and for the distinctions between the public and the private spheres. This was termed "publicized privacy" by Sloop and Gunn (2010). More than other new media technologies, social networking coincides with the blurring of public and private, the mixing of the intimacy and specificity of the personal, the anonymity and generality of the public, and everything in between (Vitak, 2012). Because of this, researchers found that social media users engage in status updates and tweets as, on one hand, forms of self-presentation and social validation to a mass public, and, on the other hand, as forms of self-disclosure and/or self-expression to specific/intimate users (see Bazarova & Choi, 2014; Marwick & boyd, 2011). On Twitter, such forms of direct and intimate address (as in the tweet "at" somebody) occur in the context of a public audience, which creates tensions for self-presentation and identity management. As Marwick and boyd (2011) wrote, "the [communicative] requirement to present a verifiable, singular identity makes it impossible to differ self-presentation strategies" to public and private audiences or in "diverse" contexts (p. 122). Users often risk disclosing too much or the wrong kind of information given the public/private nature of social media.

It is precisely this indeterminacy of audience and context within social media that can help to explain, in part, the objectionable tweets about Davuluri. The context collapse of Twitter and the blending of public and private communication meant that tweeters were addressing "flattened" audiences/contexts and thus could not be sure who they were addressing, even if their tweets were directed at specific, ideal or intimate audiences of followers. The offensive tweets were seen by all users and circulated in the public sphere, creating social sanction and backlash against the offending users that may not have been anticipated. At the same time, the context collapse and publicized privacy of Twitter meant that observers trying to interpret the tweets (including we as scholars) could not be sure of the "correct" reading or "intention," whether sincere or sarcastic, because the tweets were acontextual forms of communication. Were the tweets "meant" to be racist? Does that matter? On the one hand, the intention of the Twitter users is irrelevant to the impact of the tweets because, whether intending to or not, they represented "racist violations" that enacted old forms of racism and upheld white supremacy (Holling et al., 2014). On the other hand, the difficulty in determining whether or not the tweets were "meant" to be racist is precisely the point. It is difficult if not impossible to determine intention not only because of the difficulty of getting "inside" the tweeters' heads, but also, more importantly, because of the acontextual, publicized privacy of social media culture. One cannot say whether the tweets were directed at an audience of like-minded racists or were meant as a sarcastic and tongue-in-cheek joke to an otherwise "color-blind" audience? The context collapse of Twitter meant that, in either case, the tweets were seen by invisible and/or unintended audiences who themselves evaluated the tweets acontextually (for example, as "sincerely" racist expressions rather than as tongue-in-cheek, or as expressions of "private" identity and beliefs that were read by a public audience). These features of social media help to explain the tweets' polysemy and how they created controversy and backlash. According to Marwick and boyd's (2011) survey of Twitter users, many respond to context collapse by imagining the audience "as [composed of] its most sensitive members" so as to limit themselves to "topics that are safe for all possible readers" (pp. 125–126). In contrast, these particular users addressed messages to too-specific audiences and/or overlooked the flattening of the audience/context of Twitter, which resulted in the expression of unsanctioned forms of discourse.

Context collapse and publicized privacy also draw attention to the highly enthymematic nature of these tweets, which was exacerbated by the already-truncated nature of Twitter. Whether meant as sincere expressions of racist attitudes or as sarcasm, the objectionable tweets drew on culturally latent racist beliefs, stereotypes and attitudes of difference, deviance, and threat. Both those tweets that drew upon explicit racist stereotypes (e.g., 1–5, 10–13; 21–24) as well as those that constructed Davuluri's deviance through a rhetoric of whiteness and "American values" (e.g., 6–9, 14–16) worked through an enthymematic logic because racism and whiteness were working in the background (see Jackson, 2006). Yet, the anonymity and ease of online communication and the influence of context collapse and publicized privacy contributed to the violation of prohibitions against explicitly racist speech.

This discussion illustrates that understanding the cultures of new media communication are necessary to develop a fuller picture of the types of communication occurring online (Shuter, 2011, 2012). It was not only the cultural logics of race and whiteness, working enthymematically and hegemonically in the broader culture, but also the specific cultural features of social media, and Twitter specifically, that contributed to the offending tweets and broader controversy about Davuluri's Miss America victory. Yet, as Sloop and Gunn (2010) noted, the culture of freedom of expression that is often wrapped around social media masks the surveillance that accompanies it until the very moment of disciplining. It was only after being confronted with the backlash over their tweets that many of the users in question got defensive and, more times than not, removed their Twitter accounts (Greenhouse, 2013).

Celebrating Davuluri and Criticizing Racist Tweets

As we mentioned above, the tweets in question sparked a backlash on social media and broader controversy in mainstream media outlets. Briefly considering this debate can help to illuminate the cultural significance of discourses of race and new media. Above we mentioned some of the ways in which Twitter users attacked, shamed, and corrected those tweeting offensive or racist comments (see tweets 17–20). Some of those exchanges featured anger and condemnation, while others escalated to attacks and harassment (Greenhouse, 2013). On other Internet platforms, such as blogs and Tumblrs, the offending Twitter users were publicly shamed for their remarks. Similarly, except for a few sources that took a broader approach to understanding the controversy (e.g., Ling, 2013), much of the news media coverage of these objectionable tweets framed them as the ranting of a few pathological, racist bigots who were out of touch with the new, multicultural America. Reporters framed the tweeters as "yahoos" (Abcarian, 2013) and "rednecks" (Virtual world no less prejudiced than real, 2013), as "uneducated" (Le Tellier, 2013) and a "bigoted minority" (Bucktin, 2013; Rajghatta, 2013). Through these sorts of remarks, commentators generally worked to minimize the tweets as the ignorant outbursts of a few backward, anachronistic, and uneducated individuals.

This could be contrasted with a broader discourse of racial progress, post-racialism, and multicultural diversity, which news media used to interpret Davuluri's win. Her crowning as Miss America was "the ideal answer to racism" and a symbol of the new, multicultural, and increasingly post-racial America (Hetrick, 2013; see also Beauty and the beasts, 2013; Vyavahare, 2013). Davuluri, whose Miss America platform was "Celebrating Diversity Through Cultural Competency," was fêted as the embodiment of the multicultural American citizen and as evidence for the continued hope in a colorblind society (Tandon, 2013). As an opinion piece on September 17 in the newspaper *Newsday* proclaimed, "There she is, Miss America. There she is, our ideal" (p. A26).

In efforts to minimize and marginalize the tweets and make meaning of Davuluri's win for racial politics, other Twitter users and media commentators engaged in their own neo-racial logics by reasserting norms of post-racialism, colorblindness, and neoliberal multiculturalism around Miss America (Banet-Weiser, 1999; Parameswaran, 2004). Discourses of individualization and post-racialism are characteristic of "new racism" or "colorblind racism," which work to minimize struggles for racial equality and to replace anti-racism with anti-racialism (Bonilla-Silva, 2010). While Twitter users engaged one form of racist expression, news sources and bloggers presented Miss America as part of the "new face" of a multicultural America, what some scholars have called "neoliberal multiculturalism," or the idea of U.S. identity as the most universal, inclusive, and multicultural identity (Jones & Mukherjee, 2010). In this case, portraying the social media users as "rednecks" or "yahoos" framed racism as aberrant and uncommon, recentered whiteness as the invisible and default ideal, and suggested that multiculturalism was the preferred mode of combatting racism and inequality. The celebration of the pageant as a groundbreaking moment and as a validation of a multicultural/diverse America also sustained this form of neoliberal racism.

It is not that commentators found the tweets offensive *because* they violated "colorblind" logics but rather that their disciplining of these tweets had the effect of *shoring up* neoliberal whiteness and color-blind multiculturalism. As Archana A. Pathak (2013) stated, "in naming diversity" in a "palatable" way, "we've reinforced the white/non-white binary in which whiteness continues to hold the place of the mythical norm" (para. 24). In other words, by accepting Davuluri as the embodiment of the new, multicultural U.S. American "ideal," diversity and its performance (in appropriate and sanctioned ways, such as in a pageant) could continue to serve the cause of "color-blind" racism. By marginalizing the tweeters, commentators could "prove" their anti-racism and validate a "color-blind" norm. Importantly, these competing cultural logics about race are not logical but rather must be rearticulated and recentered through shared communicative interactions. Thus the invocations of Davuluri as a "new ideal" or an "answer to racism" also worked enthymematically by drawing on cultural logics of neoliberal multiculturalism (which is indexed to whiteness in the broader culture, see Jones & Mukherjee, 2010). Both the circulation of "old" forms of racist expression and their policing contributed to logics of racialization and racial exclusion. In the conclusion, we consider some of the implications of this case study for scholarship on new media, race, and intercultural communication.

Conclusions

The preceding analysis has sought to unpack the Twitter controversy in response to Nina Davuluri's victory of the 2014 Miss America Pageant as an expression and example of continuing controversies about racist discourse on social media. We advanced three specific arguments. First, the racist tweets about Davuluri after her crowning as Miss America circulated "old school" forms of racist expression—relying on difference, deviance, and threat—that entrenched white supremacy, the association of whiteness with a particular "ideal" national identity and culture, and the racialization of "brown" people as threatening and deviant. Intentionally or not, these discourses not only responded to the crowning of Davuluri as the first Indian American Miss America but also seemed to express broader cultural anxieties about race, culture and national identity. Second, we argued that these offensive tweets should be contextualized in the broader cultures of social media, such as publicized privacy and context collapse, which contributed both to the tweets themselves as well as to the broader backlash and controversy that they engendered. The expression of latent strands of racist expression that persist in our contemporary "post-racial society" were facilitated by and refracted through the media cultures of social networking in general and Twitter in particular. Third, brief consideration of the popular backlash against such tweets demonstrated that, by marginalizing and pathologizing the offending tweeters, and by celebrating Davuluri as a neoliberal, multicultural, U.S. ideal, some news commentators actually reasserted norms of whiteness and "post-racialism"—the idea that Davuluri's victory was an expression of racial progress, that her crowning as "Miss America" was itself a solution to what were lingering expressions of racism. "New" and "old" logics of racism and racist expression fed off of each other here, as both the violation of "post-racial" norms and their policing reasserted whiteness, racialization, and racial exclusion. To conclude, we want to emphasize three implications of this case study.

First, the Twitter controversy surrounding Miss America 2014 demonstrates the perseverance and evolution of explicitly (a.k.a. "old") racial logics and racist discourse in spite of popular claims to "color-blindness" and "post-racialism." This analysis lends support to scholars who argue that racist violations persist, belying pronouncements of a shift to "color-blind" or "post-racial" ideology (e.g., Cresswell, Whitehead, & Durrheim, 2014; Holling et al., 2014; Klein, 2012). While positioned as aberrant in the broader culture, such forms of racist expression demand continued critical attention precisely because they form the foil and justification for the purportedly "post-racial" era.

In fact, this case study suggests that the two strands of discourse about race considered above are intimately connected; therefore, the second implication we wish to highlight: the connection between "old" and "new" racisms and the way that they feed off of each other. The policing and marginalization of one shores up the other. In this case, by marginalizing the tweeters as aberrant individuals and celebrating a multicultural norm, those who contested the tweets reasserted "color-blindness" and the insignificance of race, except as a validation of specific neoliberal, "post-racial" values. The racist tweets and their suppression worked as a "double whammy" (Holling et al., 2014, p. 19) because both the explicitly racist violation and the reassertion of the "color-blind" or "multicultural" norm assert a racial logic. Thus it behooves scholars not only to consider the discourses of racial neoliberalism or inferential racism but also to analyze explicit discourses of racism and how they feed off of each other. In fact, this relationship between "old" and "new" racisms, between the avowal and disavowal of race, may be one of the dynamics of contemporary racial discourse.

A third and final conclusion we wish to draw relates to the call for scholars to explore the ways in which new media affect intercultural communication as well as how culture affects new media communication (Smith Pfister & Soliz, 2011; Shuter, 2011, 2012). As noted in the introduction, this controversy surrounding Davuluri's victory in the 2014 Miss America Pageant is only one in a regularly recurring pattern of such controversies of racist speech on social networking. Such controversies appear to be episodic, arising during events that seem to violate a set of expectations or norms about racial/ethnic or national identity, and resulting in a popular backlash against these individuals and a rejection of what is seen as aberrant communication. Such conflicts are not only episodic but highly contingent because only some receive national media attention while others quickly fade away. Their persistence signals the growing importance of social media for evolving forms of racial discourse, and suggest the need to extend scholarship on race on social networking platforms, which provide unique challenges and contexts for critical race studies. Tweets such as those directed at and in defense of Davuluri work to explicitly transgress, reassert and negotiate norms of racial and national identity; as such they signal evolving modes of communication influencing how race is articulated in contemporary culture.

Analysis of discourses of race in new media contexts must also attend to the cultural dimensions of new media and the ways in which they impact norms of intercultural communication. In fact, we cannot fully understand the controversial tweets directed at Davuluri in the wake of her victory without taking into consideration factors such as context collapse, publicized privacy, and the formulaic requirements of Twitter, each of which contributed to the creation and circulation of these tweets and the ensuing controversy. All of these factors demonstrate that Twitter and other social media provide particular and increasingly important micro- and macro-level communication that articulates racial identity and perpetuates racism. In this essay, we provided a preliminary exploration of some of the cultural factors of social media that influence discourses of race online, as well as the interacting "new" and "old" cultural logics that continue to influence public discussion about race. This analysis augurs the potential for critical race studies to attend to the ways that social media technologies express and reinforce cultural logics of race and the articulation of racism, the connections between new media culture and intercultural communication.

Acknowledgments

The authors would like to thank the editors of the special issue, Dreama Moon and Michelle A. Holling, as well as the anonymous reviewers, for their help strengthening the manuscript. We also thank Nate Stormer for hosting the writing retreat at Schoodic Point where much of this manuscript was written.

Notes

[1] Our use of this word reflects its prevalence in the literature on "new racisms" and is not meant to evoke any negativity toward visually impaired people.

[2] Our analysis is based on a sample of 100 tweets that were collected from a variety of web and news stories that covered the Twitter controversy, including Binder (2013a, 2013b), Broderick (2013), Hafiz (2013), and others (Greenhouse, 2013; "Miss America Faces Abuse," 2013; "Miss America 2014 Win," 2013; Zara, 2013). We have selected representative tweets for the analysis, a full list of which can be found in Appendix A. We have chosen not to include the screen names of the Twitter users so as to focus on the discourse itself, but we do quote some of the representative tweets because they are all publicly reproduced and archived, and this decision is consistent with recommended practice when conducting research involving Twitter (see Rivers & Lewis, 2014). Our study is not meant to provide a comprehensive, quantitative analysis of all the tweets about the pageant, or to make any claims that the objectionable tweets represent a broader consensus, attitude, or ideology.

[3] Although outside the purview of this essay, it is interesting to note the specific post-feminist subjectivity posited for Vail here, who purportedly both transgressed but also reasserted traditional gender roles (see Banet-Weiser & Portwood-Stacer, 2006).

[4] Based on a LexisNexis search of the terms "Miss America," "Davuluri," and "Twitter or tweet," we found over 400 English-language news stories over a 2-month period of time, from September 15, 2013, the day of the Pageant final, to November, 30, 2013.

References

Abcarian, R. (2013, September 16). *Miss America pageant*: Always a few steps behind. *Los Angeles Times*. Retrieved from http://latimes.com/local/lanow/la-me-ln-miss-america-pageant-always-a-few-steps-behind-20130916,0,314469.story

Ahmed-Ghosh, H. (2003). Writing the nation on the beauty queen's body: Implications for a "Hindu" nation. *Meridians: Feminism, Race, Transnationalism, 4*, 205–227.

Atkinson, J.D., Rosati, C., Berg, S., Meier, M., & White, B. (2013). Racial politics in an online community: Discursive closures and the potentials for narrative appropriation. *Journal of Communication Inquiry, 37*, 171–185.

Banet-Weiser, S. (1999). *The most beautiful girl in the world: Beauty pageants and national identity*. Berkeley, CA: University of California Press.

Banet-Weiser, S., & Portwood-Stacer, L. (2006). "I just want to be me again!": Beauty pageants, reality television and post-feminism. *Feminist Theory, 7*, 255–272.

Bartlett, J., Reffin, J., Rumball, N., & Williamson, S. (2014). *Anti-social media*. London: Demos. Retrieved from http://www.demos.co.uk/files/DEMOS_Anti-social_Media.pdf

Bazarova, N.N., & Choi, Y.H. (2014). Self-disclosure in social media: Extending the functional approach to disclosure motivations and characteristics on social network sites. *Journal of Communication, 64*, 635–657. doi:10.1111/jcom.12106

Beauty and the beasts; Bigots hound Miss America on her ancestry. (2013, September 20). *Pittsburgh Post-Gazette*, p. A-14. LexisNexis.

Binder, M. (2013a, September). *Americans call first Indian American Miss America winner a terrorist*. Public Shaming [Tumblr] Retrieved July 19, 2014, from http://publicshaming.tumblr.com/post/61388585374/americans-call-first-indian-american-miss-america

Binder, M. (2013b, September). *Americans figure out new Miss America's actual ethnicity, are still racist*. Public Shaming [Tumblr]. Retrieved July 19, 2014, from http://publicshaming.tumblr.com/post/61639541662/americans-figure-out-new-miss-americas-actual

Bonilla-Silva, E. (2010). *Racism without racists: Color-blind racism & racial inequality in contemporary America* (3rd ed.). Lanham, MD: Rowan & Littlefield.

boyd, d. (2010). Social network sites as networked publics: Affordances, dynamics, and implications. In Z. Papacharissi (Ed.), *Networked self: Identity, community, and culture on social network sites* (pp. 39–58). New York, NY: Routledge.

boyd, d.m., & Ellison, N.B. (2007). Social network sites: Definition, history, and scholarship. *Journal of Computer-Mediated Communication, 13*, 210–230.

Brock, A. (2009). "Who do you think you are?": Race, representation, and cultural rhetorics in online spaces. *Poroi, 6*(1), 15–35.

Brock, A. (2012). From the blackhand side: Twitter as a cultural conversation. *Journal of Broadcasting & Electronic Media, 56*, 529–549.

Broderick, R. (2013, September 16). *A lot of people are very upset that an Indian-American woman won the Miss America Pageant*. Retrieved from http://www.buzzfeed.com/ryanhatesthis/a-lot-of-people-are-very-upset-that-an-indian-american-woman

Brown, C. (2009). WWW.HATE.COM: White supremacist discourse on the internet and the construction of whiteness ideology. *Howard Journal of Communications, 20*, 189–208.

Bucktin, C. (2013, September 19). No beauty in racism row. *Western Mail*, p. 29. LexisNexis.

Byrne, D.N. (2008). The future of (the) 'race': Identity, discourse, and the rise of computer-mediated public spheres. In A. Everett (Ed.), *Learning race and ethnicity: Youth and digital media* (pp. 15–38). Cambridge, MA: MIT Press.

Cresswell, C., Whitehead, K.A., & Durrheim, K. (2014). The anatomy of 'race trouble' in online interactions. *Ethnic and Racial Studies, 37*, 2512–2528. doi:10.1080/01419870.2013.854920

Dow, B.J. (2003). Feminism, Miss America, and media mythology. *Rhetoric & Public Affairs, 6*, 127–149.

Flores, L.A., Moon, D.G., & Nakayama, T.K. (2006). Dynamic rhetorics of race: California's Racial Privacy Initiative and the shifting grounds of racial politics. *Communication and Critical/Cultural Studies, 3*, 181–201.

Fredrickson, G.M. (2002). *Racism: A short history*. Princeton, NJ: Princeton University Press.

Gajjala, R. (2007). Shifting frames: Race, ethnicity, and intercultural communication in online social networking and virtual work. In M. B. Hinner (Ed.), *The role of communication in business transactions and relationships* (pp. 257–276). New York, NY: Peter Lang.

Gallagher, C.A. (2003). Color-blind privilege: The social and political functions of erasing the color line in post-race America. *Race, Gender and Class, 10*(4): 22–37.

de Gobineau, A. (2011). *The inequality of the human races*. Burlington, IA: Ostara. (Originally published 1853).

Goldberg, D.T. (1993). *Racist culture: Philosophy and the politics of meaning*. Malden, MA: Blackwell.

Goldberg, D.T. (2009). *The threat of race: Reflections on racial neoliberalism*. Malden, MA: Wiley-Blackwell.

Greenhouse, E. (2013, September 20). Combatting Twitter hate with Twitter hate. *The New Yorker*. Retrieved from http://www.newyorker.com/online/blogs/elements/2013/09/combatting-twitter-hate-with-twitter-hate.html

Grumet, J.L. (2013, September 15). #MissAmerica racist tweets. *I Am Not the Babysitter* [Web log comment]. Retrieved from http://www.iamnotthebabysitter.com/miss-america-racist-tweets/

Hafiz, Y. (2013, September 16). Nina Davuluri's Miss America 2014 win prompts Twitter backlash against Indians, Muslims. *Huffington Post*. Retrieved from http://www.huffingtonpost.com/2013/09/16/nina-davuluri-miss-america-religion_n_3934428.html

Hetrick, B. (2013, September 23). There she is, Miss America, an ideal answer to racism. *Indianapolis Business Journal*. LexisNexis, 42.

Highfield, T., Harrington, S., & Bruns, A. (2013). Twitter as a technology for audiencing and fandom. *Information, Communication & Society, 16*, 315–339.

Holling, M.A. (2011). Patrolling national identity, masking white supremacy: The Minuteman Project. In M.G. Lacy & K.A. Ono (Eds.), *Critical rhetorics of race* (pp. 98–116). New York, NY: New York University Press.

Holling, M.A., Moon, D.G., & Jackson Nevins, A. (2014). Racist violations and racializing apologia in a post-racism era. *Journal of International and Intercultural Communication, 7*, 260–286. doi:10.1080/17513057.2014.964144

Howard, R.G. (2008). The vernacular web of participatory media. *Critical Studies in Media Communication, 25*, 490–513.

Jackson, M. (2006). The enthymematic hegemony of whiteness: The enthymeme as antiracist rhetorical strategy. *JAC, 26*, 601–641.

Jones, B., & Mukherjee, R. (2010). From California to Michigan: Race, rationality, and neoliberal governmentality. *Communication & Critical/Cultural Studies, 7*, 401–422.

Josey, C.S. (2010). Hate speech and identity: An analysis of neo racism and the indexing of identity. *Discourse & Society, 21*, 27–39.

Klein, A. (2012). Slipping racism into the mainstream: A theory of information laundering. *Communication Theory, 22*, 427–448.

Le Tellier, A. (2013, September 16). The new Miss America is not Muslim—But so what if she were? *Los Angeles Times*. Retrieved from http://latimes.com/opinion/opinion-la/la-ol-new-miss-america-not-muslim-20130916,0,2872062.story

Ling, C.S. (2013, September 19). Not so social world of social media. *New Straits Times*, p. 14. LexisNexis.

Loke, J. (2012). Public expressions of private sentiments: Unveiling the pulse of racial tolerance through online news readers' comments. *Howard Journal of Communications, 23*, 235–252.

Loke, J. (2013). Readers' debate a local murder trial: "Race" in the online public sphere. *Communication, Culture, & Critique, 6*, 179–200.

Marwick, A.E., & boyd, d. (2011). I tweet honestly, I tweet passionately: Twitter users, context collapse, and the imagined audience. *New Media & Society, 13*, 114–133.

McEwan, B., & Sobre-Denton, M. (2011). Virtual cosmopolitanism: Constructing third cultures and transmitting social and cultural capital through social media. *Journal of International & Intercultural Communication, 4*, 252–258.

Miss America faces abuse over Indian descent. (2013, September 23). *Sky News*. Retrieved July 22, 2014, from http://news.sky.com/story/1142271/miss-america-faces-abuse-over-indian-descent

Miss America 2014 win prompts racist Twitter backlash, followed by (some) Twitter apologies. (2013, September 16). *Huffington Post*. Retrieved July 22, 2014, from http://www.huffingtonpost.com/2013/09/16/miss-america-2014-win-racist_n_3935800.html

Nakamura, L. (2008). *Digitizing race: Visual cultures of the Internet*. Minneapolis, MN: University of Minnesota Press.

Nakayama, T.K., & Krizek, R.L. (1995). Whiteness: A strategic rhetoric. *Quarterly Journal of Speech, 81*, 291–309.

Omi, M., & Winant, H. (1994). *Racial formation in the United States: From the 1960s to the 1990s*. New York, NY: Routledge.

Parameswaran, R. (2004). Global queens, national celebrities: Tales of feminine triumph in post-liberalization India. *Critical Studies in Media Communication, 21*, 346–370.

Pathak, A.A. (2013). Miss America is Indian-American: Yay, I think. Or not. *The Feminist Wire*. Retrieved from http://thefeministwire.com/2013/09/miss-america-is-indian-american-yay-i-think-or-not/

Rajghatta, C. (2013, September 17). Racist tweets mar sweet moment for Nina Davuluri, first Miss America of Indian origin. *The Times of India*. Retrieved from http://timesofindia.indiatimes.com/nri/us-canada-news/Racist-tweets-mar-sweet-moment-for-Nina-Davuluri-first-Miss-America-of-Indian-origin/articleshow/22631169.cms

Rivers, C.M., & Lewis, B.L. (2014). Ethical research standards in a world of big data. *F1000 Research*, p. 1. Retrieved from http://f1000research.com/articles/3-38/v1

Schlarmann, J. (2013, September 16). *An open letter to the racist fucks on Twitter bashing Miss America Nina Davuluri*. Retrieved July 22, 2014, from http://www.politicalgarbagechute.com/an-open-letter-to-the-racist-fucks-on-twitter-bashing-miss-america-nina-davuluri/

Shuter, R. (2011). Introduction: New media across cultures—prospects and promise. *Journal of International & Intercultural Communication, 4*, 241–245.

Shuter, R. (2012). Intercultural new media studies: The next frontier in intercultural communication. *Journal of Intercultural Communication Research, 41*, 219–237.

Silva, K. (2014). Browning our way to post-race: Identity, identification, and securitization of brown. In A.A. Barreto & R.L. O'Bryant (Eds.), *American identity in the age of Obama* (pp. 133–51). New York, NY: Routledge.

Simpson, J.L. (2008). The color-blind double bind: Whiteness and the (im)possibility of dialogue. *Communication Theory, 18*, 139–159.

Sloop, J.M., & Gunn, J. (2010). Status control: An admonition concerning the publicized privacy of social networking. *The Communication Review, 13*, 289–308.

Smith Pfister, D., & Soliz, J. (2011). (Re)Conceptualizing intercultural communication in a networked society. *Journal of International & Intercultural Communication, 4,* 246–251.

Sultan, A. (2013, September 22). When Miss America gets ugly racist comments are just the tip of the pageant iceberg. *St. Louis Post-Dispatch,* p. H1. LexisNexis.

Tandon, S. (2013, September 18). Indian-origin Miss America shows evolving US ideal. *Gulf Times.* Retrieved from http://www.gulf-times.com/opinion/189/details/366187/indian-origin-miss-america-shows-evolving-us-ideal

Terrace, V. (2013). *Television specials: 5336 entertainment programs, 1936–2012.* Jefferson, NC: McFarland.

Van Dijk, T.A. (1987). *Communicating racism: Ethnic prejudice in thought and talk.* Newbury Park, CA: Sage.

Virtual world no less prejudiced than real. (2013, September 18). *New Indian Express.* Retrieved from http://www.newindianexpress.com/editorials/Virtual-world-no-less-prejudiced-than-real/2013/09/18/article1789872.ece

Vitak, J. (2012). The impact of context collapse and privacy on social network sites. *Journal of Broadcasting & Electronic Media, 56,* 451–470.

Vyavahare, R. (2013, September 18). Why these racial slurs? Nina belongs to America. *The Times of India.* Retrieved from http://timesofindia.indiatimes.com/life-style/people/Why-these-racial-slurs-Nina-belongs-to-America/articleshow/22662065America/articleshow/22662065

Weaver, S. (2011). Jokes, rhetoric and embodied racism: A rhetorical discourse analysis of the logics of racist jokes on the Internet. *Ethnicities, 11,* 413–435.

Zara, C. (2013, September 16). Nina Davuluri Twitter fiasco: Critics shamed off Twitter following racially charged Miss America insults. *International Business Times.* Retrieved from http://www.ibtimes.com/nina-davuluri-twitter-fiasco-critics-shamed-twitter-following-racially-charged-miss-america-insults

Zhang, Y., Gajjala, R., & Watkins, S. (2012). Home of hope: Voicings, whiteness, and the technological gaze. *Journal of Communication Inquiry, 36*(3), 202–221.

Zook, M. (2012, November 8). *Mapping racist tweets in response to President Obama's re-election.* Retrieved from http://www.floatingsheep.org/2012/11/mapping-racist-tweets-in-response-to.html

Appendix A. Table of tweets

Tweet #	Text
1	And the Arab wins Miss America. Classic
2	How the fuck does a foreigner win miss America? She is a Arab!#idiots
3	9/11 was 4 days ago and she gets miss America?
4	@ABC2020 nice slap in the face to the people of 9-11 how pathetic#missamerica
5	Congratulations Al-Qaeda. Our Miss America is one of you
6	I swear I'm not racist but this is America
7	Asian or indian are you kiddin this is america omg
8	Miss New York is an Indian … With all do [sic] respect, this is America
9	This is America. Not India
10	Miss America? You mean Miss 7-11
11	Miss America is brought to by their sponsors PF Changs and 7-11
12	Miss New York looks like a dot head without a dot
13	I hope the next snake she tries to charm bites the shit out of her
14	Man our president nor [sic] our new Miss America isn't even American I'm sorry but Miss Kansas I salute you your [sic] the real American#MissAmerica
15	Darn … I wish Miss Kansas would've won! Real American woman!!
16	The liberal Miss America judges won't say this—but Miss Kansas lost because she actually represented American values. #missamerica
17	Wow America, you've really embarrassed yourselves now! Racist pieces of crap! #MissAmerica is American, not Muslim or a terrorist. #Idiots
18	A country full of racists. That is America. #MissAmerica
19	This world is so ignorant. #MissAmerica Indian or not had every right to gain the title of MissAmerica. This is why I want to leave America
20	So Indians and Arabs are the same now? O for sure … #MissAmerica
21	#MissAmerica ummm wtf?! Have we forgotten 9/11?
22	Miss America is a terrorist. Whatever. It's fine
23	Miss America, footlong buffalo chicken on whole wheat. Please and thank you
24	Miss Arab wins Miss America and the score of the Seattle/SanFran game is 5-0 at the half? What is life?

(Net)roots of Belonging: Contemporary Discourses of (In)valuability and Post-Racial Citizenship in the United States
Megan Elizabeth Morrissey

Neoliberalism has gained a foothold in U.S. policy and practice, and maintains the advantages of those already privileged within the global community. In this essay, I argue that national discourses of (in)valuability, informed by and in the service of neoliberalism and post-racial citizenship, (1) establish cultural understandings that invest the (white) U.S. nation with increasing levels of worth, (2) demonstrate migrants' value as investors and protectors of such privilege, and (3) devalue U.S. minorities. Ultimately, many migrants' personal stories about their value participate in national narratives assigning worth to some bodies and burden to others in ways that reinforce existing social hierarchies.

Within recent decades, discourses of race and racism have morphed into a host of alternate narratives that cast the disenfranchisement and struggles of many within language that eclipses the ideological and material considerations of race. Narratives of personal responsibility, memoirs about the content of one's character, and heroic tales of tenacity color the impressions many U.S. citizens have about the opportunities afforded by the United States. In spite of a steady media diet affirming the United States' liberal and progressive attitude toward race, the United States is still dominated (politically and culturally) by whiteness, and protected by racism and antiracialism (Goldberg, 2009). Contextualizing contemporary U.S. conversations about race, Flores (2014) offered, "Historically and today, the meanings around race, racialization, racism—though complex, contradictory, and multiple—circulate in and through the alleged truth of the racially marked body" (p. 95). Thus, for raced individuals to be understood as abiding post-racial citizens of the nation—indeed for them to be included within its folds—they must make careful arguments about their *value* to the nation.

In the past decade, the Internet has emerged as a primary discursive space for marginal communities to share personal stories about their experience. Since the early 1990s, storytelling has been used by social movement groups seeking recognition and support for their cause. Indeed, many social movement groups have seen value in a formula that solicits, collects, and archives personal narratives of experience—an interest evidenced by the swell of storygathering/storytelling campaigns to recently gain traction online.[1] More recently, storytelling has been deployed within civic pedagogy as a political tool to create a sense of group identity and collective action (Rand, 2014). Nevertheless, as a method for social change, this rhetorical strategy is still criticized as creating emotionally charged narratives that distract attention from institutional and systemic forms of injustice (Chávez, 2013; Nair, n.d.). Nevertheless, Fisher (1984) explains, narrative (generally) and narrative theory (specifically) insists that people can and do judge the stories that are told for and about them. According to Fisher, human communication should be viewed as "historical and situational, as stories competing with other stories constituted by good reasons, as being rational when they satisfy the demands of narrative probability and narrative fidelity as inevitably moral inducements" (p. 2). In this way, migrant video participants in the We Are America campaign produce narratives they believe demonstrate their national belonging. U.S. publics then evaluate these narratives to determine if migrants' stories can earn them a place alongside themselves as U.S. community members.

What many of us come to value—as individuals, communities, and as a nation—is a product of the stories that we tell. Regularly, people narrate stories to demonstrate that which matters most in their lives—their friends and family, their personal property, their freedom—and with each iteration, those stories assign *value*. So what about those things that are not named in our stories? Do people assume that they have no value? As I argue, within the "post-racial" United States it is that which remains largely *unnamed* that wields the greatest power of all; indeed, what is worth most—what is *invaluable*.

In 2011, the year that material for this project was collected, the Center for Community Change's (CCC) We Are America campaign (renamed "Keeping Families Together" in 2013[2]) organized one of the largest social movement group archives of personal stories available at the time. Notable for its expansive collection of video testimonials (comprised of both content generated specifically for this campaign, and material sourced from other organizations[3]), as well as for its self-described purpose to show the "diversity and compelling human faces of real immigrants while countering the opposition's narrative," the We Are America campaign prioritizes the role of storytelling as a political tool for (raced) migrant bodies to argue for inclusion (We Are America stories, n.d.).[4] Available as an archive to be accessed, the We Are America campaign's primary audiences are those individuals looking for other people/communities with which to identify, and/or activists looking for resources or content that could be distributed to local media to help put "a human face" on immigration.

We Are America's compilation of personal narratives is representative of a contemporary movement within immigration reform that centers storytelling as a means of claiming U.S. citizenship and belonging. Reviewing the campaign's aims, it is apparent that their efforts are decidedly normative/inclusionary (Chávez, 2013)—attempting to claim a space for migrants within existing modes of U.S. citizenship. As such, the politics of location that orient these story-gathering efforts are inclined toward reinforcing neoliberal citizenship structures rather than challenging them. Recognizing this, and after exploring the migrants' narratives, I argue that their personal stories imbue the United States with some of its value. This tension between *value* and *invaluability* (something that I discursively demarcate as "(in)valuability") underscores many migrants' stories of belonging, revealing that post-racial U.S. citizenship requires a constant balance of race, gender, sexuality, and social class, often tipping the scales so as to (silently) reproduce and protect whiteness and devalue other U.S. minority identities.

Within the United States, (in)valuability plays an important function, marking some identities as being worth more than others, and generating and maintaining criteria for that worth along the lines of race, class, gender, and sexuality. As Omi and Winant (1994) described, the United States has long engaged in a practice of racial dictatorship that has resulted in the construction of a color line whereby U.S. identity has primarily been understood as white (masculine, heterosexual, and middle/upper-class) and where black/brown bodies of varying social classes, genders, and/or sexualities have been eliminated from the sphere of politics. Recognizing the continued influences of whiteness in the United States, participants in the We Are America campaign entering into this U.S. social hierarchy distance themselves from U.S. minorities and appeal for inclusion into the (white) nation by preserving the *invaluability* of whiteness—a construct that is performed, enacted, protected, and resisted through discourse (Nakayama & Krizek, 1995). As I will argue, because (in)valuability is premised on U.S. whiteness, migrants often remain liminal owing to the ways they are racialized. In spite of this, however, by crafting discourses that demonstrate their *value* to/for whiteness, they participate in reproducing and protecting the category, allowing them conditional inclusion into some (white) national spaces and limited access to certain privileges.

Neoliberal logics of privatization and personal responsibility couch the advancements of some U.S. subjects and the decline of others within discourses that inconspicuously work in the service of whiteness, downplaying the role of race within U.S. culture (see, e.g., Enck-Wanzer, 2011; Goldberg, 2009). Ansell (1997) explained this relationship between race, governmentality, and capital as *racial neoliberalism*, noting that this social ideology and practice is:

> concerned less with notions of racial superiority in the narrow sense than with the alleged "threat" people of color pose—either because of their mere presence or

because of their demand for "special privileges"—to economic, socio-political, and cultural vitality of the dominant (white) society. (p. 21)

Extending this conversation about neoliberalism's multifaceted and intersecting impacts, Duggan (2003) explained that the neoliberal spin on cultural projects such as public assistance and law and order "was the removal of explicitly racist, misogynistic language and images, and the substitution of the language and values of privatization and personal responsibility" (p. 16). This emphasis on personal responsibility scapegoats minorities, women, and people of lower socio-economic status (among others) who, owing to systemic forms of disenfranchisement, cannot compete within the neoliberal social-scape.

To unpack these complex relationships, this essay first engages in a brief discussion about the relevance of logics of (in)valuability and what has given rise to them, suggesting that the turn toward neoliberalism, as well as the United States' historical privileging of whiteness, have worked to code different bodies as *invaluable*, *valuable*, and *unvaluable*. That material is followed by a discussion of video narratives uploaded and curated by the Center for Community Change. In these video clips, I focus on how migrants' personal stories foreground their *white*-collar dreams, their interest in home/business ownership, and their commitment to pay (national) dues. Finally, I turn my attention toward how, in crafting these narratives, video participants discursively construct national understandings of (in)valuability that predicate national inclusion and exclusion along racial lines, and explore the ways this constructs, protects, and preserves whiteness within the United States.

Constructing a Framework of (In)valuability

There is a difference between that which is valuable and that which is invaluable. The *Oxford English Dictionary* (n.d.-b) listed among its definitions of *value* something that has "considerable importance or worth," is of "great benefit," or, if referring to a person, references someone who is "entitled to consideration or distinction; worthy, estimable." Concurrently, that which is *invaluable* is described as something "that cannot be valued; above and beyond valuation; of surpassing or transcendent worth or merit; priceless, inestimable," as well as "too great to be estimated; incalculable" (*Oxford English Dictionary*, n.d.-a). Seeing the nation's population as "living resources" (Ong, 2006, p. 6), neoliberalism instantiates the significance of value within the United States by creating a hierarchy of (in)valuability, and marking certain bodies as more or less valuable—value that is (silently) assigned, among other things, by race, gender, sexuality, and economic contribution. Indeed, each of these subjectivities colludes (with whiteness) to produce contemporary conceptions of neoliberal citizenship.

Neoliberalism, embedded within discourses of colorblindness and multiculturalism (Goldberg, 2009; Enck-Wanzer, 2011), gender (Bailey, 2011; Hasinoff, 2008), and labor (Duggan, 2003; Ong, 2006), influences national narratives of belonging by investing whiteness (a social status that, historically, has been privileged) with *invaluability*. Racial minorities and/or new citizens may be *valuable* to the nation but they may not be *invaluable*, for that status suggests a greater degree of power and authority reserved for white U.S. community members. In a post-racial United States, migrants (and U.S. minorities) who claim that they are *invaluable* national community members threaten the control and authority of whiteness, as such a label intimates that the nation would not function without the presence and contribution of its *invaluable* citizens—citizens who are white.

The United States is fundamentally invested in whiteness, as evidenced by a wealth of scholarship that traces historical protections that the nation has put into place to maintain a particular racial order, with whiteness being dominant (see, e.g., Bailey, 2011; Enck-Wanzer, 2011; Jacobson, 1998; Puar, 2007). To orient this discussion, I move beyond an understanding of whiteness that is tied exclusively to phenotypical characteristics and, instead, comprehend it as a representation of a privileged nexus of inclusion/belonging that marks race, sexuality, gender performativity, geographic location, nation, and social class (see, e.g., Lipsitz, 2006).

Recognizing that whiteness has value—indeed, as I argue, *(in)valuability*—by extension has been seen as something that individuals possess as private property (Crenshaw, 1997; Feagin, Vera, & Batur, 2001; Harris, 1993). As Lipsitz (2006) wrote, "Whiteness has a cash value" (p. vii) and consequently can be understood as something one can possess. Just as U.S. vigilante groups such as the Minutemen coalesce around the emphatic privatization of the nation, as demonstrated in vocal claims such as "This is *my* America" (Goldberg, 2009, p. 336), other U.S. insiders might *indirectly* assert that "This is *my* whiteness," further investing this identity category with invaluability and identifying it as something that requires protection. It is this protection, I argue, that temporarily affords certain raced/classed/gendered bodies a place in the post-racial United States as *protectors* of whiteness, but that, nevertheless, continues to marginalize subjects who do not or cannot discipline their difference. This analysis then specifically demonstrates how migrants from the We Are America campaign are positioned within a historical legacy of U.S. exclusion that has used the standards of whiteness to marginalize other communities such as southern Europeans and/or the Japanese.

Whiteness and the people benefiting from its privileged position struggle to shore up its perimeters and protect its interests. Goldberg (2009) explained, "Fear of a black state is linked to worries about a black planet, of alien invasion and *alienation*, of a loss of the sort of local and global control and privilege long associated with whiteness" (p. 337). Within neoliberalism, this fear translates to a construction of black men as violent, aggressive, and homophobic (see, e.g., Bailey, 2011), and black women as the central cause of poverty, criminality, and disorder (see e.g., Duggan, 2003). As such, black bodies (specifically) and raced bodies (generally) are positioned as marginal neoliberal citizens whose differences must be carefully managed [within narratives of (in)valuability].

Migrants' discursive moves to frame themselves as *protectors* of whiteness deliberately shift historical and contemporary public discourse about racial minorities away from narratives that mark them as diseased, burdensome, or otherwise unfit for inclusion and/or citizenship. Much communication scholarship has theorized the damaging ways that language choices and naming have scarred nonwhite communities and argued for the need to be more rhetorically responsible (see, e.g., Cisneros, 2012; Flores, 2003). Adding to this conversation, I consider how *migrants* code themselves as more or less valuable to (white) U.S. institutions in an effort to access national inclusion. These efforts afford migrants conditional belonging into otherwise inaccessible national communities and spaces, but nevertheless reproduce whiteness.

The Nation's Possessive Investment in Whiteness

How migrants narrate their educational preparation, professional goals, and family values, reveals a complicated nexus of race, gender, sexuality, and citizenship that informs a sense of U.S. national identity and belonging that highlights how value is (discursively) constructed, (materially) treated, and (ideologically) measured. First I will look at the *white*-collar dreams and aspirations that are captured in video participants' personal stories, followed by an exploration of how migrants talk about ownership as an investment in the nation, and the ways paying dues balances the national tensions of (in)valuability. Each of these storylines suggest the ways (in)valuability works to delineate the nation's ideological and material racial borders, as well as demonstrate how migrants' stories of belonging contribute to such constructions.

White-collar Dreams

Migrants use their stories to narrate and perform *white*-collar aspirations, lightening and bringing themselves closer to the coveted U.S. status of whiteness while also distancing themselves from the shadows occupied by U.S. minorities. These efforts help them demonstrate their national value and expose how national discourses of (in)valuability, although hinging upon notions of material worth, work to assemble complicated hierarchies of privilege through vocabularies that mask the nation's possessive investment in whiteness (Lipsitz, 2006). As I have argued, these hierarchies are stitched together from neoliberal principals that afford (racial) minorities access to logics of personal responsibility, privatization, and individual merit, and that detract attention from deviant public embodiments and performances of race (see, e.g., Bailey, 2011; Duggan, 2003; Goldberg, 2009).

Throughout the We Are America videos, migrants express their desire to work as engineers, physicians, architects, and other skilled and educated professionals, allowing migrants to frame their intersecting racial, gendered, and national identities in ways that elevate their material value to the nation and that positions them in clos(er) proximity to whiteness (in spite of their differences). Highlighting these *white*-collar ambitions, migrants construct personal stories that locate themselves as individuals with *value* who can financially strengthen the nation. Simultaneously, these narratives challenge the stigma that particularly raced, classed, and gendered groups are figured as being "unable to scale the skills ladder or measure up to the norms of self-governing" within the neoliberal social-scape (Ong, 2006, p. 502).

Highlighting their white-collar aspirations separates migrant bodies from the stereotype that they are a transient population, performing manual, low-paid labor, only to earn a wage that they then send home to be reinvested in their nations of origin—a narrative of exploitation that further entrenches the perceived threat posed by "free-loading" U.S. minorities. Indeed, these discursive efforts also work to distance migrant populations from the U.S. black community who continues to be systematically and institutionally marginalized from white-collar spaces. Even though many video participants appearing in the We Are America campaign might be read as nonwhite, their race is never mentioned. Instead, migrants highlight their professional aspirations (and, by extension, social class) through the impressions communicated by their business casual attire, or their clear (often unaccented) English. Migrants' material value is derived from (seeking to) populate middle- or upper-class, *white*-collar professional categories that demonstrate a degree of material worth and *value* to which stigmatized migrant bodies and/or U.S. minorities, owing to (historical) U.S. discourses, do not (and cannot) contribute.

Demonstrating their desire to occupy white cultural spaces, migrant video participants express their interest in keeping their talents and their (future) capital within the United States. For example, Durham, North Carolina resident Palma-Guifarro (facing deportation after recently being arrested trying to cross the border between states) discussed his desire to go to college and be a pediatrician (18 year-old Durham Resident, n.d.). Similarly, Juan articulated his interest in going to college, saying, "My dream has always been to become an aerospace engineer, to work for NASA one day. Design satellites and shuttles" (Juan's Story, n.d.). In addition to these snippets, other migrants speak of owning businesses, becoming educated "professionals," or serving as U.S. Congresspersons, and each of these statements are spoken from the classed, raced, and gendered body.

In each of these instances, young migrant men speak of their desires to excel in the U.S. public sphere—the workplace—and the attendant ways they will perform a normative (white) masculine role of laborer/provider/protector within U.S. society—a narrative that once again stands in contrast to discourses that stigmatize U.S. minorities (generally) and black men (specifically) as lazy and emasculated for inappropriately depending on public assistance and not caring for their own families (Feldstein, 2000). In the We Are America campaign, migrants manage their intersectional differences by using their well-groomed, articulate, and stiffly managed bodies to construct a challenge to those narratives that have already marked them (their brown-ness, their masculinity, their national status) as burdensome, or as doing harm to the nation (Chávez, 2010; Cisneros, 2012; Flores, 2003). Working against the affective economies that code brown bodies as dangerous and/or threating, and that mobilize visceral negative reactions in those who encounter them (Cisneros, 2012), migrants enact a disciplined subjectivity that implies their ability to perform docile citizenship. Storytellers' efforts to engage in *appropriately* gendered labor for U.S. institutions such as NASA, the government, or within the U.S. white-collar world, assert the invaluability and influence of whiteness. Indeed, migrant narrative participants recognize the intersecting elements of their identity (as young, non-white, migrant, presumably heterosexual men) and work to represent these elements in the most effective manner, resulting in a performance of docile citizenship that constructs, protects, and preserves whiteness.

Efforts to frame themselves as bodies who labor (or desire to labor) on behalf of the nation redirects negative cultural attitudes about migrants' *burden* on the nation to highlight how they are national *assets*, and discursively distance themselves from cultural tropes that mark U.S. racial minorities as welfare queens and/or deadbeat dads. Engaging in American dream discourses, migrants ideologically align themselves with foundational U.S. concepts—in particular, with post-racial, neoliberal discourses that suggest people who work hard always will find success in the United States [and success, by extension, equates to *access* to (white) U.S. belonging]. For many culture bearing individuals (Hasinoff, 2008), neoliberalism requires that their race, gender, and/or class differences be safely contained (see, e.g., Bailey, 2011). Those who cannot manage their differences (those who require public assistance, take up identity politics, or charge discrimination) are presented as pathological bigots unable/unwilling to progress with the rest of U.S. society beyond the nation's racist past. In migrants' stories, individuals who demonstrate their willingness to work hard—following the nation's logic—can gain entrance to same (white) spaces of privilege and belonging. These discursive efforts create a situation whereby U.S. cultural insiders must recognize the legitimacy of migrants' arguments, lest they acknowledge flaws in their social system and, potentially, the invisible privilege of whiteness.

Although the American dream is not explicitly a dream of whiteness, in many ways it has stood to benefit only those who could access this privileged social category (Jacobson, 1998). If migrants use American dream discourses to demonstrate they (can) occupy culturally privileged categories, such as the middle- or upper-class, and/or professional *white*-collar positions, they increase the cultural capital of such categories by demonstrating their desirability. As Raul Zamora (n.d.) expressed:

> I just want to stay here [in the United States]. I just want to reach for what I wanted to do since the time I was a little kid, which was attend UT. Finish my education, try to get a masters in architecture. I just want to give something back to Austin, in particular, and this great country that is America.

Zamora, highlighting his desire to "give back" to the nation and the city he loves, speaks from a position of relative privilege. His male, college-educated, able-bodied perspective allows Zamora to easily see himself as valuable within the U.S. neoliberal marketplace and make it relatively simple for him to argue an American dream story. Indeed, this narrative is not as easily accessible to women, LGBT/Q individuals, black U.S. citizens, and differently abled people who, in spite of presumably similar efforts, have encountered myriad systemic and institutional discrimination that have limited their access to university education or high-paying jobs that might allow them to demonstrate their contribution. Anguiano and Chávez (2011) explained, in a cultural and political climate that is hostile to immigrants, "it is not surprising then, that they [migrants] surrender to the pervasive, mainstream discourse, and the naturalization of the myth of the American dream" (p. 83), as doing so becomes a way for (raced) individuals to identify with and to engage in stories of national belonging that reference the *value* of social class and the *invaluability* of social class mobility that neoliberal logics extend.

Further suggesting the significance of American dream narratives, Yves Gomes (n.d.), a young man who was brought to the United States as a child, shares his heart-wrenching story of watching his mother and father, at separate times, be deported back to India. The tearful memory of his family's separation across national borders creates an affective response—both in the speaker, and in the viewer who witnesses young Yves alone on the screen (and alone in the United States), needing to be strong in the face of adversity. Managing a *national affect* (Muñoz, 2006) shaped by "the English language, public displays of nationalism, and certain markers of socio-economic status and race" (Cisneros, 2012, p. 133), Yves both narrates and performs his American-ness through an American dream story that allows him to embody good U.S. citizenship (and national affect) as well as potentially shift the way he is coded within nationalist narratives that mark him as other. Now, describing his current situation, he affirms his love for the United States and his desire to stay and pursue a *white*-collar career. In this featured video, the clip opens to reveal Yves sitting alone against a white background as the patriotic sound of trumpets quiets and the cacophony of voices claiming "I am America" recedes. Facing deportation, Yves explains:

> Whatever happens, I know it'll be difficult, but I'm going to have to keep doing what I'm doing. I'm going to have to keep pushing, do good in school, and, eventually, get to that point where I want to be, which is to become a doctor. (Yves Gomes, n.d.)

Yves engages in a story of belonging that showcases his desire to work hard to achieve his professional goals (aligning himself as an independent, productive male citizen) and, foregrounding particular personality traits that affirm his value: being hard-working, tenacious, and disciplined. In accordance with American dream stories, each of these qualities should allow Yves' upward social class mobility—movement that emphasizes his personal responsibility and that discursively distances his non-white body from other stigmatized U.S. minorities whose public entitlement, dependency, and irresponsibility are the source of the neoliberal United States' social ills (Duggan, 2003). Certainly, Yves can go to medical school and become a doctor in many other countries; therefore, his *American* dream must be understood as emphasizing the particular value of the United States—indeed, the *invaluability* of the United States.

Ownership as an Investment

Although previous examples highlight how white-collar dreams and aspirations locate migrants within the folds of neoliberal discourses of value, there are other instances where migrants narrate their value to/for the nation as business and/or home*owners*. In particular, migrant ownership protects and invests the material and ideological structures that give rise to whiteness, asserting their own class privilege and distancing themselves from marginalized non-white U.S. minorities who will not/cannot do the same. As Duggan (1993) explained, identity construction (and the appeals for belonging that identity formation necessitates) is "a process in which contrasting 'stories' of the self and others—stories of difference—are told, appropriated, and retold as stories of location in the social world of structured inequalities" (p. 793), leading to distinctions between people and groups.

Discussing his success in business, Alberto's story begins with a text over that reads, "In 1993, Alberto took over the ownership of Don Juan Restaurant in the Mt. Pleasant neighborhood of Washington, DC." Alberto, a well-groomed older man, dressed in a simple button down shirt and one of the only storytellers to speak in Spanish, explains:

> Things started going well; the business was making money. We started to invest more money in order to remodel and expand the restaurant, until we were able to buy the house where now live. My children were growing up, and soon they started helping out at the restaurant, and such was the story of our family. Hard work to earn what we have now. (Alberto, n.d.)

Humbly crafting his testimonial to demonstrate his masculine role as family provider and his relative class privilege, Alberto highlights his investment in the nation. Specifically, Alberto's narrative performance implies that the nation has given him an *invaluable* opportunity to discover this potential (as a man, as a father, and as a citizen). Narrating his story in Spanish and growing emotional to the point of tears, Alberto, in spite of his racial/ethnic background, embodies the (white) American dream.

Alberto, demonstrating the cultural value he possesses as a male, able-bodied, middle class person, contains his racial/ethnic/linguistic difference within a docile and humble performance of appreciation for the opportunities afforded him by the United States. Alberto's very public narrative not only beneficially frames his efforts as valuable, but also casts ownership and investment as conditions of belonging. Further, such conditions of belonging do the disciplinary work of marginalizing culture-bearing U.S. minorities who are consequently indexed as unactualizable neoliberal U.S. citizens owing to their inability to contribute to the nation and support their family. Though migrants' narratives may create for themselves a conditional space within the nation (as valuable protectors and/or investors in whiteness), their belonging can never be entirely fulfilled because the stories they tell reproduce whiteness.

Expressing similar success in business, Atour Eyvazian discusses his meteoric rise up the management chain at the popular fast-food restaurant Jack in the Box. Transitioning from earning just $3.35 an hour to owning more than 100 restaurants, Atour's story is the quintessential American dream story. Atour's narrative (which, actually, is a news segment) begins with a reporter explaining:

> I recently met Atour Eyvazian at this Jack in the Box, which he owns. He worked his way up the corporate ladder, until he became the owner of this Jack in the Box, and this one, and this one. In fact, Atour Eyvazian owns 117 Jack in the Boxes, more than anyone else in the country. (Atour Eyvazian, n.d.)

As the extended video title indicates, Atour is Iranian, and his material body presents as Middle-Eastern, a phenotypical appearance that is contrasted with his very white-collar performance as a U.S. business owner. Atour, a self-made man, begins his narrative by carefully describing opportunities he took advantage of upon arriving in the United States. Describing himself in the appropriate neoliberal model of citizenship, Atour talks about himself as industrious, disciplined, and committed—qualities that stand in contrast to the national stigma of the Arab man as a "monster terrorist fag" that has haunted the U.S. imaginary since September 11 (Puar & Rai, 2002). Even though Atour's narrative is one of prideful professional growth, it also is a story of whiteness, capitalism, and (Western) masculinity. Atour's exceptional rise up the management chain granted him access to privileged national, white-collar spaces that invaluably fuel the nation's worth and that some phenotypically nonwhite bodies participate in reinforcing. In this way, some U.S. minorities and migrants can reposition themselves within post-racial narratives as valuable protectors of whiteness—indeed as protectors who ironically defend (white) national institutions against the lingering threat that their *stigmatized* bodies and identities pose.

Citizens of the U.S. nation state have discursively constructed an understanding of the U.S. economy that suggests it will not rise or fall with the successes or failures of nonwhite migrants (specifically) and U.S. minorities (broadly), as implying such admits the precariousness of whiteness to protect and reproduce itself, rupturing the neoliberal, post-racial narrative that circulates in the United States. Even though this is the case, nonwhite migrants cannot be seen as threatening the position that whiteness occupies (something that could be perceived if migrants and/or racial minorities claimed invaluability to the nation); instead, they prove their willingness to invest in (and, subsequently, protect) these white spaces. Not unlike the efforts of the Irish or other new immigrants who successfully claimed a space for themselves in the United States (see, e.g., Jacobson, 1998), these efforts provide *valuable* labor for the nation. Specifically, migrants participate in historical and post-racial narratives of the United States that suggest there is a place for all people as long as they work hard—further stitching together whiteness, (masculine forms of) labor, and neoliberal citizenship and enhancing their invaluability.

Paying Dues

In addition to migrants' American dream discourses and in their comments of home and business ownership, their stories of (in)valuability suggest that paying one's dues to the nation creates a degree of entitlement that other narratives of (in)valuability—those that utilize white-collar aspirations, as well as business and/or homeownership—do not. Harvey (2005) explained, "Evidence strongly suggests that the neoliberal turn is in some way and to some degree associated with the restoration or reconstruction of the power of economic elites" (p. 19)—economic elites that are disproportionately white (Lipsitz, 2006) and that directly benefit when others pay into the system. Liliana Ramos, talking about being arrested by Immigration and Customs Enforcement (ICE), noted:

> But you live a good life. One tries to live a peaceful life. You avoid trouble so as to not have run-ins with the law. You really feel humiliated because you know that you haven't done anything. You know that you have tried to live a peaceful life. You've been working. You've paid your taxes. (Liliana Ramos, n.d.)

Liliana's experience of feeling "humiliated," coupled with the rights and entitlements that come from paying taxes, do the neoliberal work of marginalizing U.S. minorities who take advantage of the public services Liliana's tax dollars create and situate Liliana as an appropriately gendered minority. In Liliana's example, the ideal female citizen-subject is a woman who does not take advantage of the system, but who is invested in the affective/emotional national landscape and interested in maintaining the United States as a safe space where someone can live in peace, not be humiliated, and can have a good life.

Another way that some migrant video participants condition U.S. national belonging is by positioning themselves as owing a debt to whiteness. In one video, award-winning journalist, Jose Antonio Vargas defines his understanding of what it means to be "American," saying that an American is, "someone who works really hard, someone who's proud to be in this country and wants to contribute to it. I'm independent. I pay taxes. I'm self-sufficient. I am an American. I just don't have the right papers" (Jose Antonio Vargas, n.d.). Vargas, using his credentials as a Pulitzer Prize winning journalist, narrates his story in unaccented English and directs the audience to become frustrated by his experience as he performatively relives the emotional experience of his marginalization. As the full version of this segment implies, the interpersonal connections that Vargas is able to call on for assistance were key. Referencing his reliance on an entire network of (white) teachers, school administrators, and neighbors who assisted him, Vargas expresses his indebtedness. As he notes, Ms. Denny, his choir teacher, was the first member of his "Underground Railroad," a comment that discursively invokes a historical legacy of slavery and the (white) individuals who risked their lives and security to provide for the safety and security of nonwhite individuals—a sacrifice he has translated into personal success. In part, because he is phenotypically nonwhite and, in part, because he is discursively represented as always already *owing a debt to whiteness* (by virtue of the white U.S. citizens who sacrificed themselves for him), Vargas remains a valuable commodity for the nation, but not an invaluable asset. Nevertheless, Vargas favorably positions himself against *unvaluable* U.S. minorities who are cast as ungrateful and unsuccessful in caring for themselves and contributing (back) to the nation. Indeed, by contrasting Vargas' deliberate and disciplined masculinity against the failing, wayward, and disorganized gender performativity of U.S. minorities who are of lower socio-economic status, Vargas performs as an appropriate citizen subject, containing his difference and tapping into core national values that reinforce the value of whiteness.

Although most migrants who engage in larger national discourses of (in)valuability assert their value to/for the nation, far fewer *critique* the United States for how they have been *devalued*. To call negative attention to the nation in this way risks marking the speaker as a threat and ruptures the grand narrative of a post-racial United States.

Chris, however, a phenotypically white, male, gay, U.S. citizen does just this when he discusses his partner's inability to acquire a Green Card. Speaking from a position that foregrounds his white neoliberal citizenship status, Chris makes transparent the difficulty (if not impossibility) that migrants experience in this country as they attempt to build a home in the United States:

> From the start of this country, where it was limited to white men in origin to become a citizen in its early years, it was expanded. You know, over and over again, but at the same time, there have also been occasions, like the Chinese Exclusion Act of 1870 [sic], which followed on the heels of the Gold Rush, in which Chinese immigrants were very welcome in this country, until the gold market flattened out, and all of the sudden, there wasn't enough work, and all of the sudden, the immigrants were demonized, and all of the sudden, they were not allowed to come to this country and were sent out of the country, and we keep repeating the same mistake over and over again. The fact of the matter is our economy depends on it, the soul of the country is derived from immigrant history, and I would like to see the country come face-to-face with that and see the importance of immigrants. (Chris's Story, n.d.)

Chris, performing in his own neoliberal labor, contains his cultural difference by calling upon his white male privilege to wage this critique that the United States does not recognize the value of immigrants. These comments momentarily make visible the relationship between race and value in this nation. When Chris notes that he would like the United States to "see the importance of immigrants to the nation," he directly correlates immigrant, nonwhite bodies with national *value* and leaves the value and contribution of U.S. minorities unmarked and *unvalued*—a discursive move that positions U.S. minorities in stark relief to laboring migrant bodies.

When Whiteness is Discursively Visible

Although value oftentimes is understood as being derived from material worth, it is less often understood as being derived from whiteness. In spite of this less familiar association, as I have shown, whiteness remains an integral component in how (in)valuability is conceived within the United States. Recognizing that neoliberalism is a kind of non-politics or "a way of being reasonable, and of promoting universally desirable forms of economic expansion and democratic government around the globe" (Duggan, 2003, p. 10), it becomes clear how whiteness (and attendant intersecting axes of privilege) are protected through discursive silences. There are many examples across the We Are America campaign where, by virtue of video, viewers might code participants as white or nonwhite, but, in keeping with post-racial narratives of the United States, it is infrequently the case that these individuals discursively reference their race. In *only three instances* across the 87 videos sampled for analysis is the value of whiteness, or the challenges presented by one's nonwhite racial status, explicitly referenced.

When whiteness *is* discursively visible in these testimonials, it is often commented on in negative ways that suggest how whiteness must construct a nonwhite other, who often is cast as violent, aggressive, free-loading, and/or sexually deviant (see, e.g.,

Bailey, 2011). Such discourses lead to dominant cultural narratives about the difficulties that migrant and/or minority bodies bring on the nation, linking the stigma of this group with *burden* (which might be seen as the opposite of *value*). For instance, Muhammad Zahid Chaudhry, appearing alongside his military honors in a wheelchair, performs his veteran status, foregrounding his physical labor for the nation and his courageous and self-sacrificing masculinity. Chaudhry's limited physicality is both visually evident in his video, and discursively marked at other points in his testimonial, positioning Chaudhry as a committed and nonthreatening patriot, and works against U.S. narratives that code the Arab male body as a threat (Puar, 2007). He commented about his nonwhite racial appearance:

> In 2001, I became a legal permanent resident, but since then, every possible barrier has been erected between me and my dream to achieve U.S. citizenship. In fact, instead of stepping closer to citizenship, I am now fighting deportation. Because my name is South Asian, "Muhammad," background name checks have been indeterminable. The suspicion around a South-Asian man living, primarily in agricultural area of Eastern Washington, has been overwhelming. (Muhammad Zahid Chaudhry, n.d.)

Although he references his dream to become a U.S. citizen, his faithful military service to the nation, and his resulting paralysis, Chaudhry breaks his calm and dutiful demeanor to momentarily comment on the nation's racism. The isolated nature of his comment, as well as the critique he levels against the United States that he concurrently claims to love and admire, is a moment where viewers see how whiteness, although normally invisible, is exposed as a U.S. insider status and, subsequently, as a privileged (and invaluable) U.S. identity category. Chaudhry is one of only a few participants who discursively marks whiteness and its value, and succeeds because, in spite of the affective economy that marks him as threatening, his embodied performance is appropriately self-disciplined and he appears on screen as physically non-threatening—a successful management of his intersecting subjectivities.

Articulating similar concerns, another group of migrant day laborers reference race and its construction, expressing frustration over a new piece of immigration legislation that targets undocumented workers. As a man explained in Spanish with English subtitles:

> I've personally been affected by the law. Those who used to hire me are now afraid to. They are trying to get rid of us. Since 285G was passed, for the last 2 years, I've had no work. Companies don't want to lose their licenses. They now prefer to hire somebody white or with papers, even if their work isn't good. (Voices of Day Laborers, n.d.)

When people are read as white, opportunities that nonwhite bodies in the United States do not experience present themselves—revealing a paradox of neoliberalism. Ong (2006) explained, "The shift toward neoliberal technology of governing holds that the security of citizens, their well-being and quality of life, are increasingly dependent on their own capacities as free individuals" (p. 501); however, as this day laborer suggests, his capacity as a free individual is always already constrained by his racialized body and limited communication skills. This day laborer's story might then suggest that the nation understands male, nonwhite migrant bodies as disposable (without *value*), and male, phenotypically white bodies as always potentially *invaluable* for the mobility they can access. Regarding the feminine experience, Maria notes:

> At 4, my family came to East L.A., the first place I called home, hoping to find the American dream. According to my mother, I had an advantage because I was smart and I looked American. "The only good thing the Spanish ever left us," she said. (No Place, n.d.)

Stressing the value of her phenotypical appearance, Maria's comments further suggest the cultural capital of whiteness, foregrounding how her ability to pass as white affords her access to the American dream—something she benefits from because of her appearance, as long as she remains silent about race. Unlike masculine stories of social class mobility, Maria's narrative enforces her *feminine* value to/for the nation as someone who can appropriately capture the male gaze, highlighting the phenotypical value of whiteness.

Rhetorical scholars have traced careful arguments between whiteness and silence, suggesting the complicit ways in which silence functions to protect and preserve privileges afforded by whiteness (see, e.g., Crenshaw, 1997). In spite of this silence, race echoes loudly in the migrants' stories and in the isolated examples where one's (racialized) status is discursively marked and physically captured through video. Extending the argument introduced by other whiteness scholars (see, e.g., Crenshaw, 1997; Nakayama & Krizek, 1995), silence is what allows whiteness to remain (in)valuable to/for the nation and indeed, what perpetuates the myth of the post-racial United States, marking individuals who dare tell stories about race or racism as pathological and problematic.

Conclusion: (Re)producing Whiteness

It has been theorized that storytelling is an effective way for social movement groups to craft identity, create community, and increase social commitment because it functions to orient people to others (Fisher, 1984). Migrant testimonials from the We Are America campaign demonstrate this capacity of storytelling within social movement campaigns by suggesting how narratives both constitute and maintain social categories. Specifically, through their efforts to (1) invest the (white) nation with increasing levels of worth, (2) demonstrate their value as investors and protectors of whiteness, and (3) devalue U.S. minorities, migrant storytellers highlight how certain types of storytelling work to protect and reproduce whiteness. Opt (1988) explained, "The stories we tell are part of a larger pattern of continuity and change the way in which we make sense of human experience" (p. 308). Migrants, seeking to shift the ways they are coded within U.S. experience, use the power of narrative to reframe themselves in relation to whiteness and depend on those who view their videos to legitimize them as U.S. cultural insiders.

As a political tool, storytelling functions through form and content to communicate and construct social conditions. As I have demonstrated, migrants' We Are America stories contribute to national structures of valuation and have important implications that contour national expectations for invaluability that are closely tied to economics, gender, sexuality, and race. In particular, migrants' personal stories construct the invaluability of whiteness and, in so doing, carve out conditional inclusion for *some* marginal subjectivities. As McKinnon (2009) has discussed, the narrative structure that marginal individuals use to petition for inclusion (or in her case, asylum) must both establish credibility for the speaker, and accommodate the normative social structures that exist in the United States if their appeals will be favorably considered. In other words, national inclusion demands that people who seek access speak well, speak rationally, and speak evenly (McKinnon, 2009, p. 218). This requires that migrant video participants, in order to earn national credibility, approximate (white) U.S. standards of discursive and material expression that are premised on the white, masculine, heterosexuality of the nation.

In their efforts to establish credibility, migrant video participants manage their intersecting subjectivities in ways that service (U.S. national) whiteness and reproduce the value of the category. In addition to establishing credibility, individuals desiring national inclusion also construct narratives that resonate as truthful with/for U.S. American audiences. McKinnon (2009) explained that the conventions of "'good speech,' narrative rationality, and embodied emotion derive from assumptions about the subjectivity of proper potential citizens of the U.S. state—that proper subjects are political, modern and rational actors" (p. 218). As such, migrants negotiate complex subjectivities, at once informed by the various intersections of their embodied experience, as well as by the historical and social contexts that shape national attitudes, ultimately positioning themselves as protectors, investors, and/or champions of U.S. citizenship (and whiteness).

The intersecting elements of migrant video participants' identities position each individual in slightly different ways to/with the U.S. nation and, as we see, are carefully managed in migrants' appeals for inclusion. Focusing on the intersections of citizenship status, race, gender, and sexuality provides a comprehensive way to engage how U.S. social relations are constructed (Crenshaw, 1997) as well as migrant's participation in them. Indeed, the multiple identities that migrant video participants enact in their narratives both manage their own difference and simultaneously reproduce other sites of oppression that stem from the normative influences of U.S. national whiteness (Delgado & Stefanic, 2012). As such, unpacking the ways that migrants' intersectional subjectivities inform the narrative structures they use and the content they relay reveals the complex workings of whiteness by suggesting how bodies can be both oppressed (themselves) and oppressive (of others). Fisher (1984) reminds us that:

> to consider that public-social knowledge is to be found in the stories that we tell one another would enable us to observe not only our differences, but also our commonalities, and in such observation we might be able to reform the notion of the "public." (p. 15)

Nevertheless, migrant storytellers narrate and perform their American-ness in ways that do not subvert normative notions of the public, but instead demonstrate the ways whiteness reproduces itself.

As I have argued, whiteness remains a powerful influence, shaping U.S. political and cultural structures and informing social relationships. McKinnon (2009) explained, "Key gatekeepers to U.S. citizenship, those I call the audience of the potential citizens, read the body in order to determine whether non-citizen-subjects deserve access to belonging" (p. 208). We Are America video participants narrate and perform their national merit by accounting for whiteness (the whiteness of their audience) in careful ways. Specifically, by demonstrating the *valuable* role they play in protecting the influence of whiteness, participants reproduce its *invaluability* within the U.S. social sphere and beyond.

Notes

[1] A few examples of such efforts spanning a variety of social movement interests, include campaigns such as Testimony: Take a Stand, It Get's Better, Define American, and Welcoming stories.

[2] Though the name of the storytelling campaign has since changed to "Keeping Families Together," I use the original name of the campaign, "We Are America," throughout this paper, as this was the phrasing under which all stories I analyze were collected.

[3] Other organizations whose stories are available through the We Are America campaign include: I am From Driftwood, Welcoming Stories, Shelbyville Multimedia, SEIU Faces of Immigration Reform, Restore Fairness and Define American.

[4] Because I was interested in collecting narratives that broadly addressed immigration (and the desire for citizenship), I did not draw from the website's smaller collections with narrow topical themes (such as "Deportation Stories," or "Dream Stories,"). Instead, I opted for the two largest and most general collections: "Immigration Stories Archive," and "Featured Video Archive."

References

18 year-old Durham resident. (n.d.). *18 year-old Durham resident Fausto Palma-Guifarro faces deportation* [Video file]. Retrieved from www.weareamericastories.org/videos/18-year-old-durham-resident-fausto-palma-guifarro-faces-deportation/

Alberto. (n.d.). *Alberto: Hard work builds a successful business* [Video file]. Retrieved from www.weareamericastories.org/videos/albertos-story-hard-work-builds-a-successful-business/

Anguiano, C.A., & Chávez, K.R. (2011). DREAMers' discourse: Young Latino/a immigrants and the naturalization of the American dream. In M.A. Holling & B.M. Calafell (Eds.), *Somos de una voz? New directions in Latina/o communication* (pp. 81–100). Lanham, MD: Lexington Books.

Ansell, A.E. (1997). *New right, new racism: Race and reaction in the United States and Britain*. New York: New York University Press.

Atour Eyvazian. (n.d.). *Atour Eyvazian: Business owner finds success in the US after escaping Iran in the 1980s* [Video file]. Retrieved from www.weareamericastories.org/videos/atour-eyvazian-business-owner-finds-success-in-the-us-after-escaping-iran-in-the-1980s/

Bailey, C.W. (2011). Coming out as homophobic: Isaiah Washington and the *Grey's Anatomy* scandal. *Communication and Critical/Cultural Studies, 8*(1), 1–21. doi:10.1080/14791420.2010.541926

Chávez, K.R. (2010). Border (in)securities: Normative and differential belonging in LGBTQ and immigrant rights discourse. *Communication and Critical/Cultural Studies, 7*, 135–155. doi:10.1080/14791421003763291

Chávez, K.R. (2013). *Queer migration politics: Activist rhetoric and coalitional possibilities*. Urbana, IL: University of Illinois Press.

Chris's story. (n.d.). *Kept apart from partner of 17 years because of immigration policy* [Video file]. Retrieved from www.weareamericastories.org/videos/chriss-story-kept-apart-from-partner-of-17-years-because-of-immigration-policy/

Cisneros, J.D. (2012). Looking 'illegal': Affect, rhetoric and performativity in Arizona's Senate Bill 1070. In D.R. DeChaine (Ed.), *Border rhetorics: Citizenship and identity on the US-Mexico frontier* (pp. 133–155). Tuscaloosa, AL: University of Alabama.

Crenshaw, C. (1997). Resisting whiteness' rhetorical silence. *Western Journal of Communication*, 61, 253–278. doi:10.1080/10570319709374577

Delgado, R., & Stefanic, J. (2012). *Critical race theory: An introduction* (2nd ed.). New York, NY: New York University Press.

Duggan, L. (1993) The trials of Alice Mitchell: Sensationalism, sexology, and the lesbian subject in turn-of-the-century America. *Signs*, 18, 791–814. doi:10.1086/494843

Duggan, L. (2003). *The twilight of equality? Neoliberalism, cultural politics, and the attack on democracy*. Boston, MA: Beacon Press.

Enck-Wanzer, D. (2011). Barack Obama, the Tea Party, and the threat of race: On racial neoliberalism and born again racism. *Communication, Culture & Critique*, 4(1), 23–30. doi:10.1111/j.1753-9137.2010.01090.x

Feagin, J.R., Vera, H., & Batur, P. (2001). *White racism: The basics* (2nd ed.). New York, NY: Routledge.

Feldstein, R. (2000). *Motherhood in black and white: Race and sex in American liberalism*. Ithaca, NY: Cornell University Press.

Fisher, W.R. (1984). Narration as a human communication paradigm: The case of public moral argument. *Communication Monographs*, 51(1), 1–22. doi:10.1080/03637758409390180

Flores, L.A. (2003). Constructing rhetorical borders: Peons, illegal aliens, and competing narratives of immigration. *Critical Studies in Media Communication*, 20, 362–387. doi:10.1080/0739318032000142025

Flores, L.A. (2014). The rhetorical "realness" of race, or why critical race rhetoricians need performance studies. *Text and Performance Quarterly*, 34(1), 94–96. doi:10.1080/10462937.2013.849356

Goldberg, D.T. (2009). *The threat of race: Reflections on racial neoliberalism*. Malden, MA: Wiley-Blackwell.

Harris, C.I. (1993). Whiteness as property. *Harvard Law Review*, 106, 1707–1791. doi:10.2307/1341787

Harvey, D. (2005). *A brief history of neoliberalism*. New York, NY: Oxford University Press.

Hasinoff, A.A. (2008). Fashioning race for the free market on America's Next Top Model. *Critical Studies in Media Communication*, 25, 324–343. doi:10.1080/15295030802192012

Jacobson, M.F. (1998). *Whiteness of a different color: European immigrants and the alchemy of race*. Cambridge, MA: Harvard University Press.

Jose Antonio Vargas. (n.d.). *Jose Antonio Vargas: Prominent American journalist comes out as undocumented* [Video file]. Retrieved from www.weareamericastories.org/videos/jose-antonio-vargas-prominent-american-journalist-comes-out-as-undocumented/

Juan's story [Video file]. (n.d.). Retrieved from www.weareamericastories.org/videos/juans-story/

Liliana Ramos. (n.d.). *Liliana Ramos: A single mother threatened with deportation* [Video File]. Retrieved from www.weareamericastories.org/written/liliana-ramos-a-single-mother-threatened-with-deportation/

Lipsitz, G. (2006). *The possessive investment in whiteness: How white people profit from identity politics* (Rev. ed.). Philadelphia, PA: Temple University Press.

McKinnon, S.L. (2009). Citizenship and the performance of credibility: Audiencing gender-based asylum seekers in U.S. immigration courts. *Text & Performance Quarterly*, 29, 205–221. doi:10.1080/10462930903017182

Muhammad Zahid Chaudhry. (n.d.). *Military veteran tells his story of being denied citizenship* [Video file]. Retrieved from www.weareamericastories.org/videos/muhammad-zahid-chaudhry/

Muñoz, J.E. (2006). Feeling brown, feeling down: Latina affect, the performativity of race, and the depressive position. *Signs*, 31, 675–688. doi:10.1086/499080

Nair, Y. (n.d.). *What's left of queer?: Immigration, sexuality, and affect in a neoliberal world*. Retrieved from www.uic.edu/jaddams/hull/immigrantcitychicago/essays/nair_leftofqueer.html

Nakayama, T.K., & Krizek, R.L. (1995). Whiteness: A strategic rhetoric. *Quarterly Journal of Speech, 81*, 291–309. doi:10.1080/00335639509384117

No Place. (n.d.). *"No Place"—Maria's story* [Video file]. Retrieved from www.weareamericastories.org/videos/no-place-marias-story/

Omi, M., & Winant, H. (1994). *Racial formation in the United States: From the 1960s to the 1990s*. New York, NY: Routledge.

Ong, A. (2006). *Neoliberalism as exception.* Durham, NC: Duke University Press.

Opt, S.K. (1988). Continuity and change in storytelling about artificial intelligence: Extending the narrative paradigm. *Communication Quarterly, 36*, 298–310. doi:10.1080/01463378809369733

Oxford English Dictionary. (n.d.-a). *Invaluable*. Retrieved from www.oed.com/view/Entry/98913

Oxford English Dictionary. (n.d.-b). *Valuable*. Retrieved from http://www.oed.com/view/Entry/221246

Puar, J.K. (2007). *Terrorist assemblages: Homonationalism in queer times*. Durham, NC: Duke University Press.

Puar, J.K., & Rai, A.S. (2002). Monster, terrorist, fag: The war on terrorism and the production of docile patriots. *Social Text, 20*(3), 117–148. doi:10.1215/01642472-20-3_72-117

Rand, E.J. (2014). ""What one voice can do": Civic pedagogy and choric collectivity at camp courage. *Text and Performance Quarterly, 34*(1), 28–51. doi:10.1080/10462937.2013.853825

Raul Zamora. (n.d.). *Raul Zamora: Austin student athlete facing deportation after being picked up for broken taillight* [Video file]. Retrieved from www.weareamericastories.org/videos/raul-zamora-austin-student-athelete-facing-deportation-after-being-picked-up-for-broken-taillight/

Voices of day laborers. (n.d.). *Voices of day laborers in the United States* [Video file]. Retrieved from www.weareamericastories.org/videos/voices-of-day-laborers-in-the-united-states/

We Are America stories. (n.d.). *We are America in the news*. Retrieved from www.weareamericastories.org/media/we-are-america-in-the-news/

Yves Gomes. (n.d.). *Maryland 17 year old to be deported* [Video file]. Retrieved from www.weareamericastories.org/videos/yves-gomes-maryland-17-year-old-set-to-be-deported-on-august-13/

Problematic Representations of Strategic Whiteness and "Post-racial" Pedagogy: A Critical Intercultural Reading of *The Help*

Rachel Alicia Griffin

The Help is argued to influence understandings of racial histories, racial in/equality, and interracial coalitions from a pedagogical stance invested in the re/production of white dominance. This essay mobilizes strategic whiteness to map the representational strategies utilized to secure the superiority of whiteness and further the momentum of "post-racial" ideology. Facilitated via white female characters, The Help's cinematic centralization of whiteness and redemption of white racists are illuminated as manifestations of strategic whiteness that operate at the expense of black women.

Introduction

In recent decades, white authored and directed narratives presumably focused upon the struggles of people of color, including *Mississippi Burning* (Zollo, Colesberry, & Parker, 1989), *Dangerous Minds* (Simpson, Bruckheimer, & Smith, 1995), *Crash* (Haggis, 2004), and *The Blind Side* (Netter, Kosove, Johnson, & Hancock, 2010), have amassed immense popularity. Similarly, *The Help* (Stockett, 2009; Taylor, Green, Columbus, & Barnathan, 2011) earned extensive acclaim first as a fictional novel authored by a white woman, Kathryn Stockett, and then as a screenplay written and directed by a white man, Tate Taylor. For some, the film is a heart-warming story of two black maids and a white female socialite who unite to expose racism in Jim Crow Jackson, Mississippi, while others are offended by its representations of race, racism, and civil rights activism (e.g., Association of Black Women Historians, 2007–2012;

Puig, 2011). Largely aligning with the latter as a biracial (black and white) black woman, I am drawn to the film precisely because of its popularity, and subsequent pedagogical influence, among everyday people.

Understanding popular culture as a site of public pedagogy[1] (Giroux, 2000; Sandlin, 2007), *The Help* (Taylor et al., 2011) cinematically influences public understandings of racial histories, racial in/equality, and interracial coalitions from a pedagogical stance invested in the re/production of white power, dominance, and superiority. By centering whiteness in this essay, I admittedly further the film's marginalization of blackness, particularly black women. Albeit a difficult choice, situating whiteness as a site of inquiry is necessary given the celebratory fanfare surrounding the novel and film. At the heart of my concern as a critical intercultural scholar is how the film centralizes, valorizes, and progressively redresses whiteness under the surreptitious guise of mass popularity and Hollywood glam.

Building upon scholarship that interrogates media representations of whiteness and racism (Chidester, 2012; Griffin, 2014; Holling, 2011; Moshin & Jackson, 2011; Rossing, 2010; Tierney, 2006), this essay mobilizes strategic whiteness (Nakayama & Krizek, 1995; Projansky & Ono, 1999) as a conceptual lens to expose *The Help* (Taylor et al., 2011) as a cinematic emblem of the "post-racial"[2] imaginary. Defined as "a belief that positions race as an irrelevant relic of the past with no viable place in contemporary thought" (Rossing, 2012, p. 45), mediated "post-racial" ideology not only antiquates racial oppression but also, in accordance with white domination, depicts white people, white culture, and racism palatably for white audiences (Moshin & Jackson, 2011; Ono, 2010).

To out *The Help* (Taylor et al., 2011) as a "post-racial" movie venture that circumvents progressive racial consciousness, I first summarize the plotline. Next, I position strategic whiteness as a conceptual lens to deconstruct the film's public pedagogy. Then, via a close reading of the storyline, character development, and dialogue, I argue that *The Help* (Taylor et al., 2011) not only centralizes whiteness but also functions as a site of apologia and redemption for white racists. I end with a discussion of the film as an endorsement of "post-racialism" that obscures the strategic labor of whiteness to "resecure the center" (Nakayama & Krizek, 1995, p. 295) at the expense of black women.

Watching *The Help*

Set in 1962, Jim Crow Jackson, Mississippi, *The Help* (Taylor et al., 2011) chronicles the lived experiences of two black women, Aibileen Clark and Minny Jackson, and one white woman, Eugenia "Skeeter" Phelan. Aibileen and Minny are black maids while Skeeter, a recent Ole Miss graduate and socialite, is living on her family's plantation and troubled by the sudden absence of their black maid, Constantine Jefferson. Aibileen is Elizabeth Leefolt's maid, while Minny, at first, is Missus Walters' maid. However, she is fired by Missus Walters' daughter, Hilly Holbrook, and then becomes Celia Foote's maid. Linking all of the women together, Hilly, Elizabeth, and Skeeter are best friends and members of the elite Jackson Junior League that Celia, unsuccessfully, tries to join. Aibileen and Minny, also close friends, are "the help" in white households and at league functions.

Aibileen, Minny, and Skeeter are united by Skeeter's desire to write a book about black maids' experiences working in white households. Initially, Aibileen and Minny are terrified by Skeeter's idea, but eventually agree to participate. Upon their agreement, they emerge as co-authors of Skeeter's envisioned book since all three women eagerly work toward its completion. However, panic sets in when Miss Stein, Skeeter's New York editor, insists that Skeeter needs 12 interviews to complete the manuscript. Consequently, Skeeter and Minny entertain the impossibility of finishing the book since 31 maids fearfully declined to interview. In response, Aibileen shares that her son Treelore, killed by white men, had dreamed of becoming a writer. She tearfully pleads, "You stop this, everything I wrote, he wrote, everything he was gonna die with him" (Taylor et al., 2011). Newly resolved to succeed, they are soon met with the turning point that fuels their manuscript to completion.

The turning point occurs when Yule Mae Davis, Hilly's maid, is violently arrested for stealing. Following her arrest, Skeeter is summonsed to Aibileen's and met by several maids newly willing to interview. Nearly finished, Skeeter approaches her mother, Charlotte Phelan, to fulfill Miss Stein's demand to "put something personal in there. Write about the maid who raised you" (Taylor et al., 2011). Skeeter then learns that her mother fired Constantine when she was embarrassed by Constantine's daughter, Rachael, entering the Phelan's home through the front door while she was hosting the Daughters of America. Having finally learned of Constantine's fate, Skeeter adds her narrative to the book just before the deadline. As the film ends, the audience discovers how each woman is impacted by the book's publication. Skeeter decides to accept her dream job offer in New York; Minny is offered a permanent maid position at the Foote's; and, less fortunate, Aibileen is maliciously fired by Hilly. In the next section, I situate strategic whiteness as a conceptual lens to critique the film's problematic public pedagogy.

Strategic Whiteness and Media Representational Strategies

During slavery, racist ideology manifested as "a conscious effort to articulate, to justify, and to propagate a universal white supremacy based on the notion of an inherent black corporeal, intellectual, and moral inferiority" (Saint-Aubin, 2002, p. 255). Then, and still now, this dichotomous construction situates whiteness as a normative identity, discourse, ideology, and structure operating to preserve and magnify its dominant status (Kendall, 2013; Nakayama & Krizek, 1995; Warren, 2009). In their landmark essay "Whiteness: A Strategic Rhetoric," Nakayama and Krizek (1995) center whiteness to "identify and critique the assemblage of whiteness" (p. 294) and compel an acute awareness of how whiteness maneuvers to uphold racist logics. Spurred by Deleuze and Guattari, Nakayama and Krizek (1995) draw upon "deterritorialization" (p. 294) to reveal how whiteness secures its centrality, maintains its invisibility, and masks the racialized privileges afforded to white people. Simply stated, deterritorialization calls for establishing a blueprint to map the representational particularities of how whiteness deliberately functions. Conceptually, this is vital to challenging unmarked [white] stories about racial histories, racial in/equality, and interracial coalitions that are presented and/or perceived as objective, neutral, innocent, universal, color-blind, raceless, and/or "post-racial." Exposing whiteness as strategic allows for a close reading of how whiteness toils to maintain its supremacy (Nakayama & Krizek, 1995; Projansky & Ono, 1999), particularly amid U.S. American society's censure against explicit racism coupled with contemporary declarations of "post-racialism."

Extending Nakayama and Krizek's (1995) conceptualization of strategic whiteness from the realm of individual rhetoric to media representation broadens our understandings of how whiteness "establish[es] and defend[s] who and what Whites can be, what others can and cannot do and/or be, and what kind of feeling and action by others is allowed or disallowed in reference to Whites" (Tierney, 2006, p. 608). In this context, media as a social institution is positioned as a conduit through which whiteness is calculatingly preserved, fortified, and disseminated as superior (Brinson, 1995; Giroux, 1997; Madison, 1999; Moshin & Jackson, 2011). Ensuring the superiority of whiteness in media are white characters cast as saviors in films ostensibly about racism. This occurs when "a white person guides people of color from the margins to the mainstream with his or her own initiative and benevolence" (Cammarota, 2011, p. 243; Madison, 1999). Serving the same purpose are empathetic representations of racists, overly generous depictions of racially conscious white people, trivial depictions of what constitutes racism, and portrayals of racism as an individual pathology rather than an oppressive system (Madison, 1999; Moshin & Jackson, 2011; Projansky & Ono, 1999).

The aforementioned representational strategies "mark out and constitute the space of whiteness" as superior (Nakayama & Krizek, 1995, p. 298); they are also pervasive—even in mediated texts that outwardly oppose racism and/or presumably position the histories and experiences of people of color as central to the storyline (Madison, 1999; Moshin & Jackson, 2011; Tierney, 2006). Case in point—although public discourses overwhelmingly bill *The Help* (Taylor et al., 2011) as a film about black women (e.g., CBS, 2012; Puig, 2011; Tauber, 2011), conceptually implementing strategic whiteness reveals that black women are centered only to the degree that they enable a "post-racial" coming of age story enamored with white womanhood. Therefore, I approach the film asking, how does *The Help* (Taylor et al., 2011) strategically center and redeem whiteness amid its purported "post-racial" aspirations? To establish a blueprint of how whiteness invisibly works in the film, I first highlight how Skeeter and Stockett anchor white womanhood at the crux of the storyline. Secondly, I situate Skeeter, Charlotte, and Hilly as racist white women who, at the expense of black women, are ultimately redeemed via the film's culmination. Lastly, I highlight how the film falls in accordance with "post-racial" ideology and "shrouds racism ... [while] subtly support[ing] racial hierarchies in and through narratives that claim to be antiracist" (Projansky & Ono, 1999, p. 156).

Helping Whiteness and Hindering Progressive Racial Consciousness

Centralizing Whiteness and White Women

 Skeeter. I experience *The Help* (Taylor et al., 2011) unequivocally as a film in "which whiteness recenters itself—even in the face of explicit attention to blackness" (Projansky & Ono, 1999, p. 151). Skeeter, as the film's protagonist, serves as a pronounced example of this representational strategy via the array of life changes she experiences. Not only does Skeeter graduate from college and get her first news column, she also dates her first boyfriend, copes with her mother's illness, learns the truth about Constantine's forced departure, co-authors a book, fulfills her dream of getting published, and accepts a journalism job in New York. The drastic changes in Skeeter's life result in her character being more complex while the character development of Aibileen and Minny is flattened despite their appearance in multiple scenes. As a result, we know very little about their lives as black women beyond their connections to white women. That they are rarely seen out of uniform strengthens the centralization of Skeeter who is often shown navigating personal, social, and professional elements of her life in a variety of different contexts, outfits, and hairstyles.

 Referred to as the "commodification of Otherness" by hooks (1992, p. 21), Skeeter can be further understood as the cultivated [white] subject of the film while Aibileen and Minny are the [black] objects of her desire—developed only insofar as Skeeter's needs require. For instance, the pivotal arc of Stockett and Taylor's storytelling depends on Skeeter's real and imagined access to blackness, which she finds alluring and useful as a means to realize her personal agency and resolve her personal struggles. Clearly objectified via this arc are Aibileen and Minny whose embodiment of objectified working-class black femininity is narratively prohibited from emerging as critical commentary on Skeeter's status as the upper-class white female protagonist. Consistent with Nakayama and Krizek's (1995) articulation of whiteness as a strategic rhetoric that functions protectively, this representational strategy safeguards Skeeter from acknowledging how her white privilege is contingent upon and necessitates Aibileen's and Minny's objectification. The film's use of motifs, defined as details that acquire significance in the plotline through repetition (Pramaggiore & Wallis, 2011), strengthens the interpretation of Skeeter as subject versus Aibileen and Minny as objects. For example, Skeeter often returns to a willow tree in her yard to remember the validation she received from Constantine as a young girl. Sitting together under the tree, Constantine reminds her of her beauty and potential despite not having been asked to a school dance. Later on, Skeeter returns to the same tree with Stuart (her soon to be first boyfriend) where he asks her out on a date, which symbolizes her growth and vindicates past romantic rejections. By comparison, fried chicken, a motif joined with Minny's character, symbolizes racist stereotypes and the relegation of black women to white kitchens.

 Heightening the perceptibility of Skeeter as the "citizen of the center" (Nakayama & Krizek, 1995, p. 293) is the film's resolute focus on her dream to become a writer. Aibileen and Minny arrive to the project fearful, suspicious, and invited by Skeeter.

Moreover, the maids are fueled by their anger at racism in comparison with Skeeter being fueled by discontent and ambition as the perfect elixir for her emergence as a white heroine tinged with a radical (for their era) sense of race consciousness. Skeeter's cardinal status is effectively advanced by her position as the conduit through which Aibileen and Minny become known, albeit minimally, beyond their role as maids. For example, the first time we see Aibileen out of uniform she is hosting Skeeter for her interview. Leading up to the interview, the shrewd power of whiteness is conveyed albeit innocently masked as kindness. This occurs when Aibileen refers to Skeeter as "ma'am" and Skeeter replies with "You don't have to call me ma'am. Not here" (Taylor et al., 2011).

Skeeter's comment must be read as more than kindness, an indication of her race consciousness, or interracial camaraderie. Rather, Skeeter's instruction enacts her white privilege since she sets the parameters for their interaction—even in Aibileen's home. Furthermore, the unnamed manifestation of Skeeter's white privilege keeps whiteness invisible, effectively "eluding analysis yet exerting influence over everyday life" (Nakayama & Krizek, 1995, p. 293). Employing "the discursive power of whiteness" to police communication (Warren, 2009, p. 81), Skeeter's authorization also indicates the steadfast degree to which their relationship remains predicated upon white superiority and black inferiority—despite her "good" intentions. Lastly, Skeeter's "Not here," implying that Aibileen should refer to her as "ma'am" everywhere else, indicates her unwillingness to publicly challenge racism. This, in turn, impedes her ability to fully humanize Aibileen and embody a genuinely progressive racial consciousness.

Troubling the interpretation of Skeeter as the foremost character is Aibileen's occasional voice-over as narrator, which outwardly centers her perspective and leads the audience to believe that we are engrossed in her lived experiences. However, returning to Skeeter as a conduit, it is important to realize that hearing Aibileen's voice is always contingent upon Skeeter's interest in writing her book entitled *The Help*. Therefore, Aibileen's voice is audible as a narrator only because her interest in sharing her experiences converges with Skeeter's interests in achieving her dream. Their "interest convergence" (Bell, 1980, p. 523), as one person with racialized power and the other without, illuminates the racialized complexity of their motivations to work together. While Skeeter certainly prioritizes her dreams without an expressed awareness of her white privilege, she is also sincerely troubled by manifestations of explicit racism. In comparison, Skeeter's book represents a means for Aibileen, joined by Minny and other maids, to subversively resist racism and they do so cognizant of the dangers at stake. However, amid the overlapping and complex motives among the women, what cannot be overlooked is the book's publication being ultimately dependent upon two white women: Skeeter and Miss Stein. This dependency for access to voice is exemplary of how whiteness strategically harvests levels of agency, power, and control for white women that are inaccessible to black women. According to Kendall (2013), white women can and do collude with white supremacy to secure status and access opportunity. Both Skeeter and Miss Stein do so, at minimum, via the absence of either woman overtly questioning the role of white privilege and black exploitation in their pursuit of literary success.

Absent consideration of whiteness' strategic labor to convey "naturalized dominance" (Nakayama & Krizek, 1995, p. 299), the interest convergence and interdependence between Skeeter and the black maids (most of whom are nameless in the film) appears comparable. Hence, Skeeter cannot write the book without the maids and the maids' perspectives cannot be published without Skeeter. Yet a critical awareness of whiteness and racism necessitates the racialized consideration of risk and vulnerability, which reveals Skeeter as not only their conduit to voice, but also their lifeline since she protects the maids' identities. As such Skeeter is positioned as a seemingly innocent, white savior. Elevated to savior status, Skeeter becomes emblematic of all that is "good" about whiteness without displaying the reflexivity and accountability that progressive racial consciousness calls for (e.g., Kendall, 2013; Marty, 1999). In this context, the "naturalized dominance" of whiteness "is not entirely hidden from view" (Nakayama & Krizek, 1995, p. 299). Skeeter's whiteness as a site of power and protection is on full display in the film. However, because she fails to expressly problematize her access to white privilege, Skeeter's embodiment of whiteness ironically helps mask the racism her book labors to expose.

Exemplary of this failure, had Skeeter, Aibileen, and Minny been outed for authoring *The Help*, Skeeter reserved the (white, upper-class) option of being perceived as a white savior with "good" intentions opposed to being deemed traitorous. By comparison, the only discursive option for Aibileen and Minny under Jim Crow would have been that of defiant and dangerous "nigras" (Taylor et al., 2011). Equally significant are explicit references to civil rights history (e.g., the White Citizens Council, Freedom Riders, and the murders of Medgar Evers and John F. Kennedy) that assist Skeeter's elevation to savior status. For example, when Skeeter is watching the news coverage of Evers' murder with Jameso and Pascagoula (the Phelans' "help"), Charlotte rushes in, turns off the television, and sharply says "Don't encourage them like that ... I won't have it!" (Taylor et al., 2011). In response, Skeeter rebelliously walks away, marking her as the racially progressive white woman of the household in comparison with her racist mother. This repetitive contrast between Skeeter and Charlotte not only secures Skeeter at the center of the storyline as a "good" (i.e., progressive) white woman, but also locks what constitutes racism into only overt articulations (e.g., "us" versus "them" logics, racial epithets, "colored" seating, etc.). Limiting racism to the overt realm disregards progressive understandings of racism as both overt and covert (Essed, 1991; Projansky & Ono, 1999) and allows for whiteness to strategically create a "post-racial" illusion of racism as an outdated, politically incorrect, and individual pathology that self-declared "progressive" white women, like Skeeter, do not partake in—all of which shields the ongoing, systemic reproduction of whiteness as superior.

Skeeter as Stockett's Surrogate. Mirroring the centralization of Skeeter, Kathryn Stockett as the author of the novel received a great deal of congratulatory attention (e.g., Couric, 2011; Denby, 2011; Tauber, 2011) that rooted her white perspective at the center of conversations about "post-racialism," rather than igniting progressive conversations about race, racism, and whiteness. In fairness, Stockett should be credited for her hard work and commended for having her novel turned into a successful film. However, her success as a white author injecting a white character at the center of black women's lives is worthy of critical attention; particularly since Skeeter functions as a surrogate for the native Mississippian in numerous ways. Stockett's articulation of her purpose in writing *The Help* (Stockett, 2009) clearly insinuates that she, like Skeeter, is a conduit through which her family's maid, Demetrie McLorn, can be known. In her epilogue entitled "Too Little, Too Late," Stockett (2009) says:

> I'm pretty sure I can say that no one in my family ever asked Demetrie what it felt like to be black in Mississippi, working for our white family. It never occurred to us to ask ... I've spent years imagining what her answer would be. And that is why I wrote this book. (p. 530)

Living between the black and white worlds Stockett transports her audience to, I struggle deeply with her motivation for doing so. Thus, similarly to Skeeter, Stockett leverages her real and imagined access to blackness to realize her personal agency (e.g., she rectifies not having asked Demetrie about her experiences by creating them herself) and resolve her personal struggles (e.g., processing childhood memories of racism, being rejected as a writer, etc.).

Bolstering my interpretation of Skeeter as Stockett's surrogate (i.e., Stockett's pathway to securing the center) are stark similarities including their dreams of becoming writers, memories of a close relationship with their black maids, books entitled *The Help*, and decisions to move to New York from Mississippi in their 20s. Additionally, Stockett wrote her memories of Demetrie into Aibileen, Minny, and Constantine's characters. For instance, Aibileen validates Mae Mobley Leefolt and Constantine validates Skeeter similarly to how Stockett remembers being validated by Demetrie as a little girl (Stockett, 2009). Also Minny, like Demetrie, is famous for her cooking and married to "a mean, abusive drinker" (Stockett, 2009, p. 525), and Aibileen and Minny, like Demetrie, had colored bathrooms outside of the white homes they worked in (Couric, 2011). Perhaps most indicative of Stockett's desire to center herself, alongside the immortalization of her memories, is the appearance of her daughter Lila in the film as a young Skeeter.

The aforementioned instances of white imposition testify to how Stockett, from the peripheral of black women's lives, exercises her white privilege to reckon with being a benefactor of racism by speaking for black women. In this context, whiteness is strategically leveraged to confine black women into the white imaginary while masking the injurious nature of doing so. Stockett does so with her whiteness as power on full display, and "the recognition of this power is often masked" (Nakayama & Krizek, 1995, p. 298) because Stockett, like Skeeter, fails to interrogate the implications of her white privilege. This is not to mark Stockett's memories of Demetrie, memorialized in the book and film, as false or trivial. Rather it is vital to underscore the political differences between a black maid speaking her truth versus the white woman she served speaking for her. Alcoff (1991) reminds us that "the practice of privileged persons speaking for or on behalf of less privileged persons has actually resulted ... in increasing or reinforcing the oppression of the group spoken for" (p. 7). With this in mind, engaging a film supposedly about black womanhood, the following questions surface: Does Stockett's storyline capture a plausible depiction of black womanhood? Yes. Does Stockett publicly acknowledge that the plausibility confines black women to the white imagination as an anesthetic for white women's guilt? No. Does Stockett publicly recognize the dangers black women face when white women speak for black women? No.

This signals Stockett's failure, accompanied by the public's failure, to remember "that a speaker's location is epistemically salient" (Alcoff, 1991, p. 7). To be clear, Stockett commonly offers all of the dis/qualifiers that whiteness strategically draws upon to appear innocuous. For example, she makes assertions such as "I don't presume to think that I know what it really felt like to be a black woman in Mississippi" (Stockett, 2009, p. 529) and, in reference to Demetrie, "it's obvious how little I knew about her ... I never once wondered what she was thinking" (Tauber, 2011, p. 103) and "I would hope if she was alive today, she would see *The Help* as a thank-you" (Tauber, 2011, p. 103). Masking the presence of whiteness as a universalized means to strategically police the representation of people of color is Stockett's inability, on display in her comments above, to reflexively center her whiteness as a site of inquiry. To counter the absence that whiteness strategically facilitates, I want to know: Why does Stockett feel the need to ameliorate her guilt about how her family treated Demetrie? Why does Stockett turn toward her real and imagined access to black femininity for relief? Why does Stockett assume that had she asked Demetrie about her experiences that Demetrie would have felt safe and comfortable enough to freely respond?

Avoiding the pitfall of criminalizing Stockett, what makes her insertion of herself and her memories monumentally problematic does not enter the debate over whether or not a white woman should have written *The Help* (Stockett, 2009) and authorized a white man to direct and produce the screenplay. Rather, I take issue with Stockett's and Taylor's failure to advocate for the novel and film to be pedagogically understood for what they are: a white man's interpretation of a white woman's interpretation of black women's lived experiences. As the author and director, Stockett and Taylor instruct the audience to understand black women in accordance with their white perceptions. What is sacrificed via Stockett's and Taylor's choices is the rich and ambivalent complexity of racial histories, racial in/equality, and interracial coalitions. In essence, they whitewashed the more fulsome narrative in favor of one that renders 1960s Jim Crow Mississippi more innocent, comfortable, and palatable for white people like themselves. Furthermore, the representational strategies deployed in the novel and film invoke "the historically constituted and systematically exercised" (Nakayama & Krizek, 1995, p. 302) power of whiteness without marking whiteness as oppressive which is peculiar given the narrative's purported "focus" on people of color and racism.

With regard to the centralization of whiteness channeled via Stockett, it is also important to mark her manipulation of whiteness as valuable property (Harris, 1995) that doubly functions as social capital (Bourdieu, 1997). More specifically Taylor, also from Mississippi, is Stockett's childhood friend. Their relationship is worthy of critical attention because, while permissible for friends to partner in business, understanding whiteness as strategic necessitates understanding business networks as racialized. Therefore, Stockett's choice to grant Taylor the screenplay rights is racialized as a business decision in which, once again, the "naturalized dominance" of whiteness "is not entirely hidden from view" (Nakayama & Krizek, 1995, p. 299). Mindful of how whiteness strategically facilitates access and opportunity for white people, while its "social functions remain hidden from analysis" (Nakayama & Krizek, 1995, p. 297), I aptly question whether or not Stockett realizes that her business decision was racialized. Likewise, I wonder if producers and directors of color had access to Stockett's social network to be considered, or if the opportunity was offered only to Taylor. According to DreamWorks Studios (2010), "Taylor and Stockett's longtime, trusting friendship formed the basis of the film's journey and along the way they added another friend, Jackson native Brunson Green." Followed by, "And it was only natural that Taylor would take the project to Producer Chris Columbus as he had known him for some time" (DreamWorks Studios, 2010). Adding a visual element to how Stockett and Taylor's social networks racially influenced who chiefly produced and directed the film is a picture of Viola Davis (Aibileen) and Octavia Spencer (Minny). In the picture, they are posing with the 2012 NAACP Image Award for Outstanding Motion Picture flanked by four of the white men who produced and directed the film.[3]

Amplifying the exposure of strategic whiteness in *The Help* (Taylor et al., 2011), the next section demonstrates how the film's centralization of whiteness allows white female characters to repent for racism without liability for their white privilege. Read closely, these redemptive opportunities become visible as a façade of white apologia opposed to genuine atonement or progressive race consciousness. Rhetorically, apologia manifests as a self-defense strategy that "enables rhetors to defend their moral character against accusation and attack ... as they deflect any recognition of wrongdoing or of the need for accountability" (Marty, 1999, p. 52; Ware & Linkugel, 1973). Additionally, apologia "allow[s] white rhetors to reject responsibility for racism and reassert their good moral standing" (Marty, 1999, p. 52). A close interrogation of Skeeter, Charlotte, and Hilly reveals how the film foregrounds whiteness and functions as a site of apologia and deliverance for racist white women.

White Women, Racism, Apologia, and Redemption

Skeeter. As the heroine of the film, Skeeter is depicted as eager to right wrongs but is never held accountable for her role in perpetuating the racialized injustice she unveils in her book. In effect, since Skeeter is the film's primary antiracist protagonist, this signals that "no representational strategy"—even an "antiracist" storyline that "centers" people of color—"is immune from the potential recuperation of white power" (Projansky & Ono, 1999, p. 152). During the opportunities for her white accountability to shine, the film instead turns toward Skeeter's exempted white savior status. For example, when Minny voices her suspicions about Skeeter's intentions, Minny quickly (in a matter of seconds) decides to interview too. Soon after, Minny, Aibileen, and Skeeter are shown laughing and cooking in Aibileen's kitchen. Quite symbolic of Aibileen and Minny's trust in Skeeter is their willingness to comically imitate white women and appear casual with their hair pinned and wrapped in Skeeter's company. Mindful of how whiteness operates strategically to shield its presence (Nakayama & Krizek, 1995; Projansky & Ono, 1999), such representations communicate the erasure of Skeeter's whiteness as a threat. Equally as troubling is *The Help*'s (Taylor et al., 2011) message that three friends led by a white woman— opposed to a social movement led by people of color—can dispel racism.

Alongside the neutralizing blossom of their "remarkable sisterhood" (DreamWorks Studios, 2010), minor black characters also affirm that Skeeter has been pardoned from her role in Jim Crow racism. For example, Henry, the waiter at the diner, risks quietly passing on the message to Skeeter that she "best head on over to Miss Aibileen's house" (Taylor et al., 2011). When Skeeter arrives, she is met by several maids who are newly willing, following Yule Mae's violent arrest, to tell her their stories. In effect, each maid's willingness representationally exempts Skeeter from white racists and the danger of white supremacy and thus "reconstitute[s] a space for white dominance without calling explicit attention to this act" (Projansky & Ono, 1999, p. 152). Another instance exempting Skeeter and heightening her savior status is when she receives the same beholden gift as Aibileen from Aibileen and Minny's church. As Aibileen presents Skeeter with a copy of their book, she says "churches over two counties signed our books. All for you and me" (Taylor et al., 2011). Functioning as a filmic parallel that emphasizes their sameness (Pramaggiore & Wallis, 2011), Skeeter's signed copy also signifies approval and that her obligation to the maids has ended. This scene, ignorant of whiteness as a strategic force, appears commonsensical since the film is winding down and must end somewhere.

In opposition, a critical stance compels a return to interest convergence to discern that the end of Skeeter's obligation to the maids conveniently mirrors the fulfillment of her interests in getting published and departing for the Harper Row position in New York. Starkly unfulfilled are the interests of Aibileen and Minny who, like all of the maids who interviewed, will remain in Jackson at risk for extreme punishment. Moreover, the maids are without tangible indication of how racist circumstances have improved. For instance, the film itself questions the significance of their book in its parallels between Aibileen, Minny, and Minny's daughter Sugar. Early on we learn that Aibileen became a maid at 14 after dropping out of school to help pay bills. Echoing her own story Aibileen's voice-over explains, "Leroy ... made Sugar quit school to help him with the bills" (Taylor et al., 2011) just before we watch Minny sternly advise Sugar, "No sass-mouthin'. I mean it" (Taylor et al., 2011). Exposing the cyclical strength of racism safeguarded by whiteness (Nakayama & Krizek, 1995; Projansky & Ono, 1999), these parallels serve as an indication that little to nothing has changed since the next generation of black women, represented via Sugar, is destined to serve as maids.[4]

Also representative of Skeeter's privileged, redemptive status is her choice between staying in Jackson or accepting the New York position. Via Miss Stein, the audience understands New York as far more progressive than the South; for example, she has her own office and staff and she uses "Negro" opposed to "colored." When Skeeter decides to accept the position, I interpret her not as a white woman who has deconstructed her white privilege and is moving forward to combat racism but rather as someone who has been offered a means to escape her racist southern town after using the experiences of black women to launch her career. Before accepting the position, Skeeter feigns refusal with "I can't just leave you two here when things are getting bad from the mess that I created" (Taylor et al., 2011). Yet once again, she is rescued from white accountability and reaffirmed as the "citizen of the center" (Nakayama & Krizek, 1995, p. 293) when Aibileen and Minny quickly intervene. Aibileen says:

> If bad things happen, ain't nothing you can do about it. And now it's for a reason we can be proud of. I don't mean to rub salt in your wound but you ain't got a good life here in Jackson. (Taylor et al., 2011)

Followed by Minny who offers:

> You ain't got nothing left here but enemies in the Junior League. You done burned every bridge there is. And you ain't never gonna get another man in this town ... So don't walk your white butt to New York, run it! Looky here Miss Skeeter, I'm gonna take care of Aibileen. And she's gonna take care of me. (Taylor et al., 2011)

Nodding in agreement and taking Skeeter's hand, Aibileen finalizes their definitive stance to ensure Skeeter's happy ending with, "Go find your life Miss Skeeter" (Taylor et al., 2011).

In this scene, with black people on a nearby porch signaling Skeeter's accepted presence in a black neighborhood, a critical interpretation highlights the manipulation of Aibileen and Minny as agents of strategic whiteness. In effect, Skeeter is let off the proverbial racist hook by two black women relegated to subservient positions and destined to continue to struggle against racism. This scene is strongly reminiscent of historical mammy caricatures (Anderson, 1997) alongside the contemporary "mammification" (Omolade, 1994, p. 54) of black women who, although no longer caged by legalized racism nor solely confined to white households, are still expected to defer to and support the interests of white women (Beauboeuf-Lafontant, 2009; Omolade, 1994). Watching Aibileen and Minny smile and nod approvingly to protect Skeeter's dreams, without a hint of concern for themselves, confirms that loyal mammification retains a stronghold in the white imagination of black womanhood and bonds the exhilaration of building a new life and chasing dreams to white womanhood. Exposing the representational strategies of whiteness "to renegotiate the centrality of white power and authority" (Projansky & Ono, 1999, p. 152) allows the audience to question why we are encouraged to root for Skeeter's bright future. Thus, if the film was genuinely concerned with Aibileen and Minny, the audience would be encouraged to root for the Civil Rights Movement, or at least wonder if Aibileen and Minny can safely remain in Jackson.

Overall, although Skeeter appears relieved from her responsibility to combat racism having published her book, I argue that she can be more accurately understood as having reproduced white supremacist exploitation. First, she benefitted from Aibileen's work experience to write the Miss Myrna column without publicly crediting Aibileen. Then, she published *The Help* without public accountability or lasting commitment to the everyday struggles of black maids in Jackson. In both instances, Skeeter personally and professionally benefits from white superiority and black inferiority without outward pause. To be fair, she does thank Aibileen and rightly divides her book advance among all of the women who interviewed, but her actions are concentrated at the micro level. This allows her to quietly repent for racism without facing the hazards of antiracist activism. Take for instance the grave sacrifices endured by white female civil rights activists Viola Liuzzo and Anne Braden. According to hooks (2013), the whitewashed representations of white femininity in *The Help* (Stockett, 2009; Taylor et al., 2011) "erase and deny the long and powerful history of the individual radical white women active in the civil rights struggle" (p. 68).

Charlotte. Another white female character afforded the opportunity to redeem her racism is Skeeter's mother Charlotte. More overtly recognizable as racist than Skeeter, there are several scenes in which Charlotte is cringeworthy. For instance, we see her physical revulsion when Skeeter, in response to Charlotte's homophobic inquiry about her marriage potential, says "Mother, I want to be with girls as much as you want to be with Jameso!" (Taylor et al., 2011). Also, when Skeeter has a date with Stuart, Charlotte chases her down their driveway to offer advice on etiquette. She screams "Don't mope! Smile! And for heaven's sakes don't sit like some squaw Indian!" (Taylor et al., 2011). Most offensive to Skeeter is when her mother explains why Constantine disappeared. Teeming with guilt, Charlotte admits having lied to Skeeter and then explains via a flashback why she fired Constantine.

During Charlotte's flashback, a troubling parallel between Skeeter and Rachael is communicated by the focus on Constantine's closet door as she packs her suitcase. Moving up the height of the door, the camera tracks the growth of both children etched over the years in pencil. Resting near the top, Constantine's aged hand regretfully pauses as it did on the screen just before Charlotte shut the Phelan's door in her face. Stripped of the anger that "'mothering' white children" (hooks, 2013, p. 63) often brought forth, this depiction dismisses the realness of race and racism by symbolizing Rachael and Skeeter as equal "daughters" on Constantine's door. This scene also leaves the audience with the impression that everyone's suffering is equivalent since Constantine, Skeeter, and Charlotte are all shown in emotional pain. Juxtaposed against Skeeter's cherished memories of Constantine, Charlotte's racist dismissal is exceptionally callous especially since Constantine died soon after being fired. In this scene, Skeeter is once again accentuated as racially progressive in comparison with her mother's cruel, overt racism.

The aforementioned scene also leverages Charlotte's bedridden desperation to resolve her strained relationship with Skeeter as an opportunity to atone for her racism. In the absence of Constantine, Skeeter needs motherly support as she navigates the life changes that position her as the main protagonist. Seizing this opportunity, Charlotte becomes a heartened protector of her daughter, which tacitly allows her to compensate for her racist maltreatment of Constantine and Skeeter's subsequent loss of a "motherly" maid. Embodying her desire to mother her daughter, Charlotte rescues Skeeter when Hilly arrives on their porch incensed by the potential of Skeeter's book to out her for having eaten Minny's shit. Charlotte says:

> Is everything okay you two? Hilly, you're a sweaty mess. Are you ill? Darling, oh, no husband wants to come home and see that [referencing her stress cankered lip]. You know Hilly, if I didn't know any better, I'd say you've been eating too much pie ... Now you get your raggedy ass off my porch. (Taylor et al., 2011)

Visibly impressed, Skeeter follows her mother inside after Hilly leaves and Charlotte, for the first time, outwardly admires her daughter. Offering Skeeter her blessing to move to New York, she says "Courage sometimes skips a generation. Thank you for bringing it back to our family" (Taylor et al., 2011). Charlotte's compliment functions paradoxically: If indifferent to whiteness, the audience can easily applaud her for finally supporting her daughter. Yet, mindful of whiteness as strategic, Charlotte's defense and support of Skeeter recompenses for her racist dismissal of Constantine without her being accountable to or confronted by a single person of color.

Sustaining this redemptive reading is Skeeter's memory of Constantine, the foremost target of Charlotte's racism, rationalizing Charlotte's behavior. Encouraging Skeeter to accept her mother, Constantine says "she didn't pick her life. It pick her" (Taylor et al., 2011). Read similarly to Aibileen and Minny's insistence that Skeeter must accept the New York position, this scene portrays another black woman being used as a communicative vehicle for strategic whiteness. Hence Charlotte's redemption, emblazoned by Skeeter's newly warm demeanor toward her, is eased by Constantine's lasting influence on Skeeter despite her being publicly humiliated and ousted from the Phelan's home. Furthermore, Charlotte also recuperates the virtuousness of white womanhood by protecting Skeeter from further pain (e.g., Hilly's rage and the absence of a mother figure) and ministering the fulfillment of Skeeter's dreams (e.g., encouraging her to go to New York). In effect, Charlotte's racism is forgiven, without an ode of reflexivity or a conscious nod toward white supremacy, because Skeeter's happiness is secured.

Hilly. Drawing upon the film's use of bathrooms and toilets as another motif, Hilly serves as a third example of a white woman delivered from her racist proclivities. Hilly also exemplifies how "whiteness attempts to elude critical attention by always remaining on our visual periphery" (Projansky & Ono, 1999, p. 156) because, like Charlotte, she is overtly racist and offers the audience opportunities to witness and decry racism without drawing critical attention to how whiteness systemically fuels racism. Unlike Charlotte, Hilly visibly enjoys the fruits of her cruelty. For example, explaining her refusal to use Elizabeth's bathroom because Aibileen uses it Hilly says,

"It's just plain dangerous. They carry different diseases than we do" (Taylor et al., 2011). Embarrassed, Elizabeth then has a colored bathroom built outside that is hot and bug infested. Smugly satisfied, Hilly basks in Aibileen's discomfort when she asks "Are you enjoying your new bathroom ... Nice to have your own, isn't it Aibileen?" and purposefully waits for Aibileen's forced "Yes ma'am. And I thank you" (Taylor et al., 2011). Additional scenes where Hilly's malevolent racism surfaces are when she fires Minny for using the inside bathroom and when she watches Yule Mae's violent arrest from afar as a satisfied voyeur. Each instance offers an exemplar of how "Whiteness, stated or unstated ... leaves one invoking ... historically constituted and systematically exercised power relations" (Nakayama & Krizek, 1995, p. 302). Hilly's racism remains poignant up until the very end of the film when she punishes Aibileen for helping Skeeter.

This scene peaks just after Hilly falsely accuses Aibileen of stealing silver she lent to Elizabeth. When Elizabeth leaves the room, Hilly nastily says, "Maybe I can't send you to jail for what you wrote, but I can send you for being a thief" (Taylor et al., 2011). Calling upon their insurance, Aibileen "talk[s] back" (hooks, 1989, p. 9) to Hilly and says "All you do is scare and lie to try and get what you want. You a godless woman. Ain't you tired Miss Hilly? Ain't you tired?" (Taylor et al., 2011) This confrontation reflects Hilly's redemptive opportunity, albeit less obvious than Skeeter's and Charlotte's opportunities. Hence, opposed to exercising her white privilege to annihilate Aibileen, Hilly emotionally crumbles and allows her to leave the Leefolt's. Through Aibileen, we are invited to read Hilly as a pathetically racist individual while she sobs conceivably in response to her depraved behavior being exposed. Reading this scene solely as empowering is tempting since Aibileen boldly confronts Hilly, yet doing so is complicated by understanding whiteness as a strategic force that is always invested in its own propriety (Projansky & Ono, 1999). Of importance is that Hilly, despite her tearful shame, maintains all of her racialized power and Aibileen's self-determination is literally (i.e., walking out of the house and not being jailed) and figuratively (i.e., taking her first steps toward her dreams) dependent upon Hilly letting her go. Moreover, a critical interpretation frames Hilly's actions as an investment in keeping her consumption of Minny's shit (i.e., blackness as a contaminant according to dominant ideologies of whiteness) a secret. Cognizant of the labor of whiteness to secure superiority on multiple fronts (Nakayama & Krizek, 1995; Projansky & Ono, 1999), even Hilly—the most repugnant racist in the film—has an admirable, albeit self-serving, final act when she lets Aibileen leave without calling the police.

Critiquing whiteness as strategic locates the redemption of Skeeter, Charlotte, and Hilly in the realm of white apologia, which discursively valorizes white culture and restores the virtue of white racists (Marty, 1999). Each woman's fulfilled opportunity to atone for racism beckons forgiveness for the pain each has inflicted upon people of color without explicit accountability toward whiteness, racism, or the people of color they have hurt. Voicing the film's decided "post-racial" shift away from accountability, actor Bryce Dallas Howard (Hilly) says, "It's not necessarily vilifying anyone, but rather vilifying certain mentalities and belief systems" (DreamWorks,

2010). Echoing Howard's stance, with an insinuation that black and white women were equally victimized in the Jim Crow South, is Taylor who, in response to public criticism, says, "People are being too critical of this film ... [Stockett] wrote a book about four women that were victims of circumstances of their surroundings. The book is about courage and love and integrity, and talking to whom you consider to be your enemy and finding common ground" (Witherspoon, 2011). Directly contradicting their sentiments with regard to the cinematic reproduction of whiteness, Projansky and Ono (1999) assert:

> Whiteness itself is not the central problem; the problem ... is representations that successfully strategize a maintenance of privileged power and the concomitant marginalization and disempowerment of highly visible "others"—while seeming to do otherwise—hence recoding domination as a virtue. (p. 171)

Challenging the Power of Whiteness and "Post-racialism"

A focus on strategic whiteness situates *The Help*'s (Taylor et al., 2011) cinematic public pedagogy firmly within the "Anti-Racist-White-Hero" (Madison, 1999, p. 399) genre of films that centralize and redeem whiteness via storylines, character development, and dialogue—despite their professed focus on people of color. Additionally, Stockett and Taylor's purposeful decisions not to explicitly challenge whiteness or racism[5] situate the film as a perfect, and profitable, revisionary "post-racial" narrative. Working against the film's romanticism of white racial consciousness and interracial coalitions in the Jim Crow South, Branch (2011) importantly articulates that:

> Domestic service for many Black women was a lifelong occupation that was physically demanding and equally, if not more, emotionally taxing ... Whites made it clear to Black women that domestic service was their highest calling and that it was to be performed with humility and deference. They were to know their place and gladly occupy it. They were expected to hide their anxieties and frustrations about serving a White family while temporarily deserting their own families with a smile and a willingness to work. (p. 69)

This reality compels curiosity as to why the novel and film became so vastly popular when previous literary, scholarly, and filmic works addressing the lived experiences of black mammies and maids did not spark such frenzied white intrigue (e.g., Anderson, 1997; Branch, 2011; Childress, 1986; Clark-Lewis, Nelson, & Nelson, 1990; Neely, 2000; Sharpless, 2010; Tucker, 1988). Drawing attention to Obama's 2008 election and the timing of Stockett's national success in the wake of 60 rejection letters (Tauber, 2011), hooks (2013) offers a politicized explanation. She says:

> Seen within the political culture and social backdrop of our time, wherein the greatest symbolic challenge to imperialist white supremacist capitalist patriarchy has occurred (the placement of a biracial black male in the White House and his black wife and children) the publication of *The Help* can only be seen as a backlash, both against the movement to end racism and the feminist movement ... had the book not been supported and fully backed by a conservative white-male-dominated

publishing and advertising empire no one would have ever heard of this work. (hooks, 2013, p. 59)

Building upon hooks, I interpret the film as a congratulatory "post-racial" salute for white women who, like Stockett and Skeeter, are on the verge of progressive racial consciousness but never fully aware of racism, how their whiteness ensures its continuance, and the difference between being a savior versus an ally. These same white women tune closely into the argument that Stockett, via Skeeter, "helps" at least some black women as perhaps she has, but fail to serve as allies who expose whiteness and fail to advocate against institutionalized racism. Thus activism, like racism, "remains individualistic, not social and certainly not structural" (Projansky & Ono, 1999, p. 158). In essence, *The Help* (Stockett, 2009; Taylor et al., 2011) is about Stockett, Skeeter, and white women like them who crave to be "good" white women minus the grueling labor that being a racially progressive white woman requires.

Absent the blueprint of how whiteness strategically functions, *The Help*'s (Stockett, 2009; Taylor et al., 2011) popular success appears innocent; merely an indication of creative genius. Yet the appeal for U.S. American society to be "post-racial" (Ono, 2010; Squires et al., 2010), coinciding with Obama's election/re-election, more complexly reveals the film as a mediated pacification of white guilt and reassurance of white superiority. More expressly, *The Help* (Taylor et al., 2011) "disavows history, overlaying it with an upbeat discourse about how things were never really that bad, are not so bad now, and are only getting better" (Ono, 2010, p. 227). As such, challenging *The Help* (Taylor et al., 2011) as a purveyor of "post-racial" public pedagogy is imperative because the film allows white people to remember an era of white cruelty more favorably, and forecasts a future where "[r]ace becomes an antiquated signifier that marks only how far the nation has come in redressing racial injustice and ignores how far we must go" (Rossing, 2012, p. 47).

The definitive moment where *The Help*'s (Taylor et al., 2011) unremitting commitment to "post-racialism" became clear is when Aibileen leaves the Leefolt home after Hilly's accusation of theft. Walking down a paved street saturated with tall, green trees and sunlight, she says:

> Mae Mobley was my last baby. In just ten minutes, the only life I knew was done. God says we need to love our enemies. It hard to do. But it can start by telling the truth. No one had ever asked me what it feel like to be me. Once I told the truth about that I felt free ... My boy, Treelore, always said we going to have a writer in the family one day. I guess its gonna be me. (Taylor et al., 2011)

This final representation of Aibileen as discovering her liberation through the feats of white women (i.e., sharing her truths via Skeeter's book and getting fired by Hilly jointly lead to her feeling free) must be troubled. In short, this scene privileges whiteness as the means through which a black woman achieves empowerment and severely undermines the autonomy that Aibileen is depicted as having achieved. Amid this peaceable ending, we must ask: What is a black woman in her fifties making less than minimum wage, whose work history reflects only domestic labor, without Social Security benefits going to do for income? How is she going to realize her dream of becoming a writer to support herself in the Jim Crow South? Furthermore with regard to Minny, is it adequate to assume that she is satisfied with her permanent maid position at the Footes' and her 14-year-old daughter working as a maid? Amid these critical questions, and innumerable others, I remain troubled by the mass celebration of the novel and film. Given their lack of transformative power, each signifies how far we have yet to go with regard to progressive racial consciousness, especially given how easily the masses ascribed to the "Obama-inspired optimism" (Teasley & Ikard, 2010, p. 413) beholden in both storylines. Of vast importance to assert is that *The Help* (Taylor et al., 2011) is by no means a film concerned with the pride and pain of black women.

Acknowledgments

The author offers sincere thanks to the reviewers and editors for their thoughtful and wise insight.

Notes

[1] Public pedagogy "refers to the education provided by popular culture; popular culture teaches audiences and participants through the ways it represents people and issues and the kinds of discourses it creates and disseminates" (Sandlin, 2007, p. 76).

[2] I place "post-racial" and "post-racialism" in quotation marks to highlight their contentious falsity in accordance with critical intercultural scholarship (Ono, 2010; Squires et al., 2010).

[3] Please see CBS (2012) for a link to the photo. Also, DreamWorks Studios (2010) lists Tate Taylor as the Director and Brunson Green, Chris Columbus and Michael Barnathan as Producers. The Executive Producers listed are Mark Radcliffe, Tate Taylor, L. Dean Jones Jr., Nate Berkus, Jennifer Blum, John Norris, Jeff Skoll, and Mohamed Mubarak Al Mazrouei. Using online resources and images, at least eight of the above appear to be white; however, I was not able to access and/or verify pictures of Jones, Blum, and Al Mazrouei.

[4] Additionally significant is the use of Aibileen's voice-over to position Leroy, a black male, solely at fault for Sugar's entry into the workforce without mention of Hilly's racist decision to fire Minny or the larger system of white supremacy that severely limits the income of black workers and their employment options.

[5] There are several examples of the purposeful choices that Stockett and Taylor make to avoid (i.e., whitewash) the realness of white supremacy and racism. Had Stockett or Taylor been invested in a racially progressive project, they could have deeply problematized the irony of white women entrusting their children to the same black women they degraded and humiliated from the perspectives of black maids rather than the safety of Skeeter's character. They also problematically relegated white men (e.g., Stuart, Robert Phelan [Skeeter's father], and William Holbrook [Hilly's husband]) to the peripheral of Southern racism which undermines the historical era the narrative attempts to speak to. Likewise, via several parallels between Aibileen and Minny and Minny and Celia, their characters seem to genuinely speak to sisterhood, but Stockett and Taylor instead forefront the "sisterhood" between Aibileen, Minny, and Skeeter. Their choice reeks of the profitability of "post-racialism" in that they cater to racially unconscious white women by fostering identification with Skeeter rather than the "colored" maids, "white trash" Celia (Taylor et al., 2011), or racist Hilly. Lastly, starkly absent is the sexual abuse that black maids endured in white households; representations of "the help" being threatened, beaten, and harassed; and discussions of what constitutes love between white children and their black female caretakers in a relationship always imbalanced by racialized power.

References

Alcoff, L. (1991). The problem of speaking for others. *Cultural Critique, 20*(20), 5–32. doi:10.2307/1354221

Anderson, L.M. (1997). *Mammies no more: The changing image of black women on stage and screen.* Lanham, MD: Rowman & Littlefield.

Association of Black Women Historians. (2007–2012). An open statement to fans of The Help. Retrieved from http://www.abwh.org/index.php?option=com_content&view=article&id=2%3Aopen-statement-the-help

Beauboeuf-Lafontant, T. (2009). *Behind the mask of the strong black woman: Voice and the embodiment of a costly performance.* Philadelphia, PA: Temple University Press.

Bell, D. (1980). Brown v. Board of Education and the interest convergence dilemma. *Harvard Law Review, 93,* 518–533. doi:10.2307/1340546

Bourdieu, P. (1997). The forms of capital. In N.W. Biggart (Ed.), *Readings in economic sociology* (pp. 280–291). Malden, MA: Blackwell.

Branch, E.B. (2011). *Opportunity denied: Limiting black women to devalued work.* New Brunswick, NJ: Rutgers University Press.

Brinson, S. (1995). The myth of white superiority in *Mississippi Burning*. *The Southern Communication Journal, 60,* 211–221. doi:10.1080/10417949509372980

Cammarota, J. (2011). Blindsided by the Avatar: White saviors and allies out of Hollywood and in education. *The Review of Education, Pedagogy, and Cultural Studies, 33,* 242–259.

CBS. (2012). *NAACP image awards: "The Help" wins big with three prizes.* Retrieved from http://www.cbsnews.com/8301-31749_162-57380561-10391698/naacp-image-awards-the-help-wins-big-with-three-prizes/

Chidester, P. (2012). "Respect My Authori-tah": South Park and the fragmentation/reification of whiteness. *Critical Studies in Media Communication, 29,* 403–420. doi:10.1080/15295036.2012.676192

Childress, A. (1986). *Like one of the family: Conversations from a domestic's life.* Boston, MA: Beacon Press.

Clark-Lewis, E., Nelson, S. (Producers), & Nelson, S. (Director). (1990). Freedom bags [Motion Picture]. New York: Filmakers Library.

Couric, K. (2011, August). Meet the woman behind the story we can't stop talking about. *Glamour,* pp. 132, 134.

Denby, D. (2011, August). Maids of honor: "The Help". *The New Yorker,* pp. 96–97.

DreamWorks Studios. (2010). The help. Retrieved from http://www.dreamworksstudios.com/films/the-help#production_notes

Essed, P. (1991). *Understanding everyday racism: An interdisciplinary tool.* Newbury Park, CA: Sage.

Giroux, H.A. (1997). Race, pedagogy, and whiteness in *Dangerous Minds*. *Cineaste, 22*(4), 46–49.

Giroux, H.A. (2000). Public pedagogy as cultural politics: Stuart Hall and the "crisis" of culture. *Cultural Studies, 14,* 341–360. doi:10.1080/095023800334913

Griffin, R.A. (2014). Pushing into *Precious*: Black women, media representation, and the glare of the white gaze. *Critical Studies in Media Communication, 31,* 182–197. doi:10.1080/15295036.2013.849354

Haggis, P. (Producer & Director). (2004). Crash [Motion Picture]. Santa Monica, CA: Bob Yari Productions-Dej Productions-Lions Gate Films.

Harris, C. (1995). Whiteness as property. In K. Crenshaw, N. Gotanda, G. Peller, & K. Thomas (Eds.), *Critical race theory: The key writings that formed the movement* (pp. 276–291). New York, NY: New York Press.

Holling, M.A. (2011). Patrolling national identity: Masking White supremacy. In M.G. Lacy & K.A. Ono (Eds.), *Critical rhetorics of race* (pp. 98–116). New York, NY: NYU Press.

hooks, b. (1989). *Talking back: Thinking feminist, thinking black.* Boston, MA: South End Press.

hooks, b. (1992). *Black looks: Race and representation.* Boston, MA: South End Press.

hooks, b. (2013). *Writing beyond race: Living theory and practice.* New York, NY: Routledge.

Kendall, F. (2013). *Understanding White privilege: Creating pathways to authentic relationships across race* (2nd ed.). New York, NY: Routledge.

Madison, K.J. (1999). Legitimation crisis and containment: The "anti-racist-white-hero"; film. *Critical Studies in Mass Communication, 16,* 399–416. doi:10.1080/15295039909367108

Marty, D. (1999). White antiracist rhetoric as apologia. In T.K. Nakayama & J.N. Martin (Eds.), *Whiteness: The communication of social identity* (pp. 51–68). Thousand Oaks, CA: Sage.

Moshin, J., & Jackson, R.L. (2011). Inscribing racial bodies and relieving responsibility: Examining racial politics in Crash. In M.G. Lacy & K.A. Ono (Eds.), *Critical rhetorics of race* (pp. 214–232). New York, NY: NYU Press.

Nakayama, T.K., & Krizek, R.L. (1995). Whiteness: A strategic rhetoric. *Quarterly Journal of Speech, 81*, 291–309. doi:10.1080/00335639509384117

Neely, B. (2000). *Blanche passes go.* New York, NY: Viking.

Netter, G. (Producer), Kosove, A.A. (Producer), Johnson, B. (Producer), & Hancock, J.L. (Director). (2010). The blind side [Motion Picture]. Burbank, CA: Warner Home Video.

Omolade, B. (1994). *The rising song of African American women.* New York, NY: Routledge.

Ono, K.A. (2010). Postracism: A theory of the "Post"- as political strategy. *Journal of Communication Inquiry, 34*, 227–233. doi:10.1177/0196859910371375

Pramaggiore, M., & Wallis, T. (2011). *Film: A critical introduction* (3rd ed.). London: Laurence King.

Projansky, S., & Ono, K.A. (1999). Strategic whiteness as cinematic racial politics. In T.K. Nakayama & J.N. Martin (Eds.), *Whiteness: The communication of social identity* (pp. 149–174). Thousand Oaks, CA: Sage.

Puig, C. (2011, August 10). "The Help": It's fine work all around. *USA Today.* Retrieved from http://web.ebscohost.com

Rossing, J.P. (2010). Critical intersections and comic possibilities: Extending racialized critical rhetorical scholarship. *Communication Law Review, 10*(1), 10–27.

Rossing, J.P. (2012). Deconstructing postracialism: Humor as a critical, cultural project. *Journal of Communication Inquiry, 36*(1), 44–61. doi:10.1177/0196859911430753

Saint-Aubin, A.F. (2002). A grammar of black masculinity: A body of science. *The Journal of Men's Studies, 10*, 247–270.

Sandlin, J.A. (2007). Popular culture, cultural resistance, and anti-consumption activism: An exploration of culture jamming as critical adult education. *New Directions for Adult and Continuing Adult Education, 115*, 73–82. doi:10.1002/ace.269

Sharpless, R. (2010). *Cooking in other women's kitchens: Domestic workers in the South, 1865–1960.* Chapel Hill, NC: University of North Carolina Press.

Simpson, D. (Producer), Bruckheimer, J. (Producer), & Smith, J.N. (Director). (1995). Dangerous minds [Motion Picture]. Burbank, CA: Hollywood Pictures Home Entertainment.

Squires, C., King Watts, E., Douglas Vavrus, M., Ono, K.A., Feyh, K., Calafell, B.M., & Brouwer, D.C. (2010). What Is This "Post-" in Postracial, Postfeminist ... (Fill in the Blank)? *Journal of Communication Inquiry, 34*, 210–253. doi:10.1177/0196859910371375

Stockett, K. (2009). The help. New York, NY: Berkley Books.

Tauber, M. (2011, August 22). Giving a voice to "The Help". *People Magazine.* Retrieved from http://web.ebscohost.com

Taylor, T. (Producer & Director), & Green, B. (Producer), Columbus, C. (Producer), & Barnathan, M. (Producer). (2011). The help [Motion Picture]. Burbank, CA: Touchstone Home Entertainment.

Teasley, M., & Ikard, D. (2010). Barack Obama and the politics of race: The myth of postracism in America. *Journal of Black Studies, 40*, 411–425. doi:10.1177/0021934709352991

Tierney, S.M. (2006). Themes of whiteness in *Bulletproof Monk, Kill Bill,* and *The Last Samurai. Journal of Communication, 56*, 607–624. doi:10.1111/j.1460-2466.2006.00303.x

Tucker, S. (1988). *Telling memories among southern women: Domestic workers and their employers in the segregated south.* New York, NY: Schocken Books.

Ware, B.L., & Linkugel, W.A. (1973). They spoke in defense of themselves: On the general criticism of apologia. *Quarterly Journal of Speech, 59*, 273–283.

Warren, J.T. (2009). Living within whiteness: A project aimed at undermining racism. In L.A. Samovar, R.E. Porter, & E.R. McDaniel (Eds.), *Intercultural communication: A reader* (12th ed., pp. 79–86). Belmont, CA: Thomson/Wadsworth.

Witherspoon, C. (2011). Director: People are too critical of "The Help". Retrieved from http://thegrio.com/2011/08/15/the-help-director-people-are-too-critical-of-this-film/

Zollo, F. (Producer), Colesberry, R.F. (Producer), & Parker, A. (Director). (1989). Mississippi burning [Motion Picture]. Santa Monica, CA: MGM Home Entertainment.

"My Family Isn't Racist—However...": Multiracial/Multicultural Obama-ism as an Ideological Barrier to Teaching Intercultural Communication

Yea-Wen Chen, Nathaniel Simmons & Dongjing Kang

We analyzed via critical discourse analysis undergraduate essays from multiple sections of an introductory intercultural communication course to interrogate underlying ideology/ies that influence intercultural communication education. "Multicultural/Multiracial Obama-ism (MMO)" is coined to expose the reconfiguration of multiracial/multicultural Americans as new signifiers of a "post-racial" utopia under the Obama presidency. The dominant ideology of MMO is constructed and reinforced through three central frames: (1) meritocracy: achieving the American dream through hard work; (2) individualism: identity as self-chosen, not born into; and (3) universalism: equality of opportunities despite privilege. We conclude with theoretical and teaching implications of MMO in a "post-racial" society.

Introduction

As globalizing forces facilitate intercultural interactions in unprecedented ways, the need for intercultural education is more critical than before (Sorrells, 2012). Yet the increasingly inequitable global contexts complicate this task. Some scholars have critiqued the field of intercultural communication as rooted in Western-centric, white, and colonial perspectives (Asante, 1987; Miike, 2003; Sorrells, 2012). Others have identified contestations of cultural identities and/or whiteness as key challenges to teaching intercultural communication (Chen, 2014a; DeVoss, Jasken, & Hayden, 2002; Hamlet, 2009; Martin & Davis, 2001; Nakayama & Martin, 2007). We situate this study in the intersection of cultural identities, whiteness, and intercultural communication pedagogy. Our effort addresses Hendrix and Wilson's (2014) critique that most communication scholars have persisted to ignore the classroom complexities stemming from negotiating multiple identities, and conclude a disturbing trend of assuming "a gender/raceless professor" in the classroom (p. 420).

At the time of the 2008 presidential campaign, sociologist Gallagher (2008) argued that we live in a racially "schizophrenic" time. Under the Obama administration, discourses of "post-racialism" signal new politics, narratives, and terrains of race relations that intensify contestations around race, identity, and whiteness (Kaplan, 2011; Logan, 2011; Orbe, 2011). Ono (2013) contends that, in the post-racial context, charges and critiques of racism are rendered "anachronistic, intrusive, or no longer relevant" (p. 315). Following Halualani (2011), we understand the post-racial era as "the period from the late 1990s to the present, during which the U.S. society invoked a neoliberal stance through which race, in all social and political matters, was to be avoided, shunned, and discarded" (p. 248). Specifically, we unpack in this study post-racial ideology/ies governing student discourses around cultural identities in a historically white institution in the Midwestern United States. Such focus has implications for advancing not just identity-based pedagogy, but also the "crisis in white identity" in a post-racial state (Logan, 2011, p. 6).

Questions of *identity* are of key concerns to intercultural communication teacher–scholars. For instance, several intercultural communication theories focus specifically on identity (e.g., Identity Management Theory, Identity Negotiation Theory, and a Communication Theory of Identity, see Gudykunst, 2005). Also, identity-based learning objectives are central to intercultural communication pedagogy (Driskill, Arjannikova, & Schneider, 2010). Yet, issues of identity and whiteness remain tricky for intercultural communication scholarship particularly in the post-racial era. Decentering whiteness—without inevitably re-centering it—is an ongoing challenge with/in intercultural communication classes (e.g., Carrillo Rowe & Malhotra, 2007; Nakayama & Martin, 2007; Warren, 2003). Martin and Davis (2001) urge intercultural communication scholars to focus on "race/ethnicity of white Americans" (p. 299). Currently, the prominence of post-racial discourses under the first black president in U.S. history calls for attention to growing racial anxieties and new racial politics (Logan, 2011). Hence, we build on existing studies by examining the ways in which post-racial ideology/ies enable and constrain student discourses of negotiating multiple identities in intercultural communication classes.

In what follows, we situate our study in relevant literature regarding identity, race, and intercultural communication, describe our methodological approach of critical discourse analysis, and present our interpretations of an emerging racial ideology under the first U.S. black president that we term "multicultural/multiracial Obama-ism (MMO)." Stemming from discourses of "post-racialism" and "colorblindness" that tout racial progress and render invisible racial inequalities, MMO signals new racial politics with a focus on *token celebrations* of miscegenation, multiculturalism, and racial diversifications as new markers of racial equality. As an indicator of this trend, *National Geographic* magazine dedicated its 125th anniversary issue to multiracial, or multiple-race, Americans and their supposedly beautiful faces arguing "race is no longer so black or white" (Funderburg, 2013).

Relevant Literature Review

We synthesize below key literature pertaining to identity, whiteness, intercultural communication pedagogy, and post-racialism, or post-racism. In this study, we use the terms "post-racialism" and "post-racism" synonymously to signify critiques of racism as irrelevant, outdated, and anachronistic.

Identity Challenges in Intercultural Communication Education

Teaching identity in intercultural communication courses can be particularly challenging for two reasons. First, the course content brings forth contestations of cultural identities within and between instructors and students (Chen, 2014a; Hamlet, 2009). Simpson, Causey, and Williams (2007) argue that cultural identities of instructors and students (such as race and gender) "are often intertwined with what occurs in the classroom" (p. 34). Second, the ongoing shifts (from functionalist perspectives to recent critical turns) in intercultural communication scholarship challenge the course's core objectives surrounding issues of identity (DeVoss et al., 2002; Martin, Nakayama, & Carbaugh, 2012). To what extent should critical issues such as racism, whiteness, and social justice be integral components of intercultural communication pedagogy? Though there is general agreement on the centrality of identity-based learning objectives in intercultural communication pedagogy (Driskill et al., 2010), pedagogical attentions, approaches, and emphases vary.

Identity challenges become especially relevant, salient, and critical in the context of teaching intercultural communication for social and racial justice. The field of (critical) intercultural communication is considered well positioned to "contribute to a world where equity and justice are the norm not the exception" (Sorrells, 2012, p. 383). For students, DeVoss et al. (2002) have named most white students' unawareness of their dominant, or privileged, group positions as the primary challenge in teaching intercultural communication. They explain "[U.S.] Americans tend to see intercultural situations through the lens of white, Protestant, middle-class, male values" (p. 76). Other challenges include: defining white identity as "cultureless," having no ties to European ancestries, cultures, or traditions (Perry, 2001, p. 58), and perceiving being white more as a cultural and economic liability than privilege (McKinney, 2008). For instructors, Perry (2008) points out a need to create safe spaces for students of color in predominately white classrooms where white teachers and students are often oblivious to how "ordinary" classroom interactions can become exclusionary and ostracizing experiences to students of color. Ultimately, both students and instructors need to increase awareness of their own and others' privileged and disadvantaged identity positions.

Whiteness and Intercultural Communication Pedagogy

Whiteness, or "the white problem" (Nakayama & Martin, 2007), is a critical issue in intercultural communication research and pedagogy. Although seldom explicitly investigated, scholars are paying increasing attention to incorporate whiteness theory and research into intercultural communication pedagogy (e.g., Cooks & Simpson, 2007; Fassett & Warren, 2007; Martin & Davis, 2001). Several scholars have offered pedagogical strategies for such examination (Endres & Gould, 2009; Martin & Davis, 2001; Nakayama & Martin, 2007). However, what is less discussed are ways in which such strategies enable instructors and students to have productive conversations about the difficult topic of race and whiteness. As an example, McPhail (2004) questions if dialogue is adequate in addressing the materiality realities of race and believes that "the symbolic resources of racial essentialism" limit our capacity to engage each other dialogically about race (p. 210). Teaching this subject within historically white institutions merits further inquiry particularly because most whites need to "continuously negotiate their recognition that race matters with their denial that race exists" (Bush, 2004, p. 98).

In essence, whiteness encompasses broadly (1) a socially constructed location and performance of structural/racial privilege; (2) a standpoint from which whites experience others, themselves, the world; and (3) a set of invisible, unnamed, and unmarked cultural practices (Frankenburg, 1993). Whiteness poses its own set of challenges for intercultural communication. On one hand, focusing on whiteness runs the epistemological risk of (re)centering whiteness as a normalizing position from which to engage intercultural communication (Nakayama & Martin, 2007); on the other hand, not attending to ways in which the race/ethnicity of whites is a sociopolitical construction risks leaving "a picture unfinished" (Martin & Davis, 2001, p. 299). To date, intercultural communication scholars have integrated whiteness and intercultural communication curriculum in several ways: (1) teaching about white privilege for anti-racism work; (2) investigating performances of whiteness with/in the classroom; (3) understanding the historical whitening of certain U.S. immigrant groups; (4) examining communication patterns of U.S. whites; and (5) analyzing representation of whiteness in popular culture (Cooks & Simpson, 2007; Endres & Gould, 2009; Martin & Davis, 2001). In particular, Warren's (2003) ethnographic investigation identifies four ways students performed whiteness inside and outside an intercultural communication class: (1) constructing sameness to erase difference; (2) constructing contradictions that challenged the privilege of whiteness while protecting it; (3) relying on stereotypes; and (4) constructing whiteness as victimhood. Building on this foundation, we identify ideology/ies embedded in students' discourses about their cultural identity positions in the hope of acquiring better pedagogical practices to promote racial justices in a post-racial era, especially within predominantly white institutions.

Communicating Post-Racial Ideology/ies

With the promise(s) of "change" in 2008, and "hope" in 2012, the election and reelection of Barack Obama have inspired many to marvel at the arrival of a "post-racial" America. Simultaneously, numerous scholars across disciplines have written about the particular challenges that the myth of a post-racial society poses for anti-racism work (e.g., Giroux, 2010; Haney-López, 2010; Logan, 2011). At its core, the term *post-racial* promotes assimilationist concepts of race that are steeped in rigid ideology, deny historical realities, and erase cultural identity and memory (Orbe, 2011; Stafford, 1996). It also suggests anxieties over histories of racism and fears about the rapid growth of racial others in the future both in terms of numbers and power (Stafford, 1996). Logan (2011) delineates the key features of the post-racial landscape in the twenty-first century including: persistent inequality, new immigrants of color, emergence of plural black identities, crisis in white identity, the global dimensions of racial anxieties, colorblind ideology, and new politics of race. Undeniably, the myth of post-racialism re-articulates, re-configures, and re-signifies "new normals" for understanding race relations today. Specifically, we agree with Haney-López (2010) that Obama's post-racialism operates as a *political* and *ideological* approach toward the continuing astringent of race, which supports our endeavor to unpack ideology/ies that structure understanding and acting in the "post-racial" America. In this study, we understand ideology as "the *basis of the social representations shared by members of a group*" (van Dijk, 1998, p. 8, emphasis in original). To van Dijk (1998), dominant ideologies are sets of beliefs adopted by the ruling class, elites, or the dominant groups to divide the non-dominant groups and maintain positions of dominance.

Communication is central in constructing racial categories and reproducing dominant ideologies that constitute a "post-racial" society. Following critical race tradition, we understand race as "an artificial construction of social identity based on an ideology of white supremacy, a belief in a racial hierarchy with white people at the top" (p. 90). Approaching post-racialism ideologically requires unpacking the underlying values, beliefs, and representations that (re)produce the racial dominance and oppression. Haney-López (2010) and Logan (2011) argue that maneuvering around race under the Obama administration must be assessed against the dominant racial ideology of colorblindness. Colorblindness renders irrelevant the difference in the lived experiences of whites and people of color and thus upholds white supremacy as normative. At the same time, Crenshaw (2011) criticizes a problematic tendency to "treat race and gender as mutually exclusive categories" and marginalize the intersection of race and sex (p. 25). Crenshaw urges those working against discrimination discourses to "embrace the complexities of compoundedness" (p. 40). Using Crenshaw's intersectional framework, Ferber (2012) argues that the ideology of colorblind racism overlaps and reinforces the ideologies of postfeminism and christonormativity, and this strand of discourses work together to reinforce and defend the culture of privilege. In our study, we are interested in such overlapping beliefs and/or ideologies that (re)produce white supremacy and related systems of oppressions.

Methods

Data Collection

This research took place in a historically white institution in the Midwestern United States. In Fall 2011, the racial composition of its student body was: 80.6% Caucasians, 7.4% internationals, 4.7% African Americans, 2.4% of Hispanics, 2.0% two or more races, and 1.0% of Asian Americans. After obtaining IRB approval, we conducted this study for one year (spring 2012 to spring 2013) across three freshmen-level intercultural communication courses. The majority of our students were 18–24-year-old, white, middle-class individuals, from major cities in a Midwestern state. Class size ranged from 30 to 76 students enrolled in each section. With student consent, we collected written assignments on cultural identities that students volunteered. We were aware of the tension involved in writing assignments as earning a grade rather than voicing truthful opinions (Simpson et al., 2007); however, we also believed that writing provided insights into how students thought about their identities and created an introspective space that could encourage self-reflexivity around challenging topics such as whiteness (Endres & Gould, 2009). As a team, we are a transnational Asian woman, a white gay American man, and a Chinese woman. We recognize that our unique subjectivities position each of us to see certain worldviews more readily than others, but all three of us are committed to social justice. Throughout this project, our similar and different identity positions enriched our analysis because they enabled us to consider perspectives that we might not have independently.

Entitled "Situating One's Cultural Identities," the assignment asked each student to describe and reflect upon three of their cultural identities that stood out within a particular context that was meaningful to their sense of self. After returning the graded assignments to students, we introduced the project, provided consent forms to each student, asked for their voluntary participation, and left the classroom. Interested students then placed their papers and consent forms on a table in the front of the room. We received 65 papers total across three sections. Among them, there were 34 females, 28 males, and 1 unidentified. Racially, 55 self-identified as White, 4 black/African American, 3 multiracial/mixed-race, 1 biracial, 1 Han Chinese, and 1 unidentified. Within these papers, students discussed their race/ethnicity ($n = 40$), gender/sexuality ($n = 31$), social class ($n = 26$), age and college student status ($n = 18$), nationality ($n = 16$), and religion/spirituality ($n = 15$) as being the most salient identities. Students spoke of their multiple and intersecting identities such as "a black woman; multi-racial, heterosexual male; or a middleclass, Caucasian woman."

Critical Discourse Analysis

Although defined and conceptualized differently across fields, discourse analysis always involves the study of particular segments of talk or text scholars use to make arguments (Tracy, 2005). For this study, we employed critical discourse analysis (CDA) to analyze ideology/ies embedded in our students' papers. Peck (1994) has argued that "it is within discourse that elements of an ideology are linked together and their relationship established" (p. 92). CDA has proven beneficial when studying culture, identity, and communication (Barker & Galasinski, 2001; Chen & Collier, 2012; van Dijk, Ting-Toomey, Smitherman, & Troutman, 1997). Rogers (2004) merged CDA and educational research, thus, revealing a growing need to ground CDA in examining issues of identity and culture in educational contexts. Throughout the different strands of CDA, discursive psychology has informed analyses of everyday talk as well as written texts about race and group relations (Augoustinoz & Every, 2007; van Dijk, 1993; Wetherell & Potter, 1992). We define *discourse* as language use in a context that constructs realities and narrates actions, identities, identity positioning, and ideologies (Wetherell & Potter, 1992).

Van Dijk's (1998) approach to CDA guided our analysis of student discourses and was useful in attending to the social construction of knowledge between and among members of different groups affiliated with different and multiple cultural identity positions (e.g., race, sex and gender, class, etc.). Much of van Dijk's work has focused on elite discourses, ethnic prejudices, and racism (van Dijk, 1984, 1993, 2008). Our approach built on Chen's (2014b) use of van Dijk's work to examine student discourses. van Dijk defines "a group" in terms of shared knowledge, objectives, problems, and social representations, and treats membership, activities, goals, values/norms, resources, positions and group relations as fundamental components that provide a comprehensive view of an ideology. Procedurally, we all read each paper to gain a holistic sense of our data. First, we recorded our preliminary impressions via a descriptive codebook in which we listed identities students claimed and noted general value statements. Second, we met multiple times to deliberate what identities students frequently discussed and what patterns of underlying beliefs we noticed throughout students' papers. We attended to frequent and repeated beliefs and interrogated dominant ideology/ies present across students' work. This process helped ensure our interpretations were guided by the participants' own words as we examined each dominant belief and/or ideology in its entirety. This helped us to see how students holistically discussed, and made sense of, beliefs and/or ideologies as they analyzed their cultural identities.

Analysis and Interpretations

In analyzing underlying ideology/ies governing student discourses about cultural identities, we identify a dominant ideology under the first black president that we term "MMO." Our analysis further identifies three central frames, or "set paths for interpreting information" (Bonilla-Silva, 2006, p. 26), for the dominant ideology, namely meritocracy, individualism, and universalism.

MMO

A number of students across the three sections evoked the belief in a "post-racial" America under Obama's presidency where racism is a thing of the past, and miscegenation and multicultural/multiracial heterogeneities are celebrated as new markers of racial equality. The term MMO captures this "post-racial" utopia and signifies new racial politics focusing on the successes of multiracial/multicultural Americans like Obama. Obama's mixed-race background hails multiracialism to the national stage and energizes beliefs that multiracialism can remake the U.S. racial order (Hochschild, Weaver, & Burch, 2012), but a new racial order "is not synonymous with progress" (p. 117). Obama in one instance self-described as a "mutt" (Fram, 2008, November), but later in his presidency he increasingly identified simply as black (Roberts & Baker, 2012). We argue that the ideology of MMO reflects complex racial terrains today in that it signifies a false optimism of racial equality by promoting token celebrations of the multicultural/multiracial experiences while masking racism.

In our context of a historically white university, both whites and some students of color shared racial optimism. A white student wrote, "To this day, Obama's race plays a factor in his political success. He has changed history and proven that Americans are more accepting and are developing more racial equality." A heterosexual, American woman echoed: "Within my birth cohort, we learned about these different equality movements that ended in success for the minority groups whether it be from school, the media, or stories from loved ones." Both white students evoked the idea of *racial equality*, which denies the reality of an unequal racial order. On the other hand, an African-American woman commented on *racial progress* that requires having overcome white supremacy. She stated: "White privilege is history's evidence that white supremacy and slavery *existed* in America" (emphasis added). For biracial and multiracial students, Obama helps to legitimize their identifications. One multiracial woman avowed: "I am African American, Irish, Blackfoot Indian, Cherokee, and some other stuff." Another biracial woman stated: "I am proud to call myself a biracial American, and I will always promote cultural differences positively." The ideology of MMO promotes false ideas of racial equality, and ignores the reality that most white Americans voted for the John McCain-Sarah Palin ticket and white supremacist hate groups surged before and after the 2008 election (Giroux, 2010).

Further, an upper/middle-class black woman even argued for a provocative idea of "*black privilege*" and remarked: "President Barack Obama awarded my identity group with an undeniable 'black privilege.' . . . His presidency grants us the ability to elect another black president and increase the presence of minority politicians." When understanding *privilege* to be systematically afforded, the term "black privilege" not only signals the end of white supremacy but also suggests a new racial order with blacks on top. Under the ideology of MMO, the socioeconomic advancement of some racial minorities is often mistaken as racial progress for all and falsely signifies racial equality (Hochschild et al., 2012). For example, this paradoxical idea of "black privilege" ignores the reality of what Alexander (2010) calls mass incarceration of black and brown young, males, and communities in the age of colorblindness.

Under MMO, though racism, white supremacy, and anti-miscegenation were largely invisible, they occasionally slipped through. One white, heterosexual student commented, "My family isn't racist—however they believe that leaders of America should be Caucasian." Comments like these suggest racial discomfort, if not fear, in dealing with the first black president. Anti-miscegenation sentiment also helps to maintain the unequal racial status quo. One biracial woman described challenges to her mixed-race background on her first day of first grade: "'Are you black?' I have always calmingly answered: 'No, I'm both black and white. I am mixed.'" Further, the persistence of racism is underscored in the following remarks about how to get rid of it from a multiracial, heterosexual male:

> Morgan Freeman said it best in a video excerpt from an episode of 60 Minutes when he was asked: "How do we get rid of racism?" Freeman's response was, "Quit talking about it." . . . I feel that this response is accurate. If people were to stop acknowledging racism and instead accept everyone for who they are as people, racism would not exist.

Besides acknowledging the reality of racism, this excerpt also evoked the authority of a black male figure like Morgan Freeman as "the savior" who shall put an end to racism as Obama was expected to do. The ideology of MMO, on the surface, attempts to promote racial progress; however, in practice, the attempts are framed through meritocracy, individualism, and universalism to mask realities of racial regression.

Meritocracy

MMO relies on and reifies the myth of meritocracy that assumes an American society with level playing fields across race and related identities, in which sheer hard work is the key to living the American dream. Under MMO, the successes of multiracial/multicultural Americans like Barack Obama and Tiger Woods reinforce the myth of meritocracy. Clark (2003) argues that the American dream is about becoming middle class and "the American dream remains a pervasive idea" because Americans want to believe that anything is possible with hard work (p. 26). Meritocracy is encapsulated in the following comments from a working-class white student: "Working hard is how you become successful in life. My parents showed me that hard work pays off." In the post-racial context, the success stories of the most racially disadvantaged such as Bill Cosby, Oprah Winfrey, and Barack Obama are so iconic and seductive that they reinforce the link between hard work and success despite systematic inequalities. A self-identified Appalachian female student quoted Oprah and commented:

> Oprah Winfrey said "where there is no struggle, there is no strength." I am a strong, hardworking, low income, [and] educated Appalachian woman. With all the struggles I have had to face, I am lucky to have a strong support system and to be able to get an education to better my future.

Oprah's words reinforced this student's belief that hard work would lead to a better future. Despite Oprah's liberal persona, Peck (1994), analyzing episodes of her 1992 show on racism, found that Oprah's particular framing was "deeply embedded in Western history" and limited understanding of the politics of race. An African-American woman wrote: "All African Americans and woman heard people telling them they could not do something . . . If they were to listen to them, Barack Obama would not have become the first black president." Here, Obama becomes a new symbolism of overcoming extreme obstacles to achieve success.

Across the student discourses, the myth of meritocracy was applied not just to race but also to gender, class, and other identity groups. The statement below from a self-identified multiracial male illustrates this:

> Like Obama's mother, my mother is a college-educated woman with strong morals and high standards for herself and her children. She worked hard to get our family to where it is today and never let her gender get in her way. I was taught to be a caring and polite man that respected women as equals.

Discourses from our students suggest the applicability of meritocracy to the interrelationships across identity positions. Ono (2010) suggests, interdiscursively, the myth of meritocracy, American exceptionalism, and post-racialism rely, reinforce, and reproduce one another. Ono argues that post-racialism simultaneously reduces the reality of racism and relies on and reproduces the mythology of American exceptionalism under capitalism that characterizes bootstrap, working hard, and not asking for help.

Individualism

Individualism, quintessentially self-made/self-willed, serves as another central frame that constructs MMO. The frame of individualism refers to the belief that an individual's cultural identity is more about choice rather than birth, lineage, or heritage. That is, individualism celebrates individual agency and uniqueness and ignores larger structural forces that constrain agency for some. Kleinman and Copp (2009) argue that students' individualistic beliefs enable them—both students in privileged and disadvantaged positions—to deny the realities of inequalities. In our study, a Caucasian woman wrote:

> I embrace all these traditions and have avowed the "Southern belle" identity to myself . . . At times this chosen identity makes me out of place because I live in a Midwestern State and those qualities are not typical. However, I have learned to embrace the relational identity of South despite my location.

This quote illustrates that individualism is about the degree of freedom to identify oneself freely based on individual pride, comfort, and choice. Discourses from several students of biracial or multiracial backgrounds affirm that. One multicultural woman with "long dark hair and olive skin tone" shared her positive attitude toward people's questioning of her nationality:

> I actually love being asked about my nationality and hearing the varied assumptions of what I might be . . . you can imagine the surprise when I reply, "Good guesses, but I am Jewish and my family came from Russia, Romania, Spain, and the Cherokee Indians of North America." I am the true definition of a "melting pot."

Similarly, a multiracial male considered his mixed backgrounds advantageous and stated: "I take pride in the fact that I have so many different ethnicities or races in my blood, and I feel that this makes me more able to associate and relate with so many different cultures." Both quotes reflect the ideal of multiculturalism, a practice that makes everyone unique but equal.

At times, individual agency is linked to group-based privilege, which functions as resistance to be defined by group memberships. One white student, who lived with international students, explained the refusal to be ascribed by others:

> In conclusion, it is clear that I refuse to be defined by any group or identity that I was born into. To define any person by something that they have no control over is stupid and just outright unfair . . . I believe that cultural identity is not shaped by appearance or group membership. Instead, it is shaped by your experiences and actions.

This explicit resistance and resentment of being defined by group membership safeguarded the belief of identity as primarily self-chosen. Similarly, a working-class student emphasized the freedom to express and choose "not to fit into" any group categories; he said:

> When you express your true colors you figure out who you are in life. I've never been the one to follow others to try to fit in. In any discussion I always express my views about the subject because I want my voice to be heard.

In other instances, discourses of individualism, particularly from white students, reinterpret "difference" narrowly as individual personalities, traits, or experiences. One white male student wrote: "Being a white, male, heterosexual, is in no way unique, what makes people unique are their personalities." Such comment exemplifies masking white privilege on the basis of individuality. The term "personality" as the representation of the "variance" in personal traits presumes a race-less world.

Further, discourses of individualism override social norms that give rise to systematic inequalities. The following excerpt from a white heterosexual student illustrates downplaying social norms: "After taking this course I'm starting to believe that word normal should be in quotations because with each person being so different from their neighbor, the word can't possibly consider ONE type of normal." Moreover, discourses in this study echo Kim's (2007) idea of cultural identity transformation. Kim understands identity as more individualized and less bounded by group categories in the increasingly multiculturalizing world. Some students emphasized their expectation of cultural fusions. An upper-middle class, white female explicitly expressed a rejection of group identities: "I am a citizen of the world. I reject much of my own culture and incorporate the aspects of other cultures." The assumption of a "culture-/race-less" person reinforces colorblindness. Also, the act of being able to "incorporate" other cultures implies agency, access, and privilege, and conjures up the colonial practice of cultural appropriation.

Under MMO, Obama's presidency is redefining the multiracial experiences in the United States. At the same time, Obama's hesitation to talk about the topic of race, especially during his first term, promotes individualism especially for minorities who idolize him. As an example, one African-American female wrote:

> I have always been able to relate to the "majority," because I pay no attention to skin color, I look at the big picture. I was never aware of how important my "blackness" was until Barack Obama became the first black president and we were all unanimously accepted into his fan club.

The excerpt exemplifies identity shifts and positive valence of "blackness" under the Obama's presidency. Individualism and MMO intersect and reinforce a romanticized notion of individual uniqueness that promote colorblindness, ignore historical pasts, and reject current inequalities.

Universalism

Students across sections demonstrate a belief in universal equality of the human experience, which ignores histories, erases difference, and privileges sameness. Warren (2003) found that both white and non-white students performed sameness between races, which kept the whiteness system pure, intact, and unchallenged. In this study, universalism refers to the belief that, despite inequalities, all humans are created equally, and such liberty and equality should be celebrated. As an example, one heterosexual woman said: "I was raised to believe that no matter how different from someone I may be, we're all human." Another white, Christian, heterosexual, male echoed: "The country will continue to grow and unite as a whole as the government makes the changes necessary to make race completely irrelevant." Universalism serves as an additional pillar for MMO as it supports the "post-racial" utopia that we are all the same and, thus, equal. Obama emerges as a token of universal equality. Love and Tosolt (2010) argue that "Obama's own rhetoric has blinded Americans to the realities of continuing racial inequities" (p. 33). Much of Obama's campaign messaging, such as "Yes, we can," features a fake "we" couched in individualism.

Rather than constructing difference to understand individual variance, universalism, in this study, constructs equality to understand similarities. For instance, in reflecting upon a conversation with a "native man" in a grocery store, a Caucasian, male atheist said: "Everyone has their own struggles and everyone deals with them in their own way." Similarly, a middle-class, white female claimed that "the world's inhabitants are unique individuals" and that: "every person has their own personal experiences to shape who they are." As supported by MMO, such statements are representative of the belief that despite having unique personal experiences, the equality of the human experience as a universal phenomenon. These statements imply that this shared experience creates commonality among humans and, therefore equality and solidarity. Our analysis highlights ways in which white and non-white students claim universalism to re-center and/or maintain the system of whiteness in the post-racial time. By claiming a lack of or no culture, Perry (2001) asserts that whites claim (intentionally or not) their racial, "normative" superiority. Both whites and students of color in our study within a historically white university supported universalism. For example, a Han-Chinese, middle-class male said: "I firmly believe that all humans are equal whatever their gender is." A multiracial male said,

> Women are often viewed as struggling in areas of school such as math and science, whereas men often struggle in English or literature classes, as well as art classes. This is frustrating to me, because I feel that men and women are equally capable of succeeding in any courses offered in school.

Such statements celebrated the diversity of human expressions while maintaining the status quo.

Universalism accomplished two primary strategies throughout our data. First, by ignoring history and claiming sameness, this belief reveals disorientation around notions of privilege/disadvantage against beliefs in universality, liberty, and equality. For instance, one white student asked: "Why do we need to have cultural identities?" That is, he meant: "Why do we need to differentiate ourselves from other cultures? Wouldn't things be much easier if things like cultures and beliefs were not so conditioned to make people believe that they are different from others?" He stated individuals should know who they are and what they believe in, but at the same time argued: "I do not personally think that it should be so stressed that people from other cultures are different than you." Within this excerpt, the student rhetorically both recognize and deny differences. This student claimed an individual should know their own culture and yet individuals should avoid making any difference known. Related, a white, straight, middle-class, man wrote that he didn't see any male-based advantages in today's society, but that "... in the past our society was a predominately male based social order that if you wanted to make any sort of impact in our world you had to be male." He further stated, "Luckily, this isn't the case today as there are plenty of powerful women holding strong decision making roles in the world; Angela Merkel, Michelle Obama, Madeleine Albright, Hillary Clinton, and Nancy Pelosi." Paralleling the rhetorical strategy using Obama to deny racial inequality, this student relied on anecdotal evidence of a few successful women (of color) to deny hegemonic masculinity at play and gender inequality in existence.

Second, throughout examples implicating this central belief, several rhetorical moves of deflecting and denying resistance were revealed. Perumal (2008) argues that student resistance assumes various guises (i.e., discounting, denying, distancing, dismay) when students' ideological framework(s) are called into question. For instance, a white, middle-class female wrote: "White people are just as much stereotyped as anyone else. I feel as if being a blonde it automatically puts in the bubble as a dumb blonde, *this is no different from stereotyping the Muslim culture*" (emphasis added). This excerpt claims an equal footing of discrimination and prejudice for all. In other words, this student claimed that we are all equal and endure hardships in the United States. However, at the same time this instance features a deflecting move in which students compared cultures in order to detract from reality. Similarly, one Caucasian, female wrote teaching intercultural communication concepts such as "white privilege" actually perpetuates inequalities. She said: "If concepts were not voiced that show that there is an obvious division between those who are white and those who are either African American or Hispanic then the division would not be as noticed." This showcases an example in which a student acknowledges inequality, but at the same time denies the importance of communicating and teaching/learning about such inequalities. Such an argument evidences that universalism is achieved if inequalities are ignored and unspoken. Another Polish-American student said white privilege frustrated him and that he wanted "everyone to simply be treated as equals, as fellow members of the human race." These students both deny the reality of modern-day inequalities and at the same time deflect the weight of their statements by offering a gross oversimplification of white privilege. Such a move served to prop up the MMO ideology by reinforcing a universal platform in which all humans dwell.

Conclusions and Implications

This research is motivated by the centrality and contestations of cultural identities and whiteness for intercultural communication pedagogy (DeVoss et al., 2002; Martin & Davis, 2001; Perry, 2008; Warren, 2003). Against the racial schizophrenias under the Obama administration, we examine post-racial ideology/ies governing student discourses about their cultural identities in a historically white institution in the Midwestern United States. Our analysis reveals a dominant ideology about new race relations in the post-racial era that we term "MMO," which celebrates miscegenation and embraces successes of multiracial/multicultural Americans as new markers of racial equality. MMO is organized by three central frames (i.e., meritocracy, individualism, and universalism) and reinforces beliefs in hard work, individual uniqueness, and racial irrelevance. Ultimately, MMO constructs a false consciousness of racial equality vis-à-vis the tokenized stories of successful (multi)racial minorities like Obama.

Theoretical Implications for "Post-Racialism"

The MMO ideology signals new race politics, represents a re-articulation of racial ideology/ies, and identifies different paths for interpreting race-based information under the Obama presidency (Haney-López, 2010; Kaplan, 2011; Ono, 2010). It is a new manifestation of the colorblind ideology under the Obama administration, arguing that anti-miscegenation is over and thus racism is over. On the surface, the idea of the United States becoming more and more racially and culturally heterogeneous seems to open up new spaces for remaking the current racial order (Hochschild et al., 2012). Like Oprah Winfrey in Peck's (1994) research, Obama becomes a powerful rhetorical vehicle for reframing race relations with particular focus on tokenized multicultural/multiracial Americans. Yet, the premature discourses of racial equality are polarizing and deceiving rather than bringing the American peoples together. As evidenced in the central frames of MMO, myths of hard work, individuality, and abstract equality for all interweave to mask the reproduction of the unequal racial status quo. Bonilla-Silva (2006) argues that "the central component of any dominant racial ideology is its frames" (p. 26). The frames of meritocracy, individualism, and universality affirm the American dream, mask anti-miscegenation discourses, and render incoherent any instances of racial inequalities by attributing sole responsibilities to the individual (a.k.a. "blaming the victim") (Bush, 2004; Kaplan, 2011; McPhail, 2004; Simpson, 2008).

Situated in a historically white university, both white majority and middle-class students of color in our study buy into the American dream that everyone who works hard could achieve middle class (Clark, 2003). By maintaining his silence about racism except four instances (i.e., the Clippers owner scandal, the shooting of Michael Brown, Trayvon Martin ruling, and the arrest of Henry Louis Gates), Barack Obama emerges as a paradoxical signifier that eases racial anxieties via calling racialized subjects to work harder, take responsibilities for their individual oppressions, and assimilate to the universal standards of humanity. Specifically, MMO touts the multiracial/multicultural experiences in the United States while keeping the racist system intact.

Further, our findings extend research on post-racism and whiteness to the instructional context. First, our findings evidence, within the intercultural communication classroom, Ono's (2010) observation that the main function of post-racial discourses is to deny the realities of racism. The MMO circulates higher education, reinforces post-racial and colorblind media discourses, and makes it difficult to discuss racial inequalities. Second, our findings affirm the importance of examining everyday discourses of race and whiteness among average whites as well as middle-class people of color by attending to multiple cultural identities (McKinney, 2008; Peck, 1994; Perry, 2001). Specifically, our analysis demonstrates the utility of understanding the ways in which students experience themselves to better teach for social and racial justices.

Overall, this study extends identity-based intercultural communication pedagogy in three ways. First, this study underscores the need to (re)think identity issues within intercultural communication pedagogy within the post-racial era. One starting point is to answer the question: *How might we make our pedagogy around cultural identities urgent and consequential for today's students?* Second, our findings suggest that unpacking MMO and its central frames can open up learning spaces for both instructors and students to better understand their multiple identities. Also, unpacking ideological barriers redirects necessary attention to how identities are interrelated through discourses and enacted through communication (Chen & Collier, 2012; Tracy, 2005; van Dijk, 2008). Third, from a dialogical standpoint, this study highlights the particular challenges of organizing meaningful dialogues about race in a post-racial era (Bush, 2004; Kaplan, 2011; McPhail, 2004; Simpson, 2008).

Implications for Teaching in a "Post-Racial" Era

Teaching is a complex and ambiguous activity (Perumal, 2008). In particular, teaching intercultural communication to address injustices is both critical and challenging. Finke (1993) reminds us that, "teaching is a practice which, proceeds not progressively through time, but through resistance, regressions, leaps, breakthroughs, discontinuities, and deferred action" (p. 26). Viewing MMO and its central frames as barriers for teaching cultural identities, we propose two strategies. First, confront the invisible dominant ideology/ies through discussions, activities, and reflections with students while raising awareness about unequal identity positions. We suggest taking a bottom-up approach to first expose and then address the central frames of meritocracy, individualism, and universalism. In the process, we maintain that it is critical to attend to how multiple identities of the instructors and students become intertwined and interact in powerful ways (Chen, 2014a; Simpson et al., 2007). As an example, Chen (2014a) concludes that (non-European) international faculty often need to negotiate racialized identity positions and address racial prejudices. In our experience, our students have responded to questions about race from each of us differently. As a white man, the second author has encountered "you know?" as a plea for racial solidarity; in contrast, the first and third authors, as immigrant others, have to learn to confront "utter silence."

Several pedagogical tools can assist in unpacking dominant ideology/ies and multiple identities: (1) Freire's (1996) critical pedagogy of problem-posing that creates spaces for dialoguing and learning from others to problem-solve a construct like MMO, and (2) classroom activities about privileged/disadvantaged identity positions and group relations such as the six-word (cultural identity) memoir (Simmons & Chen, 2014) that encourages students to critically construct a six-word narrative of at least one of their cultural identities. Used in this way, six-word memoirs encourage personal awareness of one's cultural identities and ideological beliefs. Other activities such as simulation games have proven effective in intercultural communication courses (Duerringer, 2013; Griffin & Jackson, 2011; Peeples, Hall, & Seiter, 2012). Such simulations may restructure classroom moments to render visible the central frames of MMO. Once visible, opportunities for dialogue exist.

Second, engage students in (re)thinking about how the interwoven ideological frames function in structuring and naturalizing classroom discussion, learning climate, and perceptions of both the self and others. Take advantage of student resistance as teachable moments. Ropers-Huilman (1997) argued that we should accept student resistance as an essential part of learning. Similarly, Davis (1992) contended that "some resistance is healthy; it suggests students are struggling with the issues, taking them seriously enough to be upset by them" (p. 233). At the same time, Perumal (2008) maintained that "our jobs as teachers should include active resistance to students' active resistance" (p. 222). Such resistance may take various forms such as discounting, denying, distancing, and expressing dismay (Perumal, 2008). It is important to remember that lessons may not be learned until long after our students have left our classrooms. Additionally, to increase our pedagogical strength, we must all deepen our personal knowledge and understandings of race (relations) in the United States, as well as openly share one's lived experiences and commitment to racial justice with students.

While students' written assignments are useful artifacts for unpacking ideology/ies that circulate intercultural communication courses, they are also limited because of concerns that students might write purposefully for grades. However, since ideologies predominantly function at an unconscious level (Foss, 2004), we maintain that student discourses are appropriate and useful for understanding dominant post-racial ideology/ies and central frames. We urge future research to continue this line of inquiry and suggest incorporating teaching reflections and interviews, or focus group discussions, with students. We also urge future research to attend to the changing landscape of the multiracial/multicultural America.

References

Alexander, M. (2010). *The new Jim Crow: Mass incarceration in the age of colorblindness*. New York, NY: The New Press.
Asante, M.K. (1987). *The Afrocentric idea*. Philadelphia, PA: Temple University.
Augoustinoz, M., & Every, D. (2007). Contemporary racist discourse: Taboos against racism and racist accusations. In A. Weatherall, B.M. Watson, & C. Gallois (Eds.), *Language, discourse and social psychology* (pp. 233–254). New York, NY: Palgrave Macmillan.
Barker, C., & Galasinski, D. (2001). *Cultural studies and discourse analysis: A dialogue on language and identity*. London, UK: Sage.
Bonilla-Silva, E. (2006). *Racism without racists: Color-blind racism and the persistence of racial inequality in the United States* (2nd ed.). Lanham, MD: Rowman & Littlefield.
Bush, M.E.L. (2004). *Breaking the code of good intentions: Everyday forms of whiteness*. Lanham, MD: Rowman & Littlefield.
Carrillo Rowe, A., & Malhotra, S. (2007). (Un)hinging whiteness. In L.M. Cooks & J.S. Simpson (Eds.), *Whiteness, pedagogy, performance: Dis/placing race* (pp. 271–298). Lanham, MD: Lexington Books.
Chen, Y.-W. (2014a). "Are you an immigrant?": Identity-based critical reflections of teaching intercultural communication. *New Directions for Teaching and Learning*, 2014(138), 5–16. doi:10.1002/tl.20092
Chen, Y.-W. (2014b). Pan-Asian organizing for empowerment? Unpacking nonprofit discourses across organizational status positions. *Howard Journal of Communications*, 25, 350–371. doi:10.1080/10646175.2014.924451
Chen, Y.-W., & Collier, M. J. (2012). Intercultural identity positioning: Interview discourses from two identity-based nonprofit organizations. *Journal of International and Intercultural Communication*, 5(1), 43–63. doi:10.1080/17513057.2011.631215
Clark, W.A.V. (2003). *Immigrants and the American dream: Remaking the middle class*. New York, NY and London, UK: The Guilford Press.
Cooks, L.M., & Simpson, J.S. (Eds.). (2007). *Whiteness, pedagogy, performance: Dis/placing race*. Lanham, MD: Lexington Books.
Crenshaw, K.W. (2011). Demarginalizing the itnersection of race and sex: A Black feminist critique of anti-discrimination doctrine, feminist theory, and anti-racist politics. In H. Lutz, M. T. H. Viva, & L. Supik (Eds.), *Framing intersectionailty: Debates on a multi-facted concept in gender studies* (pp. 25–42). Burlington, VT: Ashgate.
Davis, N.J. (1992). Teaching about inequality: Student resistance, paralysis, and rage. *Teaching Sociology*, 20, 232–238. doi:10.2307/1319065
DeVoss, D., Jasken, J., & Hayden, D. (2002). Teaching intracultural and intercultural communication: A critique and suggested method. *Journal of Business and Technical Communication*, 16 (1), 69–94. doi:10.1177/1050651902016001003

Driskill, G.W., Arjannikova, S., & Schneider, T. (2010). Assessing intercultural communication: Models and methods. In P. Backlund & G. Wakefield (Eds.), *A communication assessment primer* (pp. 127–143). Washington, DC: National Communication Association.

Duerringer, C.M. (2013). "They'd better hope for a lot of free parking": Using monopoly to teach about classical liberalism, marginalization, and restorative justice. *Communication Teacher, 27*(1), 11–15. doi:10.1080/17404622.2012.730619

Endres, D., & Gould, M. (2009). "I am also in the position to use my whiteness to help them out": The communication of whiteness in service learning. *Western Journal of Communication, 73*, 418–436. doi:10.1080/10570310903279083

Fassett, D.L., & Warren, J.T. (2007). *Critical communication pedagogy*. Thousand Oaks, CA: Sage.

Ferber, A.L. (2012). The culture of privilege: Color-blindness, postfeminism, and christonormativity. *Journal of Social Issues, 68*(1), 63–77. doi:10.1111/j.1540-4560.2011.01736.x

Finke, L. (1993). Knowledge as bait: Feminism, voice, and the pedagogical unconscious. *College English, 55*, 7–27.

Foss, S.K. (2004). *Rhetorical criticism: Exploration & practice* (3rd ed.). Long Grove, IL: Waveland Press.

Fram, A. (2008, November). 'Mutts like me' shows Obama's racial comfort. Retrieved from http://www.nbcnews.com/id/27606637/ns/politics-decision_08/t/mutts-me-shows-obamas-racial-comfort/#.U8rMU7HCctc

Frankenburg, R. (1993). *White women, race matters: The social construction of whiteness*. Minneapolis, MN: University of Minnesota Press.

Freire, P. (1996). *Pedagogy of the oppressed* (M.B. Ramos, Trans. 20th anniversary ed.). New York, NY: Continuum.

Funderburg, L. (2013). *The changing face of America*. Retrieved October, 2013, from http://ngm.nationalgeographic.com/2013/10/changing-faces/funderburg-text

Gallagher, C.A. (2008). Introduction. In C.A. Gallagher (Ed.), *Racism in post-race America: New theories, new directions* (pp. ix–xv). Conover, NC: Social Forces.

Giroux, H.A. (2010). *Politics after hope: Barack Obama and the crisis of youth, race, and democracy*. Boulder, CO: Paradigm Publishers.

Griffin, R.A., & Jackson, N.R. (2011). Privilege monopoly: An opportunity to engage in diversity awareness. *Communication Teacher, 25*(1), 1–6. doi:10.1080/17404622.2010.514273

Gudykunst, W.B. (Ed.). (2005). *Theorizing about intercultural communication*. Thousand Oaks, CA: Sage.

Halualani, R.T. (2011). Abstracting and de-radicalizing diversity: The articulation of diversity in the post-race era. In M. Lacy & K.A. Ono (Eds.), *Critical rhetorics of race* (pp. 247–264). New York, NY: New York University Press.

Hamlet, J.D. (2009). Engaging spirituality and an authentic self in the intercultural communication class. *New Directions for Teaching and Learning, 2009*(120), 25–33. doi:10.1002/tl.374

Haney-López, I.F. (2010). Is the "post" in post-racial the "blind" in colorblind. *Cardozo Law Review, 32*, 807–831.

Hendrix, K.G., & Wilson, C. (2014). Virtual invisibility: Race and communication education. *Communication Education, 63*, 405–428. doi:10.1080/03634523.2014.934852

Hochschild, J., Weaver, V., & Burch, T. (2012). *Creating a new racial order: How immigration, multiracialism, genomics, and the young can remake race in America*. Princeton, NJ and Oxford: Princeton University Press.

Kaplan, H.R. (2011). *The myth of post-racial America: Searching for equality in the age of materialism*. Lanham, MD: Rowman & Littlefield Education.

Kim, Y.Y. (2007). Ideology, identity, and intercultural communication: An analysis of differing academic conceptions of cultural identity. *Journal of Intercultural Communication Research, 36*(3), 237–253. doi:10.1080/17475750701737181

Kleinman, S., & Copp, M. (2009). Denying social harm: Students' resistance to lessons about inequality. *Teaching Sociology, 37*, 283–293. doi:10.1177/0092055X0903700306

Logan, E. (2011). *"At this defining movement": Barack Obama's presidential candidacy and the new politics of race*. New York, NY: New York University Press.

Love, B.L., & Tosolt, B. (2010). Reality or rhetoric? Barack Obama and post-racial America. *Race, Gender & Class, 17*(3–4), 19–37.

Martin, J.N., & Davis, O.I. (2001). Conceptual foundations for teaching about whiteness in intercultural communication courses. *Communication Education, 50*, 298–313. doi:10.1080/03634520109379257

Martin, J.N., Nakayama, T.K., & Carbaugh, D. (2012). The history and development of the study of intercultural communication and applied linguistics. In J. Jackson (Ed.), *The Routledge handbook of language and intercultural communication* (pp. 17–36). New York, NY: Routledge.

McKinney, K.D. (2008). Confronting young people's perceptions of whiteness: Privilege or liability? *Sociology Compass, 2*, 1303–1330. doi:10.1111/j.1751-9020.2008.00126.x

McPhail, M.L. (2004). Race and the (im)possibility of dialogue. In R. Anderson, L.A. Baxter, & K.N. Cissna (Eds.), *Dialogue: Theorizing difference in communication studies* (pp. 209–224). Thousand Oaks, CA: Sage.

Miike, Y. (2003). Toward an alternative metatheory of human communication: An Asiacentric vision. *Intercultural Communication Studies, 12*(4), 39–64.

Nakayama, T.K., & Martin, J.N. (2007). The "white problem" in intercultural communication research and pedagogy. In L.M. Cooks & J.S. Simpson (Eds.), *Whiteness, pedagogy, performance: Dis/placing race* (pp. 111–137). Lanham, MD: Lexington Books.

Ono, K.A. (2010). Postracism: A theory of the "post-" as political strategy. *Journal of Communication Inquiry, 34*, 227–233. doi:10.1177/0196859910371375

Ono, K.A. (2013). Mad men's postracial figuration of a racial past. In M.E.L. Goodlad, L. Kaqanovsky, & A.R. Rushing (Eds.), *Madmen, madworld: Sex, politics, style and the 1960s* (pp. 300–319). Durham, NC: Duke University Press.

Orbe, M.P. (2011). *Communication realities in a "post-racial" society: What the U.S. public really thinks about Barack Obama*. Lanham, MD: Lexington Books.

Peck, J. (1994). Talk about racism: Framing a popular discourse of race on Oprah Winfrey. *Cultural Critique, 27*, 889–126.

Peeples, J., Hall, B.J., & Seiter, J.S. (2012). The flipper debate: Teaching intercultural communication through simulated conflict. *Communication Teacher, 26*(2), 87–91. doi:10.1080/17404622.2011.643806

Perry, P. (2001). White means never having to say you're Ethnic: White youth and the construction of "cultureless" identities. *Journal of Contemporary Ethnography, 30*(1), 56–91. doi:10.1177/089124101030001002

Perry, P. (2008). Creating safe spaces in predominately white classrooms. In M. Pollock (Ed.), *Everyday antiracism: Getting real about race in school* (pp. 226–229). New York, NY: The New Press.

Perumal, J. (2008). Student resistance to and teacher normalization of radical ideologies. *International Journal of Learning, 15*(1), 211–224.

Roberts, S., & Baker, P. (2012, April). *Asked to declare his race Obama checks 'black'*. Retrieved from http://www.nytimes.com/2010/04/03/us/politics/03census.html?_r=0

Rogers, R. (Ed.). (2004). *An introduction to critical discourse analysis in education*. Mahwah, NJ: Lawrence Erlbaum Associates.

Ropers-Huilman, B. (1997). Constructing feminist teachers: Complexities of identity. *Gender and Education, 9*, 327–343. doi:10.1080/09540259721295

Simmons, N., & Chen, Y.-W. (2014). Using six-word memoirs to increase cultural identity awareness. *Communication Teacher, 28*(1), 20–25. doi:10.1080/17404622.2013.839050

Simpson, J.L. (2008). The color-blind double bind: Whiteness and the (im)possibility of dialogue. *Communication Theory, 18*(1), 139–159. doi:10.1111/j.1468-2885.2007.00317.x

Simpson, J.S., Causey, A., & Williams, L. (2007). "I Would Want You to Understand It:" Students' perspectives on addressing race in the classroom. *Journal of Intercultural Communication Research, 36*(1), 33–50. doi:10.1080/17475750701265274

Sorrells, K. (2012). Intercultural training in the global context. In J. Jackson (Ed.), *The Routledge handbook of language and intercultural communication* (pp. 372–389). London, UK: Routledge.

Stafford, W.W. (1996). If we live in a "post" era, is there a post-racism? In B.P. Bowser & R.G. Hunt (Eds.), *Impacts of racism on white Americans* (2nd ed., pp. 113–138). Thousand Oaks, CA: Sage.

Tracy, K. (2005). Reconstructing communicative practices: Action-implicative discourse analysis. In K. Fitch & R. Sanders (Eds.), *Handbook of language and social interaction* (pp. 301–319). Mahwah, NJ: Lawrence Erlbaum.

van Dijk, T.A. (1984). *Prejudice in discourse: An analysis of ethnic prejudice in cognition and conversation.* Admsterdam: John Benjamins Publishing Company.
van Dijk, T.A. (1993). *Elite discourse and racism.* Newbury Park: Sage.
van Dijk, T.A. (1998). *Ideology: A multidisciplinary approach.* London, UK: Sage.
van Dijk, T.A. (2008). *Discourse and power.* New York, NY: Palgrave Macmillan.
van Dijk, T.A., Ting-Toomey, S., Smitherman, G., & Troutman, D. (1997). Discourse, ethnicity, culture and racism. In T.A. van Dijk (Ed.), *Discourse as social interaction* (Vol. 2, pp. 144–180). London, UK: Sage.
Warren, J.T. (2003). *Performing purity: Whiteness, pedagogy, and the reconstitution of power.* New York, NY: Peter Lang.
Wetherell, M., & Potter, J. (1992). *Mapping the language of racism: Discourse and the legitimation of exploitation.* London, UK: Harvester Wheatsheaf.

Conclusion
Continuing a Politic of Disruption: Race(ing) Intercultural Communication

Michelle A. Holling & Dreama G. Moon

In the brief period since we wrote the introduction to the first special issue, we lament the deaths of more young Black men at the hands of law enforcement in the U.S.; the shootings of two police officers in New York, the massacre of women and children by Boko Haram in Baga, Nigeria that fails to garner media attention[1]; and the terrorist attacks in Paris. Likely the list of events implicating and tied to race across the globe is longer. Even so, we offer such examples as a reminder that race is and remains salient in the new year. Race is salient in the stories reported (or neglected) by international and domestic media outlets to global publics. Despite public discourse that suggest racism is over, a recent poll reveals that 58% of whites and 63% of Blacks each view race relations as "very bad."[2] These statistics are noteworthy as they serve as additional evidence of, if not play a role in, disrupting the farcical nature of a post-racial society.

The two special issues on race(ing) intercultural communication foreground several threads that unite the nine essays but that also indicate points of consideration for other scholars who wish to carry out similar work. One thread is that racism is a global problem that merits, if not urgently demands, scholars' attention. We believe that inter/cultural scholars are uniquely situated to provide insight and analysis in this area and failure to do so would seem an abdication of our responsibilities as organic intellectuals (see Milazzo, 2015; Pham, 2015). Related to the examination of racism is to account for one's subjectivity, or self-positioning, in the work and in relation to what we do (see Eguchi, 2015; Griffin, 2015; Milazzo, 2015; Nelson, 2015). In so doing, self-positioning is a critical move that gestures toward the embodied nature of scholarship but also showcases how such embodiment filters what and how we proceed in the study of race. Toward that end, any act of self-positioning must consider the aspects of reflexivity that orient scholars to remain attentive to silences, social and academic structures, and the production of knowledge (Nakayama & Krizek, 1995). A third theme regards particular values such as individualism, meritocracy, or ownership that endure despite their pernicious ramifications for addressing social relations (see Chen, Simmons & Kang, 2015; Cisneros & Nakayama, 2015; Morrissey, 2015). A final theme is the central role that whiteness plays in race(ing) intercultural communication. For example, various essays (in)directly attend to whiteness in order to expose its functioning in discourse (Cisneros & Nakayama, 2015; Griffin, 2015; Pham, 2015; Nelson, 2015) or challenge a white-Black binary (Eguchi, 2015; Mudambi, 2015). Even though whiteness was not the focus of our call for contributions to the special issues, we find that invariably whiteness and its various supportive discourses such as neoliberalism and colorblindness suffuse the study of and undergirds the race(ing) of intercultural communication. The dialectical relationship between white hegemony(ies) and global racisms is one that intercultural scholars doing race work will need to consider further.

Based on the nine essays published, we endeavored to (and, have) set in motion a politic of disruption and, it needs to remain so. We refresh readers' understandings of what we mean by a politic of disruption. "Politic" underscores scholars' balance of politics and shrewdness necessary to apprehend the connections between race and intercultural communication whereas "disruption" points to a disturbance in the norm(al) (Moon & Holling, 2015).

That is, the field of intercultural communication requires scholars who will continue to disrupt the study of intercultural communication via close analyses of race (and, its intersection with other identity categories) and through critique of postracial discourses in order to unveil what enables such beliefs to persist and to develop tactics of intervention. From where we stand, (critical) intercultural scholars appear to be in a transitional moment where old ways of thinking about and studying race surface in the discourses analyzed, yet new theorizations and ways into the racial conversation are emerging. Intercultural scholars are poised to be on the cutting edge of such shifts.

As we look ahead, we offer three directions for race(ing) intercultural communication: to broaden our attention to tensions between macro and micro forces, to conduct comparative work, and to attend to intersectionality. Of the institutions or macro structures explored by the nine authors, most often is media (e.g., film, social media, the Internet such as web campaigns or discourse), but also explored is academe, education, and vernacular discourse. What institutions do we neglect and why? How might we tease out more clearly tensions between macro and micro forces? Second, comparative work is needed. Here, we are reminded of Milazzo's (2015) essay that helps us understand how discourses permeate globally both similarly and differently. If racism is indeed global, we need to understand how it operates both within and among nations and cultural groups. Finally, scholarship that attends to intersectionality continues to be much needed. This is difficult work as it is challenging to write linearly about interconnected identities and processes. How might intercultural scholars imagine new ways of thinking through these difficult relationships? And at the end of the day, a relentless hope for doing better as peoples on the planet and an abiding desire for the full recognition of all peoples' human rights must guide our work. Are we as intercultural scholars up to this momentous challenge? Our answer to this question is an unequivocal yes.

Notes

(1) Patrick Chappatte's (2015) editorial cartoon, quips, "How many massacres does it take to be in the news around here?"
(2) *Wall Street Journal* and NBC news conducted the poll of 1,000 adults, 74% of whom are white (Hook & Ballhaus, n.d.).

References

Chappatte, P. (2015, January 16). How many massacres does it take to be in the news around here? *New York Times* Retrieved from http://www.nytimes.com/2015/01/17/opinion/patrick-chappatte-boko-haram-in-nigeria.html?_r=0

Chen, Y., Simmons, N., & Kang, D. (2015). "My family isn't racist—however ...": Multiracial/multicultural Obama-ism as an ideological barrier to teaching intercultural communication. *Journal of International and Intercultural Communication, 8*(2), 167–186. doi: 10.1080/17513057.2015.1025331

Cisneros, J. D., & Nakayama, T. K. (2015). New media, old racisms: Twitter, Miss America, and cultural logics of race. *Journal of International and Intercultural Communication, 8*(2), 108–127. doi: 10.1080/17513057.2015.1025328

Eguchi, S. (2015). Queer intercultural relationality: An autoethnography of Asian–Black (dis)connections in white gay America. *Journal of International and Intercultural Communication, 8*(1), 27–43. doi: 10.1080/17513057.2015.991077

Griffin, R. A. (2015). Problematic representations of strategic whiteness and "post-racial" pedagogy: A critical intercultural reading of *The Help*. *Journal of International and Intercultural Communication, 8*(2), 147–166. doi: 10.1080/17513057.2015.1025330

Hook, J., & Ballhaus, R. (n.d.). WSJ/NBC Poll: Mood Brightens on economy, not on race relations. Retrieved from http://www.wsj.com/articles/wsj-nbc-poll-mood-brightens-on-economy-not-on-race-relations-1418792641

Milazzo, M. (2015). The rhetorics of racial power: Enforcing colorblindness in post-apartheid scholarship on race. *Journal of International and Intercultural Communication, 8*(1), 7–26. doi: 10.1080/17513057.2015.991075

Moon, D. G., & Holling, M. A. (2015). A politic of disruption: Race(ing) intercultural communication. *Journal of International and Intercultural Communication, 8*(1), 1–6. doi: 10.1080/17513057.2015.991073

Morrissey, M. E. (2015). (Net)roots of belonging: Contemporary discourses of (in)valuability and post-racial citizenship in the United States. *Journal of International and Intercultural Communication, 8*(2); 128–146. doi: 10.1080/17513057.2015.1025329

Mudambi, A. (2015). The construction of brownness: Latino/a and South Asian bloggers' responses to SB 1070. *Journal of International and Intercultural Communication, 8*(1), 44–62. doi: 10.1080/17513057.2015.991079

Nakayama, T. K., & Krizek, R. L. (1995). Whiteness: A strategic rhetoric. *Quaterly Journal of Speech, 81*, 291–309. doi: 10.1080/00335639509384117

Nelson, C. M. (2015). Resisting whiteness: Mexican American Studies and rhetorical struggles for visibility. *Journal of International and Intercultural Communication, 8*(1), 63–80. doi: 10.1080/17513057.2015.991080

Pham, V. N. (2015). Our foreign President Barack Obama: The racial logics of Birther discourses. *Journal of International and Intercultural Communication, 8*(2), 86–107. doi: 10.1080/17513057.2015.1025327

Index

abortion 91
academic scholarship 4, 9-28
access to voice 149–50
affirmative action 13, 17; demonization of 22–3
African National Congress (ANC) 10
agency 42
aggregation 14
ak (blogger) 59
Al-Qaeda 110
Alberto 134
Alcoff, L. 48, 49, 79, 152
Alexander, B.K. 31, 39
Alvarez, M. 77
American dream 132–3, 172
anger 111
Anguiano, C.A. 132
anime, Japanese 40
Ansell, A.E. 127–8
anti-Black discourses 85–6, 87–8
anti-miscegenation 172
anti-racist-white-hero film genre 159
Anzaldúa, G. 70, 76
apartheid 16
apologia 7, 153–9
appropriation 22
Arizona: HB 2281 66, 74, 75; SB 1070 5, 46–64, 66, 74, 75; TUSD Mexican American Studies program 5, 65–82
Arpaio, J. 60, 85
Asian Americans 89, 97, 98, 99; South Asian bloggers 5, 46–64
Asian gay bars/clubs/events 30, 42
Asian gay stereotypes 40
Asian/Japanese gay male desire 4–5, 29–45
Asians 89, 97
aspirations, white-collar 130–3
autoethnography 4–5, 29–45
Ayres, T. 38

'Ballad of Gregorio Cortez' 71
Ban This: The BSP Anthology of Xican@ Literature 67–8, 72–8
Banet-Weiser, S. 109, 112
beauty pageants 105–24
Behar, J. 93–4
belonging: national 6, 7, 125–43; normative belonging strategies 60
Benatar, D. 15
Biko, S. 21–2, 24
birth certificate, Obama's 83–4, 93, 95
Birther discourses 6, 83–104
Birthers.org website 89–93, 96
Black Consciousness Movement 21
black privilege 171–2
black/white binary 48–9
Blind Side, The 144
Bloemhof water contamination child deaths 22
bloggers 5, 46–64
Bonilla-Silva, E. 16, 48–9, 108, 178
boyd, d. 114–15
Braden, A. 156
Branch, E.B. 159
Brewer, J. 66
Brown, M. 2
brownness 113; and the black/white binary 48–9; bloggers' responses to SB 1070 5, 46–64; constructions of 52–60; contesting the racialization of 57–60; and illegal immigration 49–51, 59
Buckland, F. 37
burden 138
business ownership 133–5
Buzzfeed 110

Calafell, B.M. 35, 67
Calderón, S. 73
Cambium Learning 78
Castillo, A. 71

INDEX

Causey, A. 166
Center for Community Change (CCC) 126–7
centralization of whiteness 7, 148–53
Chaudhry, M.Z. 138
Chávez, K.R. 30, 33, 132
Chávez, L. 54
Chen, Y.-W. 179
Chicanismo 70, 71
Chicana/o educational experiences 68–9
Chicana/o identities 70
Chicana/o literature 5, 67–8, 70–9
Chicano future tense (blogger) 54
Chicano Movement 70–1
China 95, 96
Chris 137
Cisneros, J.D. 46–7
citizenship 54–5, 85–6; good 54, 58; (in)valuability and post-racial 7, 125–43; natural-born 6, 85, 86–7, 90–3, 97–8, 99
civil rights movement 107, 150
Clark, W.A.V. 172
class 15–16
Clinton, W. 2
close reading 11
closet paradigm 32–3
colorblind racism *see* 'new' racism
colorblindness 2, 7, 168; Mexican American Studies 66–7, 73; South African scholarship 4, 9–28; *see also* post-racialism
Columbus, C. 153, 161
commodification of otherness 148
comparative work 185
Constitutional protection 91–3, 98–9; xenophobic 96–8
contesting the racialization of brownness 57–60
context collapse 114–16, 119
coolness 37–8
Cooppan, V. 18, 20
Copp, M. 173
Cosby, B. 172
counterstorytelling 78–9
Crash 144
credibility 140
Crenshaw, K.W. 168
critical discourse analysis (CDA) 169–70
critical race theory 11
critical rhetoric 68–79
critically compassionate intellectualism 65–6
Cronje, F. 22
Cruz, T. 96, 100
cultural deficit ideology 72

Dangerous Minds 144
Darth Paul (blogger) 57
Davis, N.J. 179
Davis, O.I. 165
Davis, V. 153

Davuluri, N. 6–7, 105, 106; racist tweets about 7, 109–19, 124; tweets celebrating Davuluri and criticizing racist tweets 116–17
day laborers 138–9
debt to whiteness 136
deflection of resistance 176–7
Delgado, R. 39
Deliovsky, K. 56
Derrida, J. 18, 21
desegregation 69
desire 4–5, 29–45
deterritorialization 146–7
DeVoss, D. 166
DevP (blogger) 54
Di (blogger) 53, 54, 59
Dick, H.P. 50
Dickinson, G. 59
direct action 69
disidentification 34
dispensation, rhetoric of 4
disruption, politic of 3–4, 185
down low (DL) 33, 39
DreamWorks Studios 153
Dred Scott case 85
Dugan, M. 72
Duggan, L. 128, 134, 137
Durban Declaration 1

economic elites 135
economic inequality 15–17
education 17; experiences of Chicana/o 68–9; higher education in South Africa 23, 24; intercultural communication education 6, 7, 164–83
El Random Hero (blogger) 52, 55
Elenes, C.A. 76
emotional outbursts 111–12
empowerment struggles 70
Enck-Wanzer, D. 68
entanglement 19–21
enthymematic logic 115–16
equality: racial 171; universalism and 175–6
Erasmus, Z. 14, 21
Evers, M. 150
Eyvazian, A. 134–5

fabulousness 37
FactCheck.org 94
feminization of Asian gay men 35
Ferber, A.L. 168
Ferguson children's video 2
film 6, 7, 144–63
Finke, L. 179
Fisher, W.R. 126, 140
Flores, L.A. 1, 125–6
forever foreigner discourses 35–6, 89, 97
formal-race unconnectedness 13

INDEX

Foster, D. 11–12, 21
Founding Fathers' intentions 91–2
Fredrickson, G.M. 107
Freeman, M. 172
Freire, P. 71
Fukino, C. 93

Gallagher, C.A. 165
Garuba, H. 12–13
gay bars and clubs 30, 34–5, 41, 42
gay communities 4–5, 29–45
gay liberation 33
gay neighborhoods 32
global problem 184
Gobineau, A. de 107
Goldberg, D.T. 87, 129
Gomes, Y. 133
good citizenship 54, 58
Gotanda, N. 13
Green, B. 153, 161
Greenhouse, E. 111
Group Areas Act (1950) 16
group-based privilege 174
Grover, S. 99
Guadalupe Hidalgo, Treaty of 70
Gunn, J. 114, 116

Halualani, R. 3, 165
Han, C.-S. 35
Haney-López, I.F. 168
hard work 132–3, 172–3
Harvey, D. 135
Hawai'i 93–4, 99
HB 2281 66, 74, 75
Help, The 7, 144–63
Hendrix, K.G. 165
'Hey White People: A Kinda Awkward Note to America by #Ferguson Kids' video 2
Hickman, F. 107
hierarchical structures 55–7, 61
higher education 23, 24
hip-hop 37–8
Hoekstra, P. 85
Holling, M.A. 4, 29, 75
home ownership 133–5
hooks, b. 156, 159–60
Horne, T. 66, 72, 73, 76
Howard, B.D. 158–9
Howard, R.G. 51
Howell, J. 99
Huerta, D. 72
humor 112–13
hybridity 20–1

identity: challenges in intercultural communication education 166; Chicana/o and Xicana/o identities 70; intercultural communication theories 165; national 113; student cultural identities 6, 7, 169–80
ignorance 12, 24
illegal immigration 49–51, 59
immigrants: fear of 96–7; (in)valuability 6, 7, 125–43
immigration legislation (SB 1070) 5, 46–64, 66, 74, 75
In Lak'ech rhetoric 68, 77–8
individualism 173–5, 178
individualization 17
inferiorization, logic of 112
inscrutability 87, 93–6, 97–8
Institute of Race Relations (IRR) 22–3
institutional racism 13, 17
intercultural communication education 6, 7, 164–83
intercultural communication pedagogy 167
interest convergence 149–50, 154
internal threat 98
intersecting subjectivities 140
intersectionality 185
(in)valuability 6, 7, 125–43; constructing a framework of 128–30
investment: ownership as 133–5; possessive investment in whiteness 12, 23, 130–9

Jack in the Box restaurants 134
Jansen, J. 13
Japan 33, 34, 36, 38
Japanese American internment 97
Jindal, B. 94, 96
Jolly, R. 14, 15, 18–19, 21
Joy Behar Show 89, 93–4

Karl, J. 89, 95–6
Keating, A. 77
Kim, C.J. 25, 88, 100
Kim, Y.Y. 174
Kinefichi, E. 34
Kitossa, T. 56
Kleinman, S. 173
Krizek, R.L. 146–7, 148

labor market 17
Lake, C. 99
Latino Politics Blog 52, 56–7
Latino/a bloggers 5, 46–64
Lee, W. 32
Lee, W.H. 97, 101
liberal humanism 14–15
Libertarians 90
Lim, E.-G. 30
Lipsitz, G. 12
literary criticism 18–20
Liuzzo, V. 156
Logan, E. 168

INDEX

logic of inferiorization 112
long-form birth certificate, Obama's 83–4, 93, 95
Lonmin platinum mine massacre 9
Lou (blogger) 52, 57–8, 60
Love, B.L. 175
Lund, J. 20

macro–micro tensions 185
Mamdani, M. 19
mammification of black women 155
Manuél (blogger) 52, 53, 54, 55, 60
Maré, G. 13–14, 23
Maria 139
Marikana massacre 9
Martin, J.N. 1, 2–3, 41, 165
Marty, D. 153
Marwick, A.E. 114–15
Mbembe, A. 10
McCune, J.Q., Jr 32, 33, 37
McKerrow, R.E. 68
McKinnon, S.L. 140, 141
McPhail, M.L. 167
media representation 146–7
meritocracy 172–3, 178
Mermin, D. 99
mestiza rhetoric 68, 71, 76–7, 78
Mexican American Citizen (blogger) 54–5, 58
Mexican American Studies (MAS) 5, 65–82
Mexicans 50, 57–8
micro–macro tensions 185
migrants' (in)valuability 6, 7, 125–43
Milazzo, M. 185
Miss America 6–7, 105–24; and 'old' and 'new' racisms 107–9; Pageant 106, 107, 109, 112; racist tweets 7, 109–19, 124
Mississippi Burning 144
Mngxitama, A. 14–15
model minority 39, 60
Molina, N. 88
Moon, D.G. 1, 2, 29
Morales, L. 95
Moreman, S.T. 35
Morrison, T. 12
multicultural/multiracial Obama-ism (MMO) 6, 7, 164–83
multiculturalism 19, 66, 174; neoliberal 117
Mundo, F. 73, 76
Muñoz, J.E. 31, 32, 34
Myerson, B. 109
mythical constructions of 'America' 74–5

Nakayama, T.K. 1, 2–3, 29, 41, 146–7, 148
narrative *see* storytelling
national belonging 6, 7, 125–43
National Day of Action 2010 photograph 60
National Geographic 166
national identity 113

Nattrass, N. 15–16
natural-born citizenship 6, 85, 86–7, 90–3, 97–8, 99
neoliberal multiculturalism 117
neoliberalism 127–8, 128–9, 132, 135; paradox of 138–9; racial 127–8
'new' racism 6–7, 106–9; and racist tweets about Miss America 116–17, 118–19
Newsday 117
Newsmax 94
Ngai, M. 54
nonracialism 10; *see also* colorblindness
normative belonging strategies 60
normativity: violent normativity of whiteness 72–4; white gay 32–4
Nuttall, S. 19–21

'O-borters' 91
Obama, B. 159, 175, 177–8; Birther discourses 6, 83–104; long-form birth certificate 83–4, 93, 95; meritocracy 172, 173; post-racialism 86, 87–90, 168, 171; *see also* multicultural/multiracial Obama-ism
'old' racism 6–7, 106–9; racist tweets about Miss America 110–14, 117–18, 118–19
Omi, M. 47, 127
Ong, A. 138
Ono, K.A. 47, 98, 159, 165, 173, 178
Opt, S.K. 139
ordering drinks 34–5
otherness: commodification of 148; shifting associations of 59–60
overlapping/shared experiences 60–1
ownership 133–5

Panche Be 77
Pathak, A.A. 117
paying dues 135–7
Peck, J. 170
Perea, J.F. 48
perpetual foreigners 35–6, 89, 97
Perry, P. 166, 176
Perumal, J. 176, 179
politic of disruption 3–4, 185
Poon, M-K-L. 40
possessive investment in whiteness 12, 23, 130–9
post-apartheid academic scholarship 4, 9–28
post-racialism 2, 107–8, 118, 165; Birther discourse and fear of a post-racial society 98–100; communicating post-racial ideologies 168–9; *The Help* 144–5, 159–61; implications of MMO for 177–8; (in) valuability and post-racial citizenship 7, 125–43; MMO 7, 164–83; Obama's 86, 87–90, 168, 171
poverty 17
Prashad, V. 60, 61

INDEX

presidential eligibility and legitimacy 6, 83–104
problem-posing 179
Projansky, S. 159
public pedagogy 145, 161
Public Shaming Tumblr 111
publicized privacy 114–16, 119

queer Asian–Black relationality 4–5, 29–45

racial categories 12–13
racial consciousness, hindered 148–59
racial equality 171
racial formations 47; brownness as a racial formation 52–5
racial neoliberalism 127–8
racial order 107
racial power 4, 9–28; defining 25; reading 12–22
'racial projects' 107
racial scripts 88–9, 97–8
racial structure 61; brownness and 55–7; three-tiered 48–9
racial triangulation 88
racialization of brownness 57; contesting 57–60
racism 172; apologia and redemption in *The Help* 7, 153–9; global problem 184; institutional 13, 17; racists positioned as outside threat 59–60
racist tweets 7, 109–19, 124
Ramos, L. 135–6
rationality, rhetoric of 98
Razib (blogger) 56, 57
redemption 7, 153–9
relational approach to race 88–9
Republican Party 84–5, 90
resistance: resistance rhetoric and Mexican American Studies 5, 65–82; student 176–7, 179
'Revisiting Apartheid's Race Categories' colloquium 12–13
rhetoric of dispensation 4
rhetoric of rationality 98
Rivera, S.J. 5, 67–8, 72–8
Rodriguez, O. 75, 77
Rodriguez, R. 74, 75, 77–8
Roediger, D.R. 75
Rogers, R. 170
Ropers-Huilman, B. 179
Ross, M.B. 33

Sachs, A. 20
Said, E. 14
same-sex relationships and marriage 39–40; *see also* gay communities
Sameer (blogger) 56
SB 1070 66, 74, 75; Latino/a and South Asian bloggers' responses 5, 46–64
Schueller, M.J. 88
Seekings, J. 15–18

segregated theory 20
segregation 16
self-assertion 70–1
self-positioning 184
Sepia Mutiny blog 52, 56
Serrano, A. 73, 78
shared humanity 14
shared/overlapping experiences 60–1
Sharma, S. 47
Sharpeville massacre 9
silence 139
Silva, K. 113
Simone, A. 72, 77
Simpson, J.L. 108
Simpson, J.S. 166
simulation games 179
'Situating One's Cultural Identities' assignment 169–80
six-word memoirs 179
slavery 146
Sloop, J.M. 47, 114, 116
social media 6–7, 105–24
social media cultures 114–16, 118
social movement groups 126
social norms 174
sociology 13–15
Soetoro-Ng, M. 100
Somfolnalco (blogger) 52, 53, 54
Soudien, C. 14, 21, 23
South African academic scholarship 4, 9–28
South African Human Rights Commission 23
South Asian American bloggers 5, 46–64
Spencer, O. 153
spiritual activism 77–8
Stefancic, J. 39
Steyn, M.E. 11–12, 21
Stockett, K. 144, 150–3, 160, 161
storytelling: counterstorytelling 78–9; We Are America campaign 7, 126–7, 129, 130–41
strategic whiteness 7, 144–63; and media representational strategies 146–7
student cultural identities 6, 7, 169–80
student mobilization 69
student resistance 176–7, 179

Taitz, O. 89–90, 93–4, 96
Taylor, T. 144, 152, 153, 159, 161
Tea Party 83, 84–5, 90, 97
teaching intercultural communication 6, 7, 164–83
Tejeda, G. 52, 55–6, 58
Tenzing (blogger) 57
This Week 89, 95–6
three-tiered racial structure 48–9
tolerance 66
Tosolt, B. 175
transformation 23

INDEX

transnational gay men 4–5, 29–45
Trump, D. 85, 89–90, 94–6
Tucson High Magnet School 72
Tucson Unified School District (TUSD) Mexican American Studies program (MAS) 5, 65–82
Twitter 6–7, 105–24; criticizing racist tweets 116–17; racist tweets about Miss America 7, 109–19, 124

undergraduate cultural identities 6, 7, 169–80
undocumented immigrants 49–51, 59
unemployment 17
United Nations World Conference against Racism (WCAR) 1–2
universalism 175–7, 178
University of Cape Town (UCT) 23, 24
untrustworthiness 87, 93–6, 97–8
Urrea, L. 74–5
USA Today 94–5

Vail, T. 111, 120
value 6, 7, 125–43
values 59–60, 184
Van Dijk, T.A. 168, 170
Vargas, J.A. 136
Vento, A. 77
vernacular discourse 46–64
Vice, S. 22
View, The 94
violent normativity of whiteness 72–4
Vivek (blogger) 52, 53, 57
voice, access to 149–50
Voices of Day Laborers 138

walkouts 69
Warren, J.T. 68, 79, 167, 175

We Are America campaign 7, 126–7, 129, 130–41
Weaver, S. 112
West, C. 3
white/black binary 48–9
white-collar aspirations 130–3
white gay normativity 32–4
white methods 16
white problem 2–3
white talk 11–12
whiteness 67, 184–5; centralization of 7, 148–53; challenging the power of 159–61; debt to 136; discursively visible 137–9; and intercultural communication pedagogy 167; (in)valuability 127, 129, 130–41; made visible in Tucson 72–5; possessive investment in 12, 23, 130–9; (re)producing 139–41; resistance rhetoric and criticisms of Mexican American Studies 5, 65–82; South Africa 11, 15; strategic 7, 144–63; violent normativity of 72–4
Williams, L. 166
Williams, V. 109
Wilson, C. 165
Winant, H. 10, 47, 127
Winfrey, O. 172–3
World Conference against Racism (WCAR) 1–2

xenophobic Constitutional protection 96–8
Xicana/o identities 70
Xicanisma 71

yellow peril discourses 89, 97
Yep, G.A. 30, 31–2
Yosso, T.J. 79

Zamora, R. 132
Zuberi, T. 16